The Romance of Thebes (Roman de Thèbes)

MEDIEVAL AND RENAISSANCE
TEXTS AND STUDIES

VOLUME 529

THE FRENCH OF ENGLAND TRANSLATION SERIES
(FRETS)

VOLUME 11

The Romance of Thebes (Roman de Thèbes)

Translated by
Joan M. Ferrante and Robert W. Hanning

FRETS Series Editors
Thelma Fenster and
Jocelyn Wogan-Browne

ARIZONA CENTER FOR MEDIEVAL
ACMRS
AND RENAISSANCE STUDIES
Tempe, Arizona
2018

THE ARIZONA CENTER FOR
MEDIEVAL & RENAISSANCE
STUDIES

Published by ACMRS (Arizona Center for Medieval and Renaissance Studies)
Tempe, Arizona

Library of Congress Cataloging-in-Publication Data
Names: Ferrante, Joan M., 1936- translator. | Hanning, Robert W., translator.
Title: The Romance of Thebes / translated by Joan M. Ferrante and Robert W. Hanning.
Other titles: Roman de Thèbes. English
Description: Tempe, Arizona : ACMRS (Arizona Center for Medieval and Renaissance Studies), 2017. | Series: Medieval and Renaissance texts and studies ; Volume 529 | Includes bibliographical references.
Identifiers: LCCN 2017029551 | ISBN 9780866985864 (hardcover : acid-free paper)
Subjects: LCSH: Roman de Thèbes. | Seven against Thebes (Greek mythology)--Romances. | Epic poetry, French--Translations into English. | Thebes (Greece)--Romances.
Classification: LCC PQ1533.T5 E5 2017 | DDC 841/.2--dc23
LC record available at https://lccn.loc.gov/2017029551

Cover Image:
MS Additional 34114, f.164r
L'Ordene de Chevalerie and Romances in French
(The 'Spalding' Manuscript')
c. 1400

∞
This book is made to last. It is set in Adobe Caslon Pro,
smyth-sewn and printed on acid-free paper to library specifications.
Printed in the United States of America

Table of Contents

Series Editors' Preface

The medieval Oedipus and Jocasta, Polynices and Etiocles, Antigone, Creon and Theseus and many other well-known figures take center stage in the story of the siege of Thebes, one of the earliest reworkings of classical material by which medieval Europe constructed its identity as successor to Greece and Rome. Questions of the nature and scope of European identity are with us as vividly as ever today and the *Romance of Thebes* has a foundational role in these questions, since it codes the Western aspects of the Mediterranean inheritance as the defining ones for Europe.

It is thirty years since the *Roman de Thèbes* received its only translation into English (a closely literal translation of Constans' 1890 text, which itself is part critical edition and part creation of an "Ur-Thebes" text), though there have been several recent translations into modern French. Joan Ferrante and Robert Hanning, distinguished comparative literature scholars, offer here a new translation that speaks to the post-nationalizing turn in literary studies and to renewed respect for individual manuscript versions. The late twelfth-century re-makings of the stories of Troy, Thebes, of Greece and Rome collectively called the *romans antiques* or *romans d'antiquité* have been primarily associated with continental France, but in recent years it has become clearer that they are better thought of as works of the Angevin realm. They are texts from the shared cultures of the *espace plantagênet*, the extensive territories on both sides of the Channel ruled over by Henry I and his successors.

Equally importantly, the *romans antiques* continued to influence medieval texts and the formation of courtly and chivalric value systems throughout the Middle Ages. Professors Ferrante and Hanning translate here the personal copy of the *Roman de Thèbes* owned by Henry Despenser (d. 1406), Bishop of Norwich, well known both for his failed crusade and his ruthless suppression of the Norwich protests in the Great Rising, also commonly referred to as the Peasants' Revolt of 1381. Ferrante and Hanning thereby contribute to the FRETS series a major work representative of literary cultures in the French of England, where francophone texts circulated from and to insular domains.

We are very grateful to these distinguished comparativists for their work, and, respecting the particular nature of this translation, we vary the usual FRETS protocols here, changing to line-by-line translation rather than translation into prose. We hope this will facilitate study of the original while also, in the provision of the translation, extending awareness of and access to this major medieval work. In addition to our gratitude to Professors Ferrante and Hanning, we owe thanks to Professor Christopher Baswell, both for his groundbreaking study of the Despenser manuscript and his characteristically generous sharing of his material, and to Carolyn Cargile, who as a Fordham Ph.D. candidate and research assistant to Jocelyn Wogan-Browne has contributed much appreciated assistance with the typescript and with typing its Appendix. At ACMRS, we thank Roy Rukkila and Todd Halvorsen for their hard work and patience, and Leslie MacCoull for meticulous copy-editing and her many constructive suggestions.

Thelma Fenster
Jocelyn Wogan-Browne

List of Abbreviations

ARLIMA	Les Archives de littérature du Moyen Âge: www.arlima.net/.
Baswell	Baswell, Christopher. "Aeneas in 1381." *New Medieval Literatures* 5 (2002): 7–58.
Constans	*Le roman de Thèbes*, ed. Léopold Constans. SATF 30. Paris: Firmin Didot, 1890, 2 vols.
Dean	*Anglo-Norman Literature, A Guide to Texts and Manuscripts*, ed. Ruth J. Dean, collab. Maureen B. M. Boulton. ANTS Occasional Publications Series 3. London: Anglo-Norman Text Society, 1999.
FRETS	French of England Translation Series.
Mora-Lebrun	*Le roman de Thèbes*, ed. Francine Mora-Lebrun. Lettres Gothiques. Paris: Le livre de poche, 1995.
MS S	London, British Library, MS Additional 34114.
ODNB	*Oxford Dictionary of National Biography from the Earliest Times to the Year 2000*, ed. H.C.G. Matthew and Brian Harrison. Vol. 15. Oxford: Oxford University Press, 2004, and online.

Introduction

I. The Poem

A. Literary Context: The *Romans Antiques* as a Twelfth-Century Phenomenon: *Roman de Thèbes*, *Roman d'Eneas*, *Roman de Troie*, Alexander Romances

During the decades between 1150 and 1170 (more precise dating is at this point impossible), and within the western European territory controlled by the Normans—including the duchy of Normandy, the kingdom of England, and subsequently (under Henry II [reigned 1154–1189]) the county of Anjou and, through Henry's 1152 marriage to Eleanor, the latter's duchy of Acquitaine—there arose a new type of narrative in the vernacular based on Latin texts inherited from classical antiquity. These Latin texts were endowed with historical and moral authority by those who studied them in the expanding network of twelfth-century monastic and cathedral schools (including the predecessors of the European university). The collective title given to the vernacular works by modern scholars is the *romans antiques* (or *romans d'antiquité*); the three primary exemplars of the category are the *Roman de Thèbes*, *Roman d'Enéas*, and *Roman de Troie*, based respectively on the *Thebaid* of Statius (published CE 92), Vergil's *Aeneid* (published after 19 BCE), and the story of the Trojan war preserved in two Latin, pseudo-eyewitness narratives ascribed to Dares Phrygias and Dictys Cretensis, Homer's *Iliad* being unknown in the West at this time. (The original Greek texts of Dares and Dictys have not survived, but scholars utilizing indirect evidence have traced both to the first century CE; the extant Latin version of Dictys is datable to the fourth century CE, that of Dares to the sixth.)[1] Alexander romances and histo-

[1] *Le roman d'Eneas*, ed. and trans. Aimé Petit, Lettres Gothiques (Paris: Le livre de poche, 1997). Benoit de Sainte-Maure, *Le roman de Troie*, ed. L. Constans, SATF (Paris: Firmin Didot, 1904–1912), 6 vols., trans. Emmanuèle Baumgartner, Bibliothèque médiévale (Paris: 10/18, 1987). Statius, *Thebaid*, in *Works*, ed. and trans. J. H. Mozley, Loeb Classical Library (London: Heinemann, Cambridge, MA: Harvard U. Press, 1928, repr. 1982). Vergil. *Aeneid*, in *Works*, ed. and trans. H. Rushton Fairclough, Loeb Classical Library (London: Heinemann; Cambridge, MA: Harvard University Press, 1950). Dares Phrygius, *De excidio Trojae historia*, ed. Ferdinand Meister (Leipzig: Teubner, 1873), trans. R. M. Frazer, *The Trojan War. The Chronicles of Dictys of Crete and Dares the*

ries were also composed in the Angevin domains on both sides of the Channel, and the *roman antique* remained an influential model for Chaucer and other writers, even when treated ironically as in the romances of Hue de Rotelande.[2]

B. The Authors of the *Romans Antiques*: Their Perspective(s) as Translators and Cultural Commentators

The process of adapting these classical texts into French was defined by contemporaries simply as rendering them *en romanz*, a phrase that might be taken to mean "in French translation" (*romanz* referring in this case to the language involved, not the genre; the association of "romance" with a particular kind of story, with love playing a central role, came later); in fact, however, the procedures involved were quite different in manner and intent from how we tend to think of translation today, i.e., as the closest possible approximation in language B of the action and thought presented in a given text in language A. Instead, a Latin classic was recreated *en romanz* as a function of (a) the age's complex intellectual response to classical antiquity; (b) its political understanding of the Anglo-Norman/Angevin state's desire to establish or support its legitimacy as inheritor of ancient imperial power, vis-à-vis similar claims by French kings or Holy Roman Emperors. That is, underlying the creation of the *romans antiques* is an intersection of the twelfth-century concepts of *translatio studii* and *translatio imperii*: the former a contention that the mantle of excellence in philosophy and other forms of learning (bunched in the French vernacular under the term *clergie*) had been passed, across the centuries, from Greece to Rome and then on to Christian Europe; the latter a similar assessment with respect to the westward transference of secular power and the martial prowess (generalized as *chevalrie*) undergirding it. (Chrétien de Troyes's romance, *Cligès*, provides the classic statement: "Ce nos ont nostre livre apris / Qu'an Grece ot de chevalerie / Le premier los et de clergie, /

Phrygian (Bloomington: Indiana University Press, 1966). Dictys Cretensis, *Ephemeridos belli Trojani libri*, ed. Werner Eisenhut (Leipzig: Teubner, 1958), trans. Frazer (cf. Dares).

[2] Alexandre de Bernay (de Paris)'s twelfth-century *Roman d'Alexandre* was reworked and incorporated into Thomas of Kent's *Roman de toute chevalerie* in the late twelfth century and other versions, variously signaled as history and romance, followed in continental and insular French and in Latin: see further, *The Medieval French Alexander*, ed. Donald Maddox and Sara Sturm-Maddox, SUNY Series in Medieval Studies (New York: State University of New York Press, 2002), and ARLIMA *s.v.* Alexandre de Paris. For Chaucer, see Barbara Nolan, *Chaucer and the Tradition of the* "Roman Antique", Cambridge Studies in Medieval Literature, 15 (Cambridge: Cambridge University Press, 1992). For Hue de Rotelande's late twelfth-century romances, *Ipomedon* and *Protheselaus*, see Ruth J. Dean with Maureen B. M. Boulton, *Anglo-Norman Literature: A Guide to Texts and Manuscripts* ANTS OPS 3 (London: ANTS, 1999), nos. 162, 163.

Puis vint chevalerie a Rome / Et de la clergie la some, / Qui or est an France venue."[3] The opening lines of the *Roman de Thèbes* link these two cultural ideals in their definition of the proper audience for the story that follows: "Let them be silent, those who work at this craft; / unless they are clerics or knights, / they can listen just as well / as asses can harp."[4] Henry II's status was bolstered by a connection between his reign and the classical stories of Thebes, Troy, Rome—a *translatio imperii.*

Beyond these two major concerns underlying the remaking of antiquity's martial narratives *en romanz* we can identify several other important components of the process, including:

- the insertion of contemporaneous details—allusions to events and characters; evocation of issues under debate and clashes of values—that configure the celebration, construction, and/or critique of ideals and traditions apposite to northwest Europe's warrior aristocracy, e.g., lord-vassal relations and tensions, heroism and bravery in battle, the imperative of defending one's honor and avoiding dishonor or shame, the primacy of noble lineage, and the accommodation of a military ethos to the conventions, rituals, and constraints of life at a royal court;

- a newfound interest in the effects of erotic desire and the nature and crises of human interiority, in part stimulated by, and responding to, the popularity of Ovid in twelfth-century scholastic and court culture;

- a recognition, direct or indirect, of the power, patronage, interests, and limitations, of the women of the nobility, most of them highly literate and well-educated (by tutors or in convents);

- a commitment to rhetorical variety and virtuosity—comprehending speeches, laments, debates, and other techniques deriving from school exercises and classical traditions of *suasoriae* and *controversiae.* (In her study of Chaucer and the *roman antique*, Barbara Nolan writes: "These forms—inherited equally from the judicial trials or *plaits* of earlier vernacular literature (and life), the oratory of Latin epic, and medieval school practices of rhetorical disputation—enter more or less centrally into the making of all

---

[3] Chrétien de Troyes, *Cligés*, ed. Alexandre Micha, CFMA 84 (Paris: Champion, 1965), vv. 28–32 ("Our books have taught us that chivalry and learning were first prized in Greece; then proceeded to Rome those chivalric ideals and that most profound learning which have now, in our day, arrived in France.")

[4] "Tout se taisent cil del mestier / si ne sont clerc ou chivaler:/ ensement poent escouter / come li asnes a harper," *Le roman de Thèbes, edition du manuscrit S (Londres, Brit, Libr., Add. 34114)*, ed. and trans. Francine Mora Lebrun, Lettres Gothiques (Paris: Le livre de poche, 1997), vv. 13–16. Line references here are to the translation in this volume.

three of the twelfth-century French *romans antiques*. . . . [T]he clerkly *romanciers* used dramatized debate and argumentation to pose circumstantial moral questions of crucial interest to their lay aristocratic public" [48].)[5]

- a predilection for ecphrases, copious verbal descriptions of objects and artifacts richly decorated with pictorial schemes reflecting the learning of the clerical authors of the *romans antiques* and their increasing presence as court functionaries, performing services of documentation central to the bureaucratization of centralized state power under Henry II (and other twelfth-century rulers).[6]

In effect, then, the *romans antiques* commemorate and celebrate the mid-twelfth-century's new, provocative intersection of the court, the school, and the battlefield.

The authors of the *romans antiques* are unknown to us, but the characteristics just catalogued indicate that they were clerics, that is, men in minor ecclesiastical orders who had been trained in the schools, attached to cathedrals or religious houses, that proliferated in the burgeoning cities and towns of northern France. They may have been writing (either with patronage or seeking to obtain it) for the court of Henry II and Eleanor, or at least within its broad cultural ambience (see below, pp. 7, 9, 10, 15–24).[7]

---

[5] See Nolan, *Chaucer and the Tradition*, 48, and see further her chapter, "*Plaits*, debates, and judgments in the *Roman de Thèbes*, the *Roman de Troie*, and the *Roman d'Eneas*," and cf. p. 54: "Public debates [in the *roman antique*] assume a novel character, typically raising complex questions about matters of feudal, family, and personal conduct. Frequently, in these debates, the consensus reached by the king's counselors does not resolve the issues raised. Furthermore, the poet often refuses to offer a definitive solution, leaving difficult prudential judgments to the audience," and further, p. 62: "If we are watching in the *Thèbes* the emergence of courtly classicizing romance, we must see in Daire's trial and its outcome [on which see below in this Introduction, pp. 8–9] an epitome of new directions. The intervention of the unexpected by means of rhetorical debate and dialogue generates a centrifugal movement away from hierarchy, certainty, and finality."

[6] As Christopher Baswell puts it, "It is a persistent habit in the romances of Antiquity to interpolate versions or icons of their own learned makers within their texts: poets, inscriptions and epitaphs, buildings and fabrics decorated with scientific and cosmological learning." See "Marvels of translation and crises of transition in the romances of antiquity," in *The Cambridge Companion to Medieval Romance*, ed. Roberta Krueger (Cambridge: Cambridge University Press, 2000), 29–44, at 30.

[7] Baswell speaks of "the role of learned clerks as mediators between abstruse Latin texts and the vernacular culture of secular aristocrats" ("Marvels of Translation," 32), men who "thereby generate a comparatively safe imaginative space within ancient story to

The *Roman de Thèbes*, based on Statius's *Thebaid*, is generally considered the earliest of the extant *romans antiques*, and is usually (and conjecturally) dated ca. 1150–55 in its (hypothetical) earliest form.[8] The *Thebaid* was well known in medieval western Europe: it is extant in over a hundred manuscripts, many copied in the twelfth century as part of the revival of classical learning at cathedral schools. The epic proved useful as an exemplar of Latin grammar and usage, composition, and rhetoric, as adduced in commentaries, florilegia, glosses, and textbooks such as Matthew of Vendome's *Ars versificatoria* (Paris, before 1175). In florilegia, the most frequent excerpts from the *Thebaid* are the laments of Argia, Ismene, Antigone, and also of Tydeus, when he eats the skull of his killer (see further note 12, below.) To quote Battles: in the formulaic introductions, or *accessus*, added to the *Thebaid* as to many other classical texts studied in the schools, "the portrait of Statius as a moral authority emerges on several levels" (7); according to these *accessus*, the examples provided in his poem were designed to head off fratricide and family squabbles—supposedly in Rome's imperial family—but are also of general moral use. The *Thebaid* was also subjected to wholesale allegorization in commentaries that deployed far-fetched (to modern ears) etymologies; one of these, the twelfth-century *Super Thebaidem*, "transforms the *Thebaid* into a *psychomachia*, each character representing a different spiritual state or concept. The struggle at Thebes becomes spiritual warfare,"[9] in which Theseus's killing of Creon becomes the triumph of piety over sin. These and other impositions of meaning on Statius's epic exemplify all the ways in which a classic is extolled as exemplary on its own terms, but in the process is in fact domesticated, even as its otherness, as a classic of the past, is recognized.

The *Roman de Thèbes* can best be understood as a part of this domestication.

C. A Comparison of Statius's *Thebaid* with the French Version (MS S) that is the Basis of this Translation

Vergil, whom Statius credits as his poetic model, is mentioned at the beginning of the French poem, along with Homer and Plato and Cicero (MS S, vv. 5–6 [hereafter, verses without accompanying identification refer to this manuscript, the source for our translation])—but Statius is not. He is mentioned only once in the poem and then as a source in the middle of an episode which he did not include in the *Thebaid*, the Dares story: "si come dit le liver d'Estaisce" [as the book by Statius puts it] (v. 8541). A character named Estaisces turns up during a

register aspects of their own time. . . . By conflating a normalized past and a mythicized present, the authors of these romances can examine complicated, often anxious transitions in contemporary society and politics" (33, 36).

[8] This paragraph depends heavily on "Statius in the Middle Ages," the Introduction to Dominique Battles, *The Medieval Tradition of Thebes* (London: Routledge, 2004).

[9] Battles, *The Medieval Tradition of Thebes*, 11.

battle; he is the rich Count of Turin, an ally of the Thebans, who kills a Phrygian (vv. 4824, 4854). This may either be a version of the name Eustache, or a sly reference to the poet, or both.

The first quarter of the French poem covers half of the *Thebaid*, though it does not include the funeral rites or the funeral games from Book 6; the bulk of the French version, MS S, relates the second half of Statius's story, with omissions, changes, and interpolations. The entire Dares episode is added (as it is in the other longer French versions, MSS A and P, discussed below; a truncated version appears in MS C). The death of Capaneus is put off to the end of the war and the poem; he is a more sympathetic figure, his defiance of the gods is omitted, and he is killed by a boulder not a thunderbolt. This French version is the only one to keep Amphiaraus's descent to hell from Statius, where he sees tortured souls, perhaps evoking a Christian description of purgatory or hell. Otherwise mythical figures and references are usually omitted, though characters may swear by their gods, "touz les diex que nous creon" [all the gods in whom we believe] (v. 3052).

The gods and allegorical figures like the Furies, the Fates, Death, Sleep, Rumor, are responsible for much of the action in Statius: the cause of a great thirst in Statius is a god, Bacchus; in the French it is a three-month drought. In the *Thebaid*, Jupiter sends Mars to urge people to stop playing at war and get on with it; in MS S a messenger comes to the king, Adrastus, to say the Thebans are on the move. The god sends Mercury disguised as Laius to incite Eteocles and warn him of Polynices's marriage; in the French, Eteocles acts from his own bad impulses. In the Latin, the Fury Tisiphone brings out the worst in people, inciting them, enflaming both armies (in Book 7), forcing the duel between the brothers (in Book 11); in the French, the brothers meet by accident on the battlefield. Human agency, treachery, deceptions, men's evil, replace divine intervention in MS S; Eteocles plots from early on, treason is in his mind from the beginning: "privement se conseille / de traïson" [and takes counsel in closed session to plan an astonishing treason] (vv. 1284–85), "grant traïson porparle a faire" [he plots a great betrayal] (v. 1286); the tower of Meleages is won by deception, the tower of Dares is taken and retaken by subterfuge; false messages are sent, branches stirred up to suggest large armies, armies and individuals are lured into traps.

Only the riddle of the Sphinx, which occurs twice, remains from myth as an active part of the narrative in MS S, and the second time the Sphinx is replaced by a devil figure (vv. 2838–47). The battle of the gods and the giants is depicted on Amphiaraus's chariot in a lengthy ecphrasis (vv. 5044–171) that includes the nine spheres of the heavens and the liberal arts, but this is not in Statius.[10] The giants in MS S are examples of arrogance, greed, and the desire to seize what

[10] Aimé Petit, *L'Anachronisme dans les romans antiques du XIIe Siècle: le Roman de Thèbes, le Roman d'Enéas, le Roman de Troie, le Roman d'Alexandre* (Paris: Champion, 2002), 188, suggests that the inspiration for this passage is Ovid's *Metamorphoses*.

one cannot have, perhaps replacing Capaneus's defiance of the gods, which MS S omits, but the whole passage certainly shows off the poet's erudition and rhetorical skills. The poet indulges in such skills in one other ecphrasis, describing Adrastus's tent (vv. 3234–71, 4299–378), wedding power to learning with a *mappamundi* [map of the world], months of the year, history of the kings of Greece, and wild animals.[11]

But for the most part, the French poem drastically reduces rhetorical flourishes like long descriptions of public rites, marriages, funeral games, catalogues of armies. Statius takes 344 lines to list and describe the Greek army (Book 4.1–344), MS S only 24 (vv. 2087–110), but the French gives more detail to the troops coming from the seven gates and their battles (Statius, Book 8.350–62, MS S, vv. 5642–725). In general, MS S gives much more detail of combats and related issues, adding an episode in which the armies' horses are being massacred by the arrows of foot soldiers and the two armies agree to a truce to get the archers on both sides to stop killing the horses. But if MS S does not focus on public rituals, it makes a great deal of public debates, consultations, arguments, among Meleager's barons, among the Thebans over whether to make a deal with Polynices (vv. 3812ff), among the Greeks about whether to leave after Amphiaraus is killed, even between Dares and his wife over whether to give up their tower to save their son. The arguments often have a feudal and legal twist, loyalty to a lord versus demands of morality or family, or self interest, technical points of when a sworn commitment must be kept or can be broken. Kings and leaders hesitate to act without the support of their vassals; vassals worry about treason, about what actions give them a right to shift loyalties.

The Dares episode is the major narrative addition to the French poem, but there are others. The pre-story of Oedipus is told in detail, to establish the sinful heritage of the warring brothers through their incestuous conceptions (vv. 27–28). We are told of Apollo's prophecy to Laius that his son, Oedipus, would kill his father, the grief of the mother, Jocasta[12] at the condemnation of her child, the rescue of the baby, his return and unwitting killing of his father in a general melee. But Oedipus is wise as well as fierce: he solves the riddle of the Sphinx and kills it, freeing the city from its power. Following the celebration in Thebes, Jocasta takes Oedipus to bed and worries how she can hold her land; her people urge her to marry Oedipus. After twenty years and four children, they discover

[11] Baswell, "Marvels of translation," 33; L. G. Donovan, *Recherches sur le Roman de Thèbes* (Paris: SEDES, 1975), 227, connects the philosophical elements of this ecphrasis to the teachings of Guillaume de Conches, a twelfth-century philosopher who taught at a cathedral school, possibly at Chartres.

[12] In the French text of MS S the form of the name is Jocaste. "Jocasta" is the form of her name in classical antiquity's versions of the Oedipus story, so we use it, as well as the classical version of all names of characters originally in the *Thebaid*, throughout this Introduction and our translation.

the truth of their relationship, he blinds himself, is mocked by his sons and curses them, and that is where the *Thebaid* begins. The riddle of the Sphinx comes up once again as the Greek army marches to Thebes and is stopped at the tower of Morgan la Fee (vv. 2801ff) by a devil disguised as an old woman who demands the answer.[13] Tydeus solves the riddle, which destroys the devil. The army encounters two more towers, medieval symbols of local power, on their march, perhaps to build sympathy for the Greeks through their various adventures, perhaps to raise feudal issues that favor Polynices. The next is at the castle of Monflor (vv. 2981ff), held by Meleages, who is a cousin of the warring brothers: "la tor en est haut et soltaigne" [its tower high and solitary] (v. 2983). Polynices claims it, since Eteocles's year is up; Mealeages is willing but his barons argue over which brother to support. Polynices hesitates, but Tydeus and Adrastus want to take it and do so, after a hard battle with war machines and Greek fire,[14] an ambush to lure the enemy out, and a Venetian who pretends to be a messenger from Eteocles.

Finally, there is Dares's tower, a long episode with courtly as well as feudal elements (vv. 8259–10370), virtually a romance within the poem. Polynices has captured Dares's son in battle and offers him freedom and land if he can deliver the tower. The son is sent home to convince his father; the mother is willing, the father is hesitant because he does not want to betray his lord, Eteocles, so he devises a plan to make Eteocles insult and strike him, thus breaking the bond between them and enabling him to allow a secret takeover. But an engineer advises Eteocles to dig a tunnel under the tower, shore it up with wood, and then burn it with Greek fire. Dares is captured and tried for treason, with lengthy arguments for and against him, and Jocasta advising against destroying him because of his powerful relations. The issue is not settled until Antigone, Eteocles's sister, brings Dares's daughter in to plead for her father, introducing a courtly element: Eteocles is in love with her but she has so far been aloof; now, as Antigone points out, he has the advantage so, ignoring his barons' arguments, he releases her father to gain her love.

The feudal and courtly and descriptive details of many episodes, anachronistic though they may be, make the story more relevant to a contemporary audience (Petit, *L'anachronisme*, 51–52). They range from brief allusions, like Morgan

[13] Morgan ("the Fairy") comes out of Arthurian legend, a half-sister of Arthur with magic powers, who appears in Geoffrey of Monmouth's mid twelfth-century fictionalized *Historia regum Britanniae* ("History of the Kings of Britain"), connected with the island of Apples (Avalon) to which the dying Arthur was brought. Morgan continued to have a presence in later Arthurian works. The use of her name here suggests an attempt to fuse classical and medieval figures with supernatural powers.

[14] Greek fire was an effective incendiary device, used in Byzantium, the Roman empire of the East, particularly in naval warfare. It involved a projection of a combination of flammable materials—the formula is no longer known—onto enemy ships or positions. In the West, it came to refer to any destructive incendiary device.

la Fee, or the smith who made Tydeus's sword, Galant, a figure from Germanic myth (v. 1675), or the legs of Eteocles's "amie" he had painted on his shield near a dent as a joke (vv. 7165–68), evoking Eleanor of Aquitaine's grandfather, Guillaume IX (more coarse than courtly perhaps, but likely to elicit a laugh), to more concentrated references to crusades and Christianity. Petit (*L'anachronisme*, 61ff) and Mora-Lebrun (*Introduction*, 15ff) note various suggestive references to the first crusade: the siege of stone castles; a comparison with the fear inspired by the sword of Godfrey of Bouillon (vv. 5184–85); connections between the Dares episode and the *Chanson d'Antioche*; the trip to Bulgaria for food (vv. 7894–8018); the presence of Venetians (vv. 3380–83; 3572–739); the son of the Duke of Chatillon (v. 11348); allusions to the Reconquista of Spain (vv. 4648–49), the Spanish Garciavarre (vv. 4758–59), the Moorish Amoraive (vv. 5972, 10580); Greek fire (vv. 3352–54; 9092–102), battle machines (vv. 3336–41, 7315–18), massacre of horses by footsoldiers (vv. 5830–33, 5870–911).

There is one probable reference to the second crusade in the mention of Laliche (v. 5748), the site of a defeat of Louis VII and heavy losses to Turks; Petit (*L'anachronisme*, 66) gives a more obscure identification, thinking that a reference to action where Eleanor was present with her first husband, Louis, would have been offensive to Henry II, but it seems more likely that Henry would have enjoyed the reminder of Louis's defeat. The crusades in Spain are suggested by the echoes of the *Chanson de Roland*: favorable comparisons of Tydeus to Roland, "de proece semble Rollant [he is like Roland in prowess] (v. 835); "colps done merveillous et granz / onc ne dona meillors Rollanz" [His blows are wondrous and great; Roland never struck better] (vv. 1788–89); of the Greek rearguard to Roland's, "l'arier garde est ordeigne; / en quatre eschieles des Rolant, dont cist jogleor vont chantant, ne fu tant bele ne tant riche" [All is in order in the rearguard; / even among the four troops of Roland, / about whom these minstrels keep singing, / there was none as handsome and richly appointed] (vv. 10610–13); and the Greek army to Charlemagne's when he conquered Spain: "ne tant n'ot Charle en sa compaignie / quant il conquist yceux d'Espaigne" [Charles did not have as many in his company when he conquered the Spanish] (vv. 4648–49); even verbal echoes of the poem as the Greeks move towards Thebes and the valleys resound with trumpets, "Granz sont les pois et les montaignes, / et les valees et les plaignes" [The hills and mountains are steep, the valleys and plains broad] (vv. 2780–81), cf. *Chanson de Roland*, "Halt sunt li pui e li val tenebrus," [the mountains are high and the valleys shadowy] (v. 814).[15] It is said of one of the young Theban allies, Nestor, son of the Duke of Châtillon, "s'il creïst Dieu et sa puissance / plius beals de lui ne portast lance" [if he only believed in God and God's power, a more attractive knight would never have borne a lance] (vv.

[15] The formulaic "Halt sunt li pui" occurs three times in the *Chanson*, each time at the beginning of a laisse: 66:814; 138:1830; 169; 2271; see *The Song of Roland, An Analytical Edition*, ed. Gerald J. Brault (University Park: Pennsylvania State University, 1978).

11355–56), which evokes Christians' admiration of their infidel enemies in the *Chanson de Roland*.

It is the Greek army which is associated with the Christians, casting the Thebans as infidels. Amphiaraus is a bishop, who has to be replaced after the earth swallows him. The election is a comment on contemporary customs; Theodamus is elected against his will and without simony (v. 5612), by the barons, not by clergy, as should have been done after Gregorian reform.[16] When the new bishop performs religious rites, leads prayers and fasting to make up for their sins, a miracle ensues, closing the earth and restoring the army's morale. Since Amphiaraus is a priest in Statius as well, replaced by another who leads a procession and prayers, the French version seems more an updating than an anachronism. But if most of the Christian connections are to the Greeks, there is a significant one among the Thebans at the end. The other sister of the warring brothers, Ismene, retires to a monastery after the death of her lover Atys. The monastery is built and endowed for her and one hundred high-born nuns, by her brother the king, certainly a reflection of twelfth-century (and earlier) practice. Perhaps Ismene's assumption of a religious life is meant to make up for the sins of her family.

D. Comparison of Characters

The tendency to favor the Greeks in MS S is reflected in the treatment of major characters, who are not only strong fighters, but dependable people who act for the good of the whole, as though the poet were moving somewhat towards a courtly world without sacrificing heroic modes. The Greek army is filled with strong and loyal vassals, serving a good king, Adrastus, while the Thebans are dominated by a treacherous king. Adrastus attracts heroic figures: Polynices, though a Theban, marries a daughter of Adrastus; he is supported by the Greeks and identified with them. Tydeus, from Calydon, also marries into the Greek royal family and becomes one of the pillars of the Greek army. Though he can be fierce, like Roland, and we are told he was exiled for fratricide, as in Statius (MS S, v. 756; Statius, Book 1, vv. 402–3), he seems more polite and reasonable in his first appearance, asking only a small space to rest until Polynices forces him to fight. They become close friends as well as brothers-in-law, establishing a clear contrast with the Polynices-Eteocles relation. Tydeus alternates between the fierce hero and the cultivated prince throughout the poem: he takes on the dangerous mission to Eteocles in Polynices's place, arriving with an olive branch, but riding into the court on his horse, presumably an aggressive gesture; his words are diplomatic until the king perjures himself, then he tries to persuades Eteocles's men to come over to Polynices (vv. 1527ff); when he is ambushed at

[16] Petit, *L'anachronisme*, 157–59, notes that English kings influenced elections directly.

the site of the Sphinx, a detail that seems to identify Eteocles and his men with the devil, God protects Tydeus and he overcomes them all. He can be courtly, playful with Hypsipyle (v. 2279), and gentle even on the battlefield, when he tries not to fight the young and beautiful Atys, until Atys forces it, then he sends the body back to the Thebans (vv. 6679ff). In Statius, Tydeus is dismissive of Atys and kills him with an "unwarlike shaft" ("imbelle . . . iaculum," Book 8, vv. 584–85). In both versions, Tydeus dies at the hands of a non-hero, by spear in Statius, by arrow in MS S. In Statius, his response is violent; he asks for the head of the spear-thrower and gnaws at the skull (inspiring a scene in Dante's *Inferno*, canto 32, v. 130, where Ugolino performs the same act on his betrayer, Ruggieri); in MS S, his men cut off the head of the archer, but there is no gnawing. In both the Latin and the French poems, Polynices wants to commit suicide out of grief for the loss of Tydeus, in both there is a fight over the corpse, which is abused by Eteocles's men in MS S. MS S also tells us that his son, Adrastus's grandson, whom the king sends to Tydeus's father to make up for the loss of Tydeus, would be the Diomedes who fought at Troy (vv. 7792ff).

In Statius, Hypomedon, one of the leaders of the Greeks, dies after raging in the terrible battle that began over Tydeus's body, almost drowning in the river Ismenus, because he had killed Ismenus's grandson, only emerging to be overcome by darts. In MS S, Hypomedon is a good leader, a clever organizer, who takes an army to Bulgaria for much-needed food, leads it through a long trip and a river battle, with strategic ploys like dragging branches to raise dust and give the illusion of a great army, until the Thebans flee and Hypomedon is able to bring the food back to the Greeks. He dies later, drowning in a river as he fights the Thebans (vv. 10845–47). Even Capaneus, another leader of the Greeks, is not as wild as in Statius. He is always ready to fight, discounting Amphiaraus's dire predictions though they will all prove to be true, because he wants the war. He is always a strong supporter of the king in MS S, but not the blasphemer he is in the Latin (though he is in MSS B and C of the *Roman de Thèbes*); he is not therefore killed by a thunderbolt from angry gods he has challenged, but by a boulder thrown down by the enemy at end of the war.

The Greek heroes all serve as respected and loyal leaders in the army Adrastus heads in MS S, and Adrastus is an effective leader, canny and conciliatory, in a twelfth-century mode. He is first introduced as a "bons reis" (v. 730), a contrast to the Theban king, Eteocles, "malveis reis" (v. 1985). Adrastus is a cultured man, as suggested by the tent described above; he can be gentle and patient as he is with the rudeness of Polynices and Tydeus when he tries to make peace between them. He rushes down to stop their battle without a cloak, perhaps suggesting a man of action rather than pomp. But he can be clever: he recognizes the two heroes as the promised husbands of his daughters and knows he can now make the marriages without expense (vv. 1128–29). In the war, he tries to cut the Thebans off from water (v. 5318), but not to kill them in their sleep as he does in Statius (Book 10); to keep the army's spirits up, the French Adrastus orders the old men to show their grey beards and fight (v. 4940) to compete with the youth. The old men are described as "sheep" presumably because of their white hair (vv. 5001, 5036) and the women who come at the end for the men's bodies also seem like sheep (v. 11675), though both fight as needed, a comment perhaps on the human side of the Greek army. When Tydeus is killed, Adrastus keeps Polynices alive by urging him to avenge the death rather than commit suicide, and he keeps Tydeus's men with the army by offering his new-born son (Adrastus's grandson) to the other grandfather, preserving his line. In the end, he loses the whole army but for three men, himself, Capaneus who will be killed in the final battle for Thebes, and one man he sends back as a messenger to Greece, which brings the Greek women to Thebes. Though Adrastus wants to kill himself, he is stopped by Capaneus, remains to the end, and sees Thebes destroyed by Theseus and the army of Greek women, and it is he, not the women as in Statius, who persuades Theseus to help. In Statius, Adrastus seems less effective and less important: he depends on omens in the choice of husbands for his daughters, and in accepting Amphiaraus's negative view of the proposed war; he does makes peace between Lycurgus and Hypsipyle after Lycurgus's son was killed in her care, but he counsels the stealthy killing of the sleeping Thebans (Book 10), in contrast to Capaneus who wants to fight openly. After he fails to separate Eteocles and Polynices, even offering his kingdom to Polynices, a good gesture but futile at that point, he flees the battle (Book 11, vv. 439ff), and dies.

There seem to be no comparable leaders on the Theban side. The man who stands out as most powerful after the king is Creon, who will take over when Eteocles dies in both poems, but he is not a much better man. He is rich and powerful in MS S, with many vassals, and speaks bluntly to Eteocles, but his motives are questionable. At first in the trial of Dares, he wants a delay for him (v. 9335), then he wants him declared innocent (v. 9371), but later he argues against him (v. 10104). He is chosen as the new king after both brothers die because he is of the royal line. In Statius, when he urges Eteocles to fight Polynices, he is accused of wanting the crown, which is apparently true. His son commits suicide on the walls of the city so his blood can purify them, a sacrifice recommended by Tiresias and accepted by Creon. He tells Oedipus, when he is grieving over the bodies of his sons, to leave the city, and refuses burial to the brothers; he will not allow any Greek to be buried, and wants to execute Polynices's widow, Argia, and his sister, Antigone, for tending to his body. Creon's cruelty is less explicit in MS S, but he lets the Greek bodies be devoured by dogs, while the Thebans are buried, and he refuses Theseus's demand for the bodies. Theseus defeats Creon in both Statius and MS S, but in the French, Theseus has his head cut off, an execution that emphasizes his criminal behavior.

Theseus, Duke of Athens, (who was mentioned in Hypsipyle's story in Statius Book 5, v. 432), appears at the end of both poems as a deus ex machina, a totally independent figure. In MS C, he is Adrastus's vassal but not in MS S, where he is en route to punish a king who was his vassal and has broken his oath of loyalty (vv. 11751–52). He tells Creon to release the unburied bodies and when Creon refuses, Theseus kills him, in battle in Statius, by execution as a criminal in MS S. He puts things right, has the bodies of the dead fighters given to the women and builds a tomb for the brothers. In Statius, Theseus is fresh from his victory over the Amazons, and brings Hippolyte in his train, which seems like a way to keep women in their place, countering the example of the Greek army of women who help him to conquer Thebes.

There are even greater differences in the treatment of the two figures who precipitate the action of the poems, the warring brothers, Polynices and Eteocles. In Statius, they are described as twin tyrants, "geminis . . . tyrannis" (Book 1, v. 34) and their actions are caused more by the gods than by their evil impulses. In MS S, they begin as similar, "deux friers" (v. 19), "felon et esragié" (v. 28) because of the sin to which they owed their life, which causes them to act against nature (v. 503), to destroy their city, their kingdom, and others. They are evil sons who mock the blinded Oedipus and trample his eyes; they are cursed by him together and doomed to discord. But the tone quickly shifts in MS S after Polynices's exile and marriage, when Eteocles plots treason ("traïson," v. 1285, "grant traïson," v. 1286) against him. Then Polynices becomes more of a hero: he is called "li frans home" [the noble brother] (v. 1288) while Eteocles is the villain and a tyrant. In both poems, the brothers agree to alternate as king, the barons choosing the elder in MS S, following the normal medieval practice; interestingly, perhaps to counter this, Tydeus will let Polynices choose the elder sister as his bride. In Statius, fate plays a larger role: Polynices loses by lot, and the Thebans do not all agree with the outcome; the shade of Laius is used by the gods to incite Eteocles to renege on his promise, in the light of Polynices's marriage, which with Greek wealth and power behind him would enable him to seize the rule permanently (*Thebaid* Book 2, vv. 108–10); meanwhile Polynices broods over his desire to hold power, and feels deserted by the gods and his friends. In MS S, the responsibility is Eteocles's; he plots treason on his own, taking the marriage as an attack on him, but knowing there will be trouble if he wrongs Polynices as he intends (1210–11). His advisors tell him to get friends, reinforce his defenses, cultivate men, govern justly and generously, all of which should be advice on how to rule well, but it is used as the way to keep power. Eteocles, knowing some of his vassals would betray him if they could (v. 3805, and again vv. 8992ff), plots the death of his brother who in MS S does not suspect him, though Tydeus does.

In both poems, Eteocles is seen as a tyrant. In Statius, he is said to be ready for any crime, with a greedy eye towards rich Argos. When Tydeus tells him he should have sent for his brother at the end of his term, Eteocles takes Tydeus's tone as evidence of Polynices's hostility and Tydeus says the crime of race works in him. In MS S, the effects of his vicious nature on his people, his bad governing, important issues to a medieval audience, are emphasized. His tyranny is revealed at first in his uncontrolled anger: his furious reaction to Tydeus's presentation of Polynices's claim, his inexcusable plot to ambush and kill the messenger.

For that act of unjustified revenge, he sacrifices fifty of his men, angering their families and weakening his own position: remembering that attack, none of his men is willing to go as a messenger to the Greek camp. Later his anger toward a powerful vassal, Dares the Red[haired] (Daires li Rous) plays into Dares's hands, giving him the excuse he wants to declare their bonds broken. His own mother, Jocasta, when asked by Adrastus why Eteocles's men stay with him, tells him they have no choice (vv. 4436ff), that he took possession as the elder, but now he keeps his men tight and holds his position by force, with little cover of right.

In the service of a bad king, men commit bad actions; fifty of Eteocles's men agree to go out to ambush the messenger, Tydeus, a horrendous crime in both cultures. In MS S, the attack is called treason, in Statius, Eteocles is condemned for plotting an unspeakable deception, "fraudis nefandae" (Book 2, vv. 482ff), against a legate, a holy name "sanctum nomen" (Book 2, v. 486) to peoples through the ages. In MS S, the comparisons with Roland make Tydeus seem a martyr and the earlier description of the Sphinx-figure as a devil connects Eteocles and his men to the Devil. The one attacker who is left alive condemns Eteocles as a bad king who should never have been born (vv. 1962, 1985) and kills himself rather than be killed by Eteocles after he had been spared by a man like Tydeus; his blood spurts on the king emphasizing his guilt. In a kind of footnote to the idea that only bad men can serve Eteocles, we later learn that someone Adrastus had expelled and disinherited, presumably for a crime, came to Thebes and became a confidante of the king, his "privez et druz" (v. 7207). Eteocles seems to want only such men around him; we are told he wants revenge upon those who disagree with him (vv. 3944, 4005). In both poems, he seems incapable of the kind of attachment Polynices has to Tydeus ("melior mihi frater," *Thebaid*, Book 9, v. 53).

Perhaps that is why Eteocles is so excessively hostile to Tydeus. There is a struggle to get Tydeus's body in both Statius and MS S; in the French, Eteocles wants to steal the corpse to feed it to dogs. Hypomedon protects it but Eteocles sends him a false message that Adrastus needs help (v. 7591); in Statius it is Tisiphone who distracts Hypomedon, letting Eteocles's men seize the corpse, which is dragged by serfs. But Eteocles's treatment of his own brother at their last encounter is the final coup. In Statius, Tisiphone wants to end the war with the brothers' duel; Jocasta tries to stop Eteocles, and Antigone to stop Polynices, but forces intervene. When Eteocles falls, he pretends to die in order to kill Polynices which is bad enough, but it is made worse in MS S by the contrast between the actions of the two brothers. Polynices and Eteocles meet by accident and Polynices fatally strikes Eteocles; then, moved by pity (v. 11421), he goes to comfort him, takes him in his arms and grieves over him. But Eteocles still has the strength and hatred to stab him with his sword.

There is a brief moment during the French poem in which we see a different side of Eteocles, when he is moved by love for Salamander, Dares the Red's daughter, in which the author might be offering us a glimpse of how courtliness might, if practiced, counter the destructive elements of the old heroic order. Eteocles rides out with two companions to do deeds of love for her. Facing Parthenopeus, Antigone's fiance, and his companion, Eteocles tries to keep his third man out of the fight, but fails, and Parthenopeus is killed. Eteocles frees Parthenopeus's companion for his sake and brings the body of Parthenopeus back to Thebes for honorable burial. But this better side of Eteocles, caused by romantic love, is completely eclipsed by his hatred for his brother. Even after death, the two cannot be reconciled. The flame from Eteocles's funeral pyre rejects Polynices in Statius; in MS S, again, the hostility is even stronger: the bodies cannot be buried together, they thrust themselves out of the ground; they cannot be burned together, the flames fight, the ashes cause their urns to fight, until Theseus has them sealed into a tomb (vv. 11993ff).

The fraternal struggle for succession to the throne held several echoes of recent English history: the armed conflicts among the three sons of William the Conqueror, Robert Curthose (the eldest, but like Eteocles the least competent), William Rufus, and Henry I (described by Orderic Vitalis in Book 11 of the *Historia Ecclesiastica*),[17] beginning during the lifetime of their father and continuing for decades until only Henry was left; and the even more recent conflict between Henry's daughter and chosen heir the Empress Mathilde, and her first cousin, Stephen of Blois. The eventual settlement gave Stephen the throne but made Mathilde's son, Henry of Anjou, his successor, as Henry II, in 1154. Henry had married Eleanor of Aquitaine, upon her divorce from Louis VII of France, a marriage which loosely linked England, Normandy, Anjou, and Aquitaine in what is sometimes referred to by modern scholars as an "Angevin empire," and created enmity between Henry and Louis.[18] Polynices, had he survived the war, would have conquered Thebes with a foreign force, but, like Henry, with a native claim to the throne.

Fraternal relations of various kinds are a letimotif through the French poem, all contrasts with the two protagonists. There is the intense mutual devotion of the brothers-in-law, Tydeus and Polynices, a clear counter to the hostile relation between the blood brothers, Eteocles and Polynices. Tydeus and Polynices begin as enemies in exile, both fratricides, one past, one future; they marry sisters, and remain devoted to each other, Tydeus taking on a dangerous mission to protect Polynices, Polynices wanting to commit suicide when Tydeus is killed; in a nasty twist, Polynices's fraternal impulse to embrace his dying brother becomes an act of [unintentional] suicide. There is the deep love between two brothers who kill each other by accident in combat (vv. 6208ff); they are on opposite sides because the elder joined Polynices, the younger stayed with Eteocles, and they do not

[17] *The Ecclesiastical History of Orderic Vitalis*, Vol. VI, ed. and trans. Marjorie Chibnall (Oxford: Clarendon Press, 1978).

[18] See Robert Bartlett, *England Under the Norman and Angevin Kings, 1075–1225*, The New Oxford History of England (Oxford: Clarendon Press, 2000).

recognize each other when they meet in battle until they have fatally wounded each other. Then they weep and grieve, each more for the other than for himself, "car molt erent de bone fei, / il s'entramoent a merveille" [for they were of very good faith and loved one another wondrously] (vv. 6249–50). Shortly thereafter (vv. 6390ff), Polynices is captured by another pair of brothers, these two working together, who present a moral contrast. They are fighting on Eteocles's side, even though they were wrongfully ("a tort") disinherited by him, because he was envious of their chivalry (vv. 6402–6). The elder argues that if they deliver Polynices to Eteocles, the war will be over and he will exile them for good and he also has an obligation to Polynices, but he refuses to accept a ransom from Polynices, much as he could use the money, because that would conflict with his feudal obligations, so they set him free.

It remains to look at a group of characters who play a much larger role in the French poem than in Statius's *Thebaid*, the women. Women for the most part work to reconcile through diplomacy, while men argue and fight, another probable reflection of contemporary culture where women played a much greater role in political life than in Roman antiquity.[19] Jocasta is the queen of Thebes at the beginning and at the end of the French poem and her grief for her children, the loss of her baby, Oedipus, and the death of her sons Polynices and Eteocles, bookends the story. She marries her son because she is worried about holding her land (v. 272) and her men advise her to take him, the hero who freed the land from the Sphinx. There is the suggestion of sexual attraction, since she sleeps with him after a night of celebration of his victory, but the emphasis seems to be on the public need. Does that remove some of the guilt of incest from her life? The sin is blamed for the actions of the men, but her actions as queen are never questioned. Jocasta, like Eleanor of Aquitaine, is older than her second husband, but has several children with him.[20] Perhaps the complications of Jocasta's sec-

---

[19] Women in power, rulers, regents, consorts, are more likely to negotiate settlements than to take military action, though they may do that as well. For general background, see Joan M. Ferrante, *To the Glory of her Sex. Women's Roles in the Composition of Medieval Texts* (Bloomington and Indianapolis: Indiana University Press, 1997), chaps. 1 and 3; for examples, see the biographies and letters of the following women in *Epistolae* (http://epistolae.ccnmtl.columbia.edu), Adela of Blois, Adelaide of Turin and Susa, Agnes of Poitiers, Empress, Beatrice of Upper Lorraine, Eleanor of Aquitaine, Matilda, Empress and Domina of England, Matilda of Boulogne, Queen of England, Matilda of Scotland, Queen of England, Matilda of Tuscany, and Theophanu, Empress of the Holy Roman Empire.

[20] Jocasta had one child with Laius and has four with Oedipus, in each case, half of Eleanor's progeny from her two marriages. In the version of the *Roman de Thèbes* found in MS A the extended description of Argia and Deiphyle, the daughters of Adrastus, contains these lines (969–72), in Léopold Constans, ed., *Le roman de Thèbes*, SATF 30, 2 vols (Paris: Firmin Didot, 1890): "Bouches ont dreites et reiaus,/ Les denz menuz , blans et egaus; / Mieus vaut lor ris et lor baisiers / Que ne fait Londres ne Peitiers [They had win-

ond marriage make Eleanor's divorce and remarriage seem less transgressive. Jocasta is a more respected and dignified figure in MS S than in Statius, where she appears disheveled when she appeals to Greeks for an agreement and then flees when battle breaks out. At the end, she tries to stop the battle of the brothers, but a fury intervenes and when she can do nothing further, she kills herself. In MS S, though she cannot finally stop the violence, she consistently works to avoid fighting and dissension, mediating between hostile parties, and on rare occasion she succeeds. When the men of Eteocles's court are afraid to go to Polynices, she takes on the mission and goes well-dressed as befits a queen, with her two daughters, the women doing what the men fail to do, "por sofraite de prodomes / iert cist messages faiz par domes" [For lack of worthy men, women will take the message] (vv. 4098–99).

That mission fails, as does her attempt to intervene between Eteocles and Creon, but when Eteocles wants to execute Dares for treason, she helps to persuade him to accept Salamander and pardon her father, who has many powerful allies, as she points out. Understanding such realities in political situations, she explains to Adrastus why Eteocles's men support him: that he began with right on his side as the elder brother, but now he governs them with fear and force (vv. 4436ff). Her judgment and authority seem to be respected on the Theban side: Meleages's men want Polynices to confer with Eteocles and his mother before they decide what to do about Monflor (vv. 3134–35). And though it will come to naught in the end, she plays what is often a woman's dynastic role in matchmaking, approving the union between Antigone and Parthenopeus, and guaranteeing Salamander's promise to Eteocles.

Jocasta's daughters, Ismene and Antigone, have somewhat larger roles in MS S, as one would expect, but they are mainly in the courtly vein. Both of them have lovers, whom they watch fighting; they laugh and dispute about them, and take pride in their deeds. Ismene, who can enjoy the company of her love, Atys, because he is Theban, loses him first. Young and reckless, he is killed because he is showing off his beautiful body without armor and insists on fighting the mighty Tydeus, who would spare him; Antigone's Parthenopeus, a Greek, is killed much later, the victim of Eteocles's desire to perform for his lady. Much

---

ning, regal smiles, their teeth small, white and even: their smiles and kisses were worth more than London or Poitiers]—a comparison that has to be taken as a reference to Eleanor. The equivalent lines in S (1070–71) are: "mielz vaut lor ris et lour baisiers / que ne fait d'autres cent milliers" [their smiles and their kisses are worth more than those of a hundred thousand others]. For a summary and critique of the use made of these lines by previous scholars in attempting to establish a date for the *Roman de Thèbes* see Aimé Petit, "*Mieus vaut lor ris et lor baisiers/ que ne fait Londres ne Peitiers*. Tradition manuscrite et critique littéraire: note sur le *Roman de Thèbes* et *Cligès*," *Bien dire et bien apprendre* 5 (1987), 123–28, repr. *Aux origines du roman*, 101–6.

is made of Ismene's grief (vv. 6937ff),[21] her desire to become a nun, and her request that Eteocles found an abbey for Atys's soul (vv. 7063–70). In Statius, the episode is more subdued: Ismene dreams of marriage with her fiance, whom she says she scarcely knew, but she can be comforted if their home can be safe, the Greeks depart, and the brothers reconciled; when she sees him dying, she closes his eyes and gives vent to sighs and tears (*Thebaid*, Book 8, vv. 634ff). Antigone flirts with Parthenopeus during her visit to the Greek camp, accepts his love, and the tokens he sends her during battle, and fears for him when she sees him fighting, but when he dies, her grief is not mentioned. The focus is instead on others: Eteocles's distress, both that one of his men was responsible and that he had lost a future brother-in-law; on the grief of his companion Dorcas, and on Parthenopeus's tender message to his young mother. Antigone's most important action in the poem seems to be to save Dares by making the match between his daughter and her brother, an act of diplomacy but within the courtly realm. She plays no role at the end of MS S, unlike her rather heroic stature at the end of Statius's poem in which she almost succeeds in stopping Polynices from fighting Eteocles, saves her father from a worse exile imposed by Creon, protects her brother's body beside his widow, Argia, and is condemned to death by Creon.

Argia and Deiphyle, the daughters of Adrastus married to Polynices and Tydeus, are also treated like "romance" heroines avant-la-lettre at the beginning of MS S, with long descriptions of their beauty and their dress, but at the end, they become part of the great army of women who besiege Thebes. When Adrastus's messenger brings the bad news back and the Greek women come to the palace to consult the two daughters, first they grieve, then they decide to go en masse to Thebes to bury their men. They set out, barefoot and disheveled, and the trip is very hard but after they meet Theseus, and Creon refuses to give them the bodies, they join in the attack on the city, climbing the walls, attacking with hammers and their own nails. We had been told at the beginning of the poem that the Greek women would destroy Thebes (vv. 519ff), so they finally accomplish, with

21 The literary lament, or *planctus*, reaches its twelfth-century apogee in six such poems by Peter Abelard, presented as the utterance of Biblical figures. See Winthrop Wetherbee, "Literary Works," in *The Cambridge Companion to Abelard*, ed. Jeffrey E. Brower and Kevin Guilfoy (Cambridge: Cambridge University Press, 2004), 60–62. With respect to the laments of Argia, Ismene, Antigone, and Tydeus, it is worth noting that medieval school boys, as part of their primary school education in Latin, frequently had to do exercises writing themselves into the position of the various classical heroes and heroines. See Marjorie Woods, "Boys Will Be Women: Musings on Classroom Nostalgia and the Chaucerian Audience(s)," in *Speaking Images: Essays in Honor of V. A. Kolve*, ed. Robert F. Yeager and Charlotte C. Morse (Asheville, NC: Pegasus Press, 2001), 143–66; Woods, "Rape and the Pedagogical Rhetoric of Sexual Violence," in *Criticism and Dissent in the Middle Ages*, ed. Rita Copeland (Cambridge: Cambridge University Press, 1996), 56–86.

Theseus's help, what their men had not been able to do. In Statius, the daughters appear at their father's command, but they are not described except for modest pallor and a blush (Book 1, v. 537) and a maidenly fear before the wedding (Book 2, v. 229). They worry for their husbands when they go off, but it is not until the end, when they come to Thebes at the head of the women of Argos, distraught with grief, that Argia takes on an independent role. She voices her plea to Thebes to give up Polynices's body, wanders through the battlefield in the dark, helped by Juno who persuades the moon to shine for her, laments over the body when she finds it, until Antigone joins her and they lament together and attempt to burn the body before they are arrested and led away in shackles (Book 12). Like Antigone, she becomes a tragic heroine at the end.

Hypsipyle is the one significant woman not directly connected to the main story, but she appears in both poems to help the Greek army when it needs water. In both she is a victim of others' mistreatment, living in exile as slave of a king, caring for his infant, but the background of the exile differs in the two stories. Dominating Book 5 of the *Thebaid*, she appears beautiful in her grief, hair disheveled, poorly dressed, but regal, and recounts the rebellion of the women of Lemnos and the murder of their men in some detail, her own God-inspired rescue of her father, the advent of Jason and his men, renewed sexual relations in Lemnos, Jason's promise of fidelity and subsequent abandonment of her and their twin sons. The twin sons appear at the end of the episode as she is to be executed for the death of the infant, and with Adrastus's help they save her, brothers making up for the sins of their father in contrast to the protagonists who compounded them. The French version omits the episode with Jason and the sons, and focuses on her attempt to save her father whom she was supposed to kill, as the other women do. This picks up the subtheme of patricide from the Oedipus story that began the poem, reminding us of the unnaturalness of the Polynices/Eteocles story, the murder of the father that led to their incestuous conceptions, the cruel treatment by them of their father and the eventual war between them. The death of the baby Hypsipyle was supposed to be tending when she went to the aid of strangers—a similar impulse of piety in MS S and/or continued susceptibility to the wiles of men, particularly in Statius?—also reminds us of the intended fate of the abandoned baby Oedipus, saved by servants and strangers. This baby is killed accidentally in Statius, in MS S it is by the act of an evil serpent.

The baby's mother appears in Statius grieving for her child, as other women do in the Latin poem, where mothers appear more often, if only in the background: if they are human, they grieve for their sons—Creon's son is mourned in Statius by his mother, who does not appear in MS S—if they are divine or nymphs, they take action or move others to action for their sons, though they cannot save them from their fate. Crenaeus's mother, a nymph, gets her father, the river Ismenos, to avenge her son's death by rising to drown Hypomedon or bring him to the point of death. Parthenopeus's mother, Atalanta, tries but fails to keep her son from going to war; a follower of Diana, she gets her help if only to win glory for him before he dies. The Thebans are moved to try not to kill him, remembering their own sons, but he attacks fiercely and is wounded; as he dies, he sends a loving message to his mother, to be broken to her gently (*Thebaid* bk. 9, vv. 885ff). In the French, too, Parthenopeus sends a tender message to his young mother telling her not to grieve too much, but the message also includes practical advice for her and their land, that she should remarry soon since she is so young —only eleven years older than he and seemed more a sister than a mother —and that she take care of his men (vv. 11087ff). The political role of women that is suggested here and depicted in Jocasta's story in S is absent from the *Thebaid*. With the exception of Amphiaraus's wife, who takes the gift of a necklace to betray her husband in Book 4 of Statius, but does not appear in MS S, individual women are examples only of suffering and devotion. Acting in groups, however, like the women of Lemnos who kill all their men, however provoked, they are condemned. There is even an implicit condemnation of the warring Amazons, who appear at the end of Statius's poem as Theseus's conquered prisoners, their queen, Hippolyte, reduced to a demure and pregnant wife. Neither group of women is allowed the heroic stature of the warring armies.

The women in MS S are never heroic, as Antigone and even Argia are at the end of the *Thebaid*, but they are present and often forceful in their mediating roles on the political scene, as women often were in medieval life, and at the end of the poem, in sharp contrast to the *Thebaid*, an army ("ost," v. 11894) of Greek women is a featured player in the final episodes, presented most sympathetically. When the message of defeat and almost complete destruction of the Greek army is brought back to Argos, the women first grieve publicly, weeping and crying out, tearing their hair, breaking their rings, some even falling dead from sorrow. But then they form an assembly (a "parlemenz," v. 11635) and go to consult the daughters of the king, the authority figures in the absence of their father, all functioning essentially as a female government by default. Together they decide to go to Thebes to find the unburied bodies; leaving barefoot and disheveled, their army cannot march very fast, but after they meet first Adrastus turning him back with them to Thebes, then Theseus who agrees to obtain the bodies, they march in ranks and attack the walls with steel mallets and tear out stones with their nails, not caring if they are wounded or killed. They inspire not condemnation, but pity and sympathy, even tears, from Theseus's army, and once they have the bodies of their fallen men, they weep and grieve over them very gently ("molt doucement," v. 11982), all passion spent. Their story is a powerful indictment of the devastating war.

E. *Courtoisie*

The political and diplomatic roles women can play in MS S, as regents for their lands when their husbands or sons are killed, as mediators between hostile forces or individuals, even as voices to be heard on public actions, are an addition to the story, not found in Statius. This is more a reflection of a different political reality in the Middle Ages than of the cultural shift towards *courtoisie*, but the two are sometimes connected in the poem offering the hope that courtly elements like romantic love might work against the male impulse to violence. When Jocasta goes to the Greek camp to seek a peaceful solution from her son Polynices, bringing her two daughters, it becomes an occasion for flirtation between them and the young men of the opposing army, and the beginning of a romance between Antigone and Parthenopeus that continues through the story and makes Antigone sympathetic to the Greeks. In the attempt to keep Eteocles from a serious political mistake, the execution of the powerfully connected Dares for treason, Antigone uses her brother's love for Dares's daughter to change his mind.

There is perhaps a civilizing aspect to the attention to courtly details, descriptions of the beauty of the young women, and some of the young men,[22] their elegant clothes and their horses' caparisons, Antigone and Salamander sitting together sewing (vv. 10965–66), the delights of lying in bed together "nu a nu," (v. 1078) ladies giving their men their sleeves to carry into battle as though it were only a tourney. But in fact, the desire to show off to their ladies also impels the men to fight more recklessly. It is said early on of the young bachelors in Eteocles's household: "Chescuns coveite pur s'amie / los de faire chevalrie" [Each one desires to win renown through chivalry for his beloved] (vv. 1268–69), they are impatient to fight to impress their ladies; the young men in the Greek army are also anxious to fight, opposed to a peace until saddles are emptied, with the girls watching (vv. 4469–74). Eteocles goes out without a hauberk to do deeds for his lady, which leads indirectly to the death of Parthenopeus; Atys goes out without armor to show off his beautiful body and insists on fighting nonetheless and is killed. Sexual and aggressive energy is often paired: the men who flee from Tydeus are taunted with: "Ou sont les granz chevaleries / dont vous vantez a vos amies?" [Where are the great blows you brag about at the hearth?] (vv. 1842–43). The young women in love take pleasure in their lovers' prowess and in watching them fight. Ismene is ready to sleep with Atys because of his prowess (vv. 4782–91), indeed, she seems to relish the idea of the fighting even during the peace mission, being "contrariose" (vv. 4475–82). One wonders if the episode of the tame viper in MS S is a comment on the complications of sex and aggression. The viper is female but also a male phallic symbol, a peaceful and cherished creature and a willing drinking companion, killed by young men of the Greek army who assume she is wild, which leads to yet another battle, breaking a truce (vv. 4604 ff). In Statius, there is a pair of tigers who had been yoked to a war chariot, but once released, they wandered tame among people and cattle. They are, like

[22] Such description was a popular subject of school exercises in accord with classical rhetoric and new treatises such as those of Mathew of Vendome (*Ars versificatoria*) and Geoffrey of Vinsauf (*Poetria nova*) and becomes a feature of twelfth-century romance texts.

the human characters in the poem, roused by a fury to their former madness and attack men until they are killed by Aconteus, who is then killed by a votary of Bacchus in revenge (*Thebaid* Book 7, vv. 564ff).

F. Feudal Issues

Women may play a role in inspiring aggressive action, as well as in mediation and diplomacy, but they do not face the complications of feudal loyalties and obligations and rivalries, of perjury and treason, that men do. Feudal bonds are complicated, there are conflicting loyalties that make it hard to take a moral stand, loyalties that may also run counter to self interest. Eteocles's refusal to abide by his promise to share rule with his brother in alternate years puts his men in an impossible bind. Those who feel a loyalty or are otherwise obligated to him are forced to perjure the oath they took to uphold that original decision: early on, Tydeus points out that Eteocles has perjured himself by refusing to hand over the realm, which would release his barons from their obligations to him (vv. 1529ff), and encourages them to come over to Polynices, but the barons, though upset, are afraid of Eteocles's wrath and do not answer. The defenders of Monflor are caught in the same bind; Meleages refuses to act without consulting his barons, but the barons loyal to Eteocles say it would be treason to their lord to give the tower to Polynices, unless Eteocles agrees.

After Monflor is taken, the Thebans argue how to proceed, Eteocles wonders if he should make a deal (vv. 3872ff); one of his men tells him not to give up without a fight, another suggests offering an agreement to share, half each, but with Polynices giving homage to Eteocles; Jocasta advises sharing rather than losing everything, but keeping the city fortifications (v. 3886). Eteocles is furious but pretends to agree; his barons do not want a wrongful war, a "guerre a tort" (v. 3916), and curse the idea of war between brothers (v. 3922). When Polynices offers to free Dares's son if his father gives up his tower, father and mother have a similar debate. Dares is concerned with fealty, the mother says he has already perjured himself to Polynices by sticking with Eteocles; the father says they have to betray one or the other brother since they swore allegiance to both (v. 8388); arguing that treason against a lord is a worse crime than perjury, he determines to provoke Eteocles so he will break their bond and thus free Dares of his obligation to him. In the course of the long legal arguments over Dares's position in court (vv. 8579ff), Dares tells Eteocles to make peace with Polynices before he loses any more of his land and his men, reminding him that he swore an oath to Polynices and that the barons who stick with him are perjuring themselves. The king's physical attack on Dares solves the immediate problem, but after the tower is given up and retaken, Dares has to face a trial for treason, where the king's right to punish is balanced against the barons' right to judge, to make sure the king does not behave tyrannically. Othon excuses Dares because of Eteocles's responsibility, reminding him of his powerful kindred, and insists on a trial or postponement, any ploy to avoid condemning him (vv. 9159ff). He also reminds him of the need to have proof of guilt if he accuses someone of treason (vv. 9223ff) but others argue it was all a scheme to free his son, that he should have challenged the king before giving up his tower (vv. 9552ff, 9730–31, 9774ff). Jocasta, like Othon, reminds Eteocles that Dares has dangerous allies, and argues for a truce (vv. 10189ff), but the resolution comes only when Antigone offers Dares's daughter instead (v. 10269) and the barons are angry that the decision has been taken out of their hands.

The legal conflicts are argued in public at councils because the lord cannot act without the consent of his vassals, his barons. And the arguments on both sides are presented as having a certain validity. In Eteocles's court there is some desire to negotiate with Polynices to share the realm; Atys argues that it would be a loss of honor for Eteocles to give it up, but Othon notes the numerical advantage of the Greeks and the folly of going to war with them. On the Greek side, many would accept the offer of realm-sharing, though they do not like the idea of doing homage to Eteocles, but Tydeus who has experienced Theban treachery, argues against it, saying that as soon as the Greeks left, the Thebans would kill Polynices and then it would be too late to get the Greek host back. He also points out the glory to be achieved by defeating Thebes, and he is supported by Capaneus and Adrastus, who rejects anything but victory over Thebes and the installation of Polynices as king in accord with the original deal between the brothers. Adrastus summons the Greek barons to decide whether to leave after Amphiaraus is killed (v. 5418); some see the act as God's will against the war, but one says if God wants to destroy us he can do it anywhere and suggests instead that they choose a new bishop to assuage God's anger.

Honor and glory, to be won or lost by winning a war or withdrawing from it, play their part in the public arguments. The heroic code is a complication within the feudal system. Men are afraid of being called cowards, seeing that as a danger of negotiations for peace. When Amphiaraus prophesies a bad end to war, Capaneus calls him a coward and the Greeks side with Capaneus. The danger of shame is ever present, alongside the need to live up to one's lineage: the leader of the ambush against Tydeus tells those who try to flee to remember the proud deeds of their ancestors, the "geste fiere, / des estors et des vasselages / que touz jours fist vostre lignages" (vv. 1851–53). They are motivated by an idealized image of a warrior aristocracy: When Polynices mourns the dead Tydeus, Adrastus scolds him, telling him not to cry, but to take vengeance: women and children weep, knights strike great blows, "femme et enfant deivent plorer, / et chevalers granz colps doner" (vv. 7459–60).

II. The Manuscript

In medieval Europe, texts became known by being read privately or read aloud (recited) in public, Latin texts such as Statius's *Thebaid* primarily by the former method, vernacular texts like the *Roman de Thèbes* by both but, we may suppose, primarily by the latter, in court settings, often involving many auditors. (Chrétien de Troyes includes in his romance, *Le chevalier au lion* [Yvain], a presumably accurate example of a more intimate practice of reading aloud, a daughter reading a romance only to her parents.)[23]

Before the advent of printing, the written transmission of texts involved their being copied one at a time, and this process inevitably resulted in changes in the text—some intended, some inadvertent—from copy to copy (a process of instability in transmission dubbed *mouvance* by French manuscript scholars and theorists). Unintentional variance includes mistakes in copying (there were/are many types) and prior damage to the manuscript being copied, due to fire, floods, mice, and other uncontrollable mishaps. Intentional revision occurred when a copyist felt the need to correct a text's grammar, rhetoric, or historical accuracy; to replace a gap (or perceived gap) owing to any of the factors just mentioned; or to add or subtract material in a move designed to make the text more concise, more compendious, more comprehensible, or just more interesting and entertaining.[24] Beyond such procedures, however, it is important to note that people frequently adapted already established texts much more extensively, in order to use them for quite different purposes and for different audiences. In such cases, adaptation is often radical and must be considered not as tampering, but as a vigorous cultural practice analogous to the modes of *translatio* (summarized on pp. 2–4, above) that governed the rendering of classical narratives *en romanz* (in vernacular adaptation).

The problem in distinguishing between additions and removals in considering the *mouvance* obvious among *Thèbes* manuscripts (to be described below) is the lack of any documented chronology of the extant versions of its text. (The respective age of the manuscripts, insofar as that can be determined, provides no guide, as all are copies of an unknown sequence of earlier copies.) For example: two of the manuscripts (see the descriptions below), related descendants of an earlier exemplar, contain near their conclusion a 750-line episode in which Capaneus, one of the Greek chieftains, leads a charge against the walls of Thebes while its inhabitants are distracted by a festival. Having breached the wall, Capaneus prepares to initiate a slaughter within the city, in the process defying its supposedly

---

23 Chrétien de Troyes, *Le Chevalier au lion [Yvain]*, ed. Mario Roques, CFMA 89 (Paris: Champion, 1965), vv. 5352–66.

24 See e.g., Sylvia Huot, "The manuscript context of medieval romance," in *The Cambridge Companion to Medieval Romance*, ed. Roberta L. Krueger (Cambridge: University Press, 2000), 60–63.

tutelary gods, a sacrilege which so arouses (and terrifies) the Olympians that they convince Jupiter, their monarch, to destroy with his lightning bolt the monstrous blasphemer (whom this episode, unlike the rest of the *roman*, depicts as a giant). This "Capaneid" within the vernacular text—based on the destruction in the *Thebaid* of a Capaneus consistently antagonistic to the gods—is generally considered by its editors and students a later addition to an earlier (original?) version of the *Roman de Thèbes* in which Capaneus is stripped of his impiety, becomes one of three survivors of the last Greek attack on Thebes, and is killed only while taking part in Theseus's mission of vengeance against Creon for the latter's refusal to allow decent burial to the Greek dead. (This is the version in the manuscript here translated; more below on the extant manuscripts.) In other words, in this interpretation of the evidence, an earlier version of the *roman* departed from the *Thebaid* by a process of subtraction, and a subsequent one "repaired" the oversight by a Statius-inspired supplement. But subsequent evidence as yet undiscovered might reverse this judgment.

A second example reveals a quite different profile: the episode centered on Dares the Red (Daires li Rous), a baronial vassal of Eteocles who, thanks to his control of one of Thebes's seven towers, plays a crucial role in its defense, and a character without prior existence in the *Thebaid*. Dares, in order to ransom his son who has been captured in battle by Polynices, must surrender his tower to the besieging army, and find a way to do this without committing treason against his lord. We discuss this episode in some detail elsewhere in this Introduction; what is relevant here is that the episode in which Dares angers Eteocles, uses this as an excuse to surrender his tower, and is subsequently tried by the Theban barons for treason at the insistence of the furious king, not only constitutes an addition to the classical source of the *roman*—one that reflects tensions about loyalty and lineage within the political imagination of the twelfth-century warrior aristocracy—but also exists in the extant manuscripts in four different lengths: 872, 1267, 2678, and 2102 lines, respectively. This last figure represents the episode's extent in manuscript S, the one here translated, which, as discussed below, has been widely considered to preserve an early version, perhaps the earliest known, of the *Roman de Thèbes*. But that judgment cannot rule out the possibility that MS S's Dares episode incorporates additions to (or revisions of) some earlier iteration. A careful comparison of all extant versions of the episode, which might shed light on their relations or sequence, is beyond the scope of this introduction, and would in any case be rendered difficult by the lack of diplomatic editions of three of the manuscripts.[25] What is safe to say is that the transmission of the *Roman de Thèbes* across time and space resulted in considerable variance in the length and impact of the episode, thanks to the interventions of an unknown number of copyist/revisers.

[25] Cf. Constans, *Roman de Thèbes*, Vol. 2, for passages from the extant manuscripts he did not consider "original."

No easy formula can completely explain the process of transmission that underlies the extant manuscripts of our text—there were doubtless many more now lost to the ravages of time and circumstance. What we have in these manuscripts are versions of the story that differ in so many ways beyond the two examples just mentioned as to make it difficult, if not impossible, to speak of a single text, and therefore, of a single poet of the *Roman de Thèbes*; it may be better to think of the *romanz* adaptation(s) of Statius's *Thebaid* as constituting a project in *translatio studii*, one that may have extended beyond the twelfth century, with the contours of each iteration, while shaped in large part by the inherited narrative, given individuality by: its idiosyncratic response to the classical past; the implied theme of *translatio imperii*; the impact of desire on behavior and decision making; and the values and anxieties of the warrior aristocracy. (Not all recopyings of a text such as the *Roman de Thebes* were revisionary in nature; some could aim simply at accurate reproduction of the manuscript being copied, in which case the inevitable *mouvance* would, as noted above, be inadvertent in nature.) At the foundation of this "project" is the special situation of a known classical Latin "original," knowledge of which might cause a copyist—here become a full-fledged reviser or de facto collaborator—to modify, add, or even subtract materials, from a few lines to a whole incident, to bring the *roman antique* more in line with (or to remove it further from) its classical inspiration.

A. Manuscripts of the *Roman de Thèbes*

The manuscripts were given letter designations by Léopold Constans, still used today; the following descriptions follow Aimé Petit's Introduction to his reissue of the edition of MS C by Guy Reynaud de Lage.

A: Paris, Bibliothèque nationale de France (BnF), fr. 375 fol. 36r-67v; 14626 ll. End of 13th c.; followed by *Roman de Troie*, *Athis et Prophilias*, and *Roman d'Alexandre*.

B: Paris, BnF, fr. 60, fol. 1–41v, 10541 ll. Middle or end of the fourteenth c., followed by *Roman de Troie* and *Roman d'Eneas*.

C: Paris, BnF, fr. 784, fol. 1–67a, 10562 ll. Middle of the thirteenth c., followed by *Roman d'Eneas*. MSS B and C represent the short version, (its putative shared source, not extant, denominated x by Constans). As Petit puts it, MS B "presents very close to the same episodes and the same text as C, although it was not copied from C" (p. 8). These two manuscripts are written in a "langue littéraire" [literary language] (Petit, 8) based on the French of the Ile de France (central France), eliminating most of the linguistic evidence of the twelfth-century French in which the first *Roman de Thèbes* would have been written. According to Constans, MSS B and C exemplify a specific redaction of the poem, fundamentally close to the (hypothetical) original but differing from it in several ways, including a considerable number of individual readings, some significant omissions, and equally important additions or re-workings such as the funeral games held after the death of the child Achemorus, the dramatic destruction of Capaneus, and the journey of the women of Argos to Athens seeking Theseus's assistance.[26]

P: Geneva, Bibliotheque Bodmer 18, fol. 185a–268a, 13296 ll. End of thirteenth c., followed by *Roman de Troie* (previously in library of Sir Thomas Phillips at Cheltenham). Together with MS A, P belongs to the long version (y) of the *Roman de Thebes* (Constans), and MS P's version, according to Petit, is the source of the story of Thebes in the *Histoire ancien jusqu'a César*, compiled 1208–1213. Like A, P is written in the Picard dialect of Old/Middle French.

D: Fragments of the poem in a manuscript in Angers, Bibliotheque Municipale 26, fol. I and Iv (221 lines). Remains of a manuscript copied between 1180 and 1220 (according to Raynaud de Lage). Written in a southwest dialect, from near the Poitou (the area around Poitiers).

S: London, British Library Add. 34114 (formerly Spalding), fol. 164a–226d, 12059 ll., written in the French of England, late fourteenth c., for Henry Despenser, Bishop of Norwich, 1370–1406. The manuscript from which the present translation has been made. Despite the manuscript's late date and English provenance, it preserves, beneath its surface—that of the French of England—an earlier linguistic state of the text, the earliest among extant manuscripts, deriving from a version of the poem written in the west of France, in the Poitou "tres voisin des regions occitanes" [very near the regions of Provence]—that is, an area within the lands Eleanor of Acquitaine brought to her marriage with the future Henry II of England in 1152.) As Constans puts it, the manuscript "most often preserves twelfth-century orthography. . .. There are very few traces of an intervening thirteenth- or fourteenth-century [continental] French stage [of transmission]." (Quoted by Mora-Lebrun, 34, who adds [following the analysis of M. Nezirovic] that "MS S preserves intact several words or archaic forms eliminated throughout the remainder of the manuscript tradition.")

B. Editions of the *Roman de Thèbes*

As already mentioned, not all of the manuscripts have been given a modern edition. Constans's groundbreaking edition of 1890 is a "critical edition" made in accord with the editorial procedures generally accepted at the time: Constans

[26] Constans, *Roman de Thèbes*, Vol. 2, Intro., li.

used manuscript S as his base text, intervening frequently to omit passages he deemed accretions to a hypothetical original and to regularize grammar and spelling. As Mora-Lebrun puts it in her Introduction, "Aware of the importance of MS S as a textual witness but also of its metrical and graphical irregularities, Constans chose it as the base text of his edition but almost entirely rewrote it, thus providing a new version [of the *Roman de Thèbes*], 'version O,' distinct from all the extant manuscripts. Such an editorial procedure would not be acceptable today" (35). Instead, current editorial practice seeks to offer accurate presentations of individual manuscripts, featuring minimal corrections, mainly of obvious scribal errors. Constans's edition contains several appendices offering passages of varying extent from the other manuscripts when they contain material not in MS S. The result is a considerable achievement, but not an easy text to use.

MS A was edited too recently for use here: see *Le Roman de Thèbes. Manuscrit A (BnF, fr. 375)*, ed. Luca di Sabatino. Textes littéraires du Moyen Âge, 42 (Paris: Classiques Garnier, 2016).

MS C was edited with introduction and notes by Guy Reynaud de Lage, *Le roman de Thèbes*. CFMA 94, 98 (Paris: Champion, 1966, 1968); this edition, with reviewed text and revised introduction and bibliography and a facing-page modern French translation was reissued by Aimé Petit (Paris: Champion Classiques, 2008).

MS S was edited with introduction, notes, and facing page modern French translation, by Francine Mora-Lebrun, Le livre de poche (Paris: Lettres Gothiques, 1995).

C. Misplaced and Missing Lines in MS S

A major lacuna in the middle of folio 182r (after v. 3354, but not noted in the manuscript)[27] has the narrative leap from its unfinished description of the Greek army's siege of the fortress of Monflor to land in the middle of Jocasta's embassy, with her daughters Antigone and Ismene, from Eteocles to Polynices, seeking a settlement of the brothers' strife after the Greek host has arrived at the gates of Thebes. Two fragments of the missing segment exist further on in MS S's narrative, embedded within the Dares episode. Mora-Lebrun explains this state of affairs by the hypothesis that "notre copiste [of MS S] avait sans doute sous les yeux un manuscrit mutilé et mal relié; mais. . . il ne s'est pas risqué à le corriger" [the scribe of MS S was doubtless working from a mutilated, improperly bound manuscript which he was unwilling to correct] (34). Lines 3355–490 in Mora-Lebrun's edition (during which the Greeks mount a trick—a phony retreat and ambush—to draw out the castle's defenders and allow Greeks to enter and take it) are missing from MS S, and supplied from Constans's "version O"; 3491–627

[27] For convenience, line numbers in our discussion from pp. 28–32 refer to Mora's edition of MS S.

are moved to this point from their placement after 8598 in MS S; 3627–862 (during which Monflor is taken and the Greeks move on toward Thebes) are missing and supplied from Constans; 3863–3998 are moved here from their misplacement immediately after the section properly belonging at 3491–627; finally, 3999–4130, missing in MS S, are supplied from Constans. We have followed More-Lebrun in this rearrangement and filling out of the text given in MS S.

D. Selective Comparison of MSS C and S

A brief comparison of the two manuscripts of the *Roman de Thèbes* available in modern editions (MSS C and S) vividly demonstrates divergences between contributors to what we are calling the "project" of this narrative. Although there is little major variation between these two versions during their first 2000 lines—we can't know how many intermediate versions might have existed between C or S and a shared narrative source—there are many minor differences in particular words, names, and numbers; often C will omit a couplet in a passage of description or narration or within a speech. And then there are the much larger divergences.

Throughout the section of the *roman* (beginning at MS S 2180, MS C 2110) that brings the drought-stricken Greek host to the land of King Lycurgus and centers on the murder of the king's infant son by a venemous serpent, the consequent plight of the boy's nursemaid, Hypsiphile (who has momentarily abandoned her charge to lead the parched Greeks to a stream of fresh water), and the vengeance taken by the Greeks on the serpent—throughout this section, S and C consistently diverge, even at the level of couplets, reflecting divergent manuscript traditions or re-writings. Besides minor details (e.g., only MS S names the child, Archemorus, and has the serpent, after killing him by sticking his rod-like tongue into the child's belly, fall asleep next to his victim: a strikingly post-coital image), there are major differences in sequence: in S the Greeks destroy the serpent, led by Capaneus, who impales the creature on a tree trunk he's uprooted, and then pleads Hypsipyle's cause before the outraged king and his distraught wife (the dead child's mother), while in C Adrastus obtains Lycurgus's forgiveness of Hypsiphile before the Greeks seek out and destroy the serpent, the climactic blow in this version being an arrow shot by Parthonopeus. In all the extant manuscripts save S, the Greeks celebrate the destruction of the monster with funeral games (modeled by Statius on the *Aeneid*, and, behind Vergil's epic, on the *Iliad*); whereas in C the games occupy 162 lines (2687–2848 in Reynaud de Lage's edition), and their mention in S takes only three (2562–64 in Mora-Lebrun's edition).

We have already mentioned the extended episode in MS C of Capaneus's assault on Thebes and challenge to the gods, leading to his destruction by Jupiter—an episode, based in Statius, lacking in MS S—and the fact that each extant manuscript of the *Thèbes,* while adding the episode of Dares the Red to its

Statian inheritance, does so at very different lengths; with respect to the latter, MS C devotes 872, lines but MS S 2102, to Dares's stratagem and the debate among Eteocles's barons as to whether it deserves punishment as treason against the king—a debate never resolved but rather usurped by Jocasta's offering the king the sexual services of Dares's daughter in exchange for her father's acquittal. As an example of a passage in MS S but not MS C: MS S 9155–260 constitutes an extended dialogue between Eteocles and his baron Othon, Dares's chief defender, in which the latter warns his vengeance-seeking lord of the risks he takes in punishing Dares, by hanging or burning at the stake, without first letting his council of barons decide whether Dares has in fact committed treason, and then acting on their advice; the passage includes Othon's careful definition of treason (*li dreis de traïson* 9224) at the king's request, and his spelling out of how Dares's extended clan of relations will consider themselves dishonored, and thus alienated from Eteocles, if their kinsman is condemned without a fair judgment exercised by his peers. By balancing the precision of legal theory against the potential resentment of a powerful social caste that defines the world via the binary of honor and shame, this passage would capture the attention and stoke the interest of both *clercs* and *chevaliers* in its original audience.

Other additions to the Dares episode in S: 8413–512 [8425 missing] [8632–36 missing, lacuna filled in from C], 8721–32; 8805–920; 8933–63; 9001–81; 9127–35; 9155–260; 9301–8; 9381–88; 9399–548; 9561–10090; 10101–12; 10225–35; 10605–18; 10939–53.

In contrast to the absence in MS S of the games marking the Greeks' triumph over the serpent who killed young Archemorus, MS S adds a good deal of material to another moment firmly based in the *Thebaid:* the death of Amphiaraus, King Adrastus's seer and the high priest of the Argians (whose role and appearance the *Roman de Thèbes* assimilates to that of a Christian bishop). Having prophesied his own death, along with that of most of the Greek host, to Adrastus before the expedition sets out for Thebes, Amphiaraus spends the last day of his life in battle outside Thebes, riding in a chariot decorated "par art et par enchantement" [by art and magic] (v. 5051), i.e., by the rhetorical skill and knowledge of a learned cleric, with images of the nine spheres comprising the universe; the earth, its lands and seas teeming with life; the seven liberal arts; and the mythological battle between the gods on Olympus and the giants who sought to oust them, storming the heavens by piling mountains atop each other. Thus far, both MS S and MS C, but MS S also includes on the chariot a vivid, literally impossible dramatization of the strife of gods and giants, with insults hurled back and forth between the combatants, and an account of the gods' conversation, a synesthesia not literally possible to portray. Then (again MS C and MS S agree), as Amphiaraus predicted, the earth opens to swallow him, his horses and his chariot, and here MS S adds seventy verses describing—in imitation of both Statius and Vergil's *Aeneid* Book 6—the priest's descent to the dark, hostile confines of the classical underworld, his passage across the river Styx and his arrival before Pluto, who avenges himself on the priest by denying him, through death, the power to foretell the future. (Is this a touch of black comedy?) The cumulative impact of these passages peculiar to MS S would seem to underscore a theme of presumption punished—the giants', the seer's—but they may perhaps also be understood as sly exercises in clerical exhibitionism.

The last section of the poem is quite different in these two manuscripts. In MS C, the messenger from Thebes come to the widows of Argos with news of the unburied Greek bodies; the women decide to appeal to Theseus and send an embassy to him at Athens. Theseus agrees to go to Thebes; only then does Theseus's army meet Adrastus, who does not go on his knees to Theseus; Theseus's army hastens to Thebes, kills Creon and destroys the city, with the help of the widows, who claw at the walls; then they bury the Greeks and find the corpses of the two brothers; those bodies are burned in one pyre but suddenly two flames separate and fight; the ashes are then put in one urn but it cannot contain them, as they keep fighting. Theseus washes his hands of them and goes home. Back in Argos, there is satisfaction at the vengeance done to Creon and Thebes by Theseus and the widows.

By contrast, in MS S the widows, learning of their dead unburied and defiled outside the walls of Thebes, set out to go there. It is very slow going; first they encounter Adrastus, and then they meet Theseus, on his way back from defeating the Amazons. Adrastus, on his knees, pleads for the duke's aid. Theseus acquiesces and leads his army to Thebes; the women attack the walls, but it is Theseus's siege machines that poke a huge hole in the walls; Creon is killed, and many prisoners brought back to Athens; but first, the duke seeks, and finds among the dead, the bodies of Polynices and Eteocles (a passage repeated twice in MS S's text, at v. 11978 and again at v. 11990 in Mora-Lebrun's edition.). Theseus has them buried, but the ground will not hold the struggling bodies; then they are burned, but the two tongues of flame fight on the pyre. Their ashes are then placed in two urns, but they escape their respective containers to continue fighting; finally, Theseus has the ashes sealed in one urn; he goes back to Athens where all live in sorrow and mourning. The ending in MS S is much darker, lacking all satisfaction, and makes the audience aware of the irreparable damage done to societies by warfare.

A list of some smaller divergences between MS S and MS C is included as an additional section to this Introduction. To give the reader of this Introduction one final idea of the divergence among all the manuscripts of the *Roman de Thèbes*, we mention here two passages found in the long, or y, version represented in MSS A and P that are not to be found in either MS S or MS C: at a point after S 4901, there is an episode in y recounting the return of Jocasta to Thebes with Parthenopeus and Polynices, where they encounter Oedipus; at a point after MS S 7832, y has an episode in which the King of Nubia arrives with 20,000 men to aid the Thebans, but Parthenopeus, warned by his *amie* Antigone, intercepts and kills them.

E. Description of MS S; Its Contents, its Owner, and his Career

BL Add. 34114 is a folio volume (37.7 x 24.4 cm) of 237 vellum leaves, with illuminated borders. According to Baswell, on whom the following sections of this Introduction heavily depend, the manuscript is written in "a single, disciplined, and rather elegant book hand, except for the added fragment [at its end]".[28] It is listed in the British Library catalogue of manuscripts [http://searcharchives.bl.uk/ our catalogues, archives and manuscripts/Spalding MS] as "a collection of Romances in French verse, as follows:

1. *Chanson de Geste* on the First Crusade; in nearly 19,000 Alexandrines. With the colophon: 'Ci finist le siege d'Antioche ouesque le conquest de Jerusalem de Godefrei de Boilion.' ff. 2–105. . . . [This is a vernacular adaptation of Baudri de Bourgeuil's *Historia Hierosolymitana*; see Baswell, 43, n. 101.]

2. *Roman d'Énéas*; in more than 10,000 octosyllabic lines. ff. 106–164. . ..

3. *Roman de Thèbes*, taken from Statius; in more than 11,000 octosyllabic lines. ff. 164–226 b. . ..

4. *Le Songe vert*: an allegorical [love vision] poem of the fourteenth century, in more than 1650 octosyllabic lines. ff. 227–236 b. . ..

5. *Ordène de Chevalerie*: the instruction in chivalry given by Hue de Tabarie to Saladin. Added in a different hand from the preceding articles. Imperfect, only about 170 octosyllabic lines remaining, some of them mutilated. If. 236 b-237 b. . .." [It's notable, and suggestive for the continuing francophone reading habits of English elite, that this is the continental version of the text; the *L'ordène de chevalerie* also has Anglo-Norman versions extant in other manuscripts, see Dean no. 706.] The manuscript is also described, and a number of its folios digitized, in the British Library Catalogue of Illuminated Manuscripts:

www.bl.uk/catalogues/illuminatedmanuscripts/record.asp?MSID=8701&CollID=27&NStart=34114

The most distinguishing feature of London, BL Add. 34114, with respect to the circumstances of its making, is (to quote the BL website again) "the arms of Spencer in two of the illuminated borders, one of the shields being within a bordure azure with bishops' mitres on it, referring to Henry de Spencer, Bishop of Norwich (1370–1406)." Or, as Baswell, puts it, "At three points, this rather large and grandly decorated manuscript includes the Despenser coat of arms, once with a small red cross. . . (fo. 1v), and twice surrounded by a blue border with bishop's mitres in it (fos. 106r, 164r). . .. Despenser's arms feature at the opening of the three poems of battle and empire, the crusade story, Eneas, and Thèbes."[29] The question presented by this manuscript is, why did a late four-

[28] Christopher Baswell, "Aeneas in 1381," *New Medieval Literatures* 5 (2002), 7–58, at 44.

[29] Baswell, "Aneas in 1381," 43.

teenth-century bishop have produced for him (as its thrice included Despenser coat of arms suggests) a manuscript the main components of which constitute, as Baswell states, "a somewhat archaic selection" of twelfth-century martial texts—relating to antiquity on the one hand, to the First Crusade on the other—in French? What clues can be found in Henry Despenser's career, class interests, and values?

Henry Despenser (usually said to have been born in 1343, though R. G. Davies argues recently for an earlier date)[30] was the scion of a noble Gloucestershire family with special connection to Tewksbury, the great abbey church of which was to be the burial place of many family members. His most illustrious (or notorious) ancestors were Hugh Despenser the Elder and the Younger, court favorites of King Edward II, who were executed after Edward's deposition and murder in 1326. Henry's early years were marked by distinctions both secular and religious: in 1354, he was made a canon of Salisbury as the result of a petition to the Pope by his older brother, Edward Lord Despenser; further papal dispensations and provisions included rectorships in Leicestershire (1361) and Cambridgeshire (1364), and the archdeaconry of Llandaff (1364) plus appointment as prebendary there in 1366. (None of these positions required residency; "they were merely sources of income to be served by deputy.") [31]

Despenser was ordained a subdeacon in 1362, but probably not a priest until just before his ordination as bishop. Meanwhile, he studied at the University of Oxford (perhaps resident at Queens College, founded by Edward III's Queen, Philippa of Hainault), and after completing an Arts course was registered as a Scholar of Civil Law in 1361, earning his Baccalaureate the same year and a Licenciate (the stage between Bachelor and Doctor) by the time of his elevation to the Bishopric of Norwich in 1370.[32] As Allington-Smith says, "There was, in fact, a compelling reason why [Despenser] should not yet be ordained priest. By the decree *Super Pecula* priests were debarred from studying civil law unless given dispensation by the Pope."[33]

By the mid-1360s, according to Davies (ODNB), "Despenser was a long term resident of the Papal curia," and with his older brother fought in the service

---

[30] *Oxford Dictionary of National Biography* (Oxford and New York: Oxford University Press, 2004), Vol. 15, 910–12, and www.oxforddnb.com/view/article/7551, accessed 16 July 2016.

[31] Richard Allington-Smith, *Henry Despenser the Battling Bishop* (Dereham, Norfolk: Larks Press, 2003), 7. For much information and bibliography concerning Bishop Despenser's career, we are indebted not only to Christopher Baswell, as mentioned above, but also to William Askins, who generously put at our disposal his extensive research on the pugnacious prelate.

[32] A. B. Emden, *Biographical Register of the University of Oxford to A. D. 1500* (Oxford: Clarendon Press, 1959), Vol. 3, 2169–70.

[33] Allington-Smith, *Henry Despenser*, 7–8; 12, note 32.

of Pope Urban V in the latter's war against the Visconti rulers of Milan. The two brothers had accompanied Prince Lionel, Edward III's third son, on his journey to Milan in 1368 to marry Violante Visconti. When Lionel died later the same year, it is thought that the Despensers, suspecting that the prince had been poisoned by his in-laws, joined the papal armies seeking vengeance. (Edward, having fought in France under the Black Prince, was awarded the Order of the Garter by Edward III in 1361; he has been identified, wearing his white Garter cape, in Buonaiuto da Firenze's fresco celebrating The Church Militant and Triumphant in the Spanish Chapel of the Dominican church of Santa Maria Novella, Florence, the supposed point of origin for Boccaccio's *Decameron.*[34] The bishopric of Norwich became vacant in August 1369, and Despenser was consecrated to it in Rome on 20 April 1370, having obtained a papal dispensation owing to his (supposed) age of twenty-seven. On 4 June of that year the Archbishop of Canterbury accepted Despenser's submission; he received the spiritualities of his office on 12 July and its temporalities—its lands and other sources of income—on 14 August.

For most of the next decade, Despenser remained in or around Norwich, attending to diocesan affairs—and feuding with the Benedictine monks of his cathedral priory; he did attend the "Good" Parliament of 1376 at Westminster, and served as one of four bishops on the "Communicating Committee" of twelve sent by the Lords to consult with the Commons on their resistance to the king's demands for taxation and attack on corruption at the royal court. Still, as William Rogers puts it, "Apparently, Despencer hefted the sword more comfortably than he did the crozier,"[35] and he was known to his contemporaries as *episcopus bellicosus*, the warlike (or, as Baswell seems first to have called him, the battling) bishop. (Perhaps the description of Amphiaraus as a warrior archbishop in the *Roman de Thèbes* was one of the attractions of the poem for Despenser.) Arrogant as well as bellicose, as Norwich's bishop Despenser aggressively defended, and even sought to expand, the considerable inherited authority of his office, an authority (like that of other secular and ecclesiastical lords, up to and including the king) that was frequently and sometimes violently challenged by both new urban and older rural constituencies during the latter part of the fourteenth century in England. In 1377, in an episode recorded in the Benedictine historian Thomas Walsingham's *Chronicon Angliae* and characterized by Baswell as "an almost emblematic encounter between emerging urban identities and entrenched aristocratic and ecclesiastical assumptions," Despenser, on a visit to the town of Bishop's (later King's) Lynn in Norfolk—a town that "tried throughout the

[34] See Sister Mary Aquinas Devlin, "An English Knight of the Garter in the Spanish Chapel in Florence," *Speculum* 4 (1929), 270–78.

[35] William E. Rogers, "The C-Revisions and the Crusades in *Piers Plowman*," in *The Medieval Crusade*, ed. Susan J. Ridyard (Woodbridge: Boydell, 2004), 145–56, at 148 (and see esp. 147, 153, 154).

fourteenth century to expand its liberties from the bishop"[36] —demanded to be preceded by the mayoral mace when in procession through the town, a privilege heretofore reserved to the mayor himself. The bishop got his way, but this "presumptious extension of ceremonial rights. . . so enrage[d] the commons of Lynn," who saw it as an infringement, however symbolic, of their liberties, "that they chased the bishop out of town in a hail of arrows."[37]

The Great Rising of 1381 in England saw attacks on monasteries and other great landholders, on lawyers (drafters and custodians of documents justifying historical inequities), and on collectors of taxes that fell most heavily on the poor; an ad hoc alliance of peasants, small rural landholders, and urban tradesmen and artisans denied full citizenship in their home cities called for freedom and justice and (at their most militant) for the suppression of all the powerful, mediating entities that stood between them and their king. In Norfolk, the leader of the rebels, Geoffrey Litster, calling himself "the king of the Commons," headed a force that imprisoned nobles, destroyed documents, and, entering Norwich, demanded payment from the city fathers to refrain from violence. Learning from afar of the disturbance in his episcopal city, Despenser quickly raised a counterrevolutionary army that crushed the rebels, meting out death sentences to many who survived his attacks.[38] Contemporary chroniclers of the Rising, overwhelmingly opposed to it, singled out Despenser for praise as a "good shepherd" for his hearing the confessions of, and comforting, the leaders of the Norfolk revolt before having them hung, drawn, and quartered(!).

Irrespective of Despenser's reactionary attitudes toward urban autonomy, his episcopal seat was a thriving mercantile city profiting from the trade in wool and textiles between England and the major towns of Flanders across the English Channel. Baswell speaks of "Norwich's rising prosperity from the worsted industry in these years [the latter decades of the fourteeenth century], and the implicit model of the wealthy cloth towns of Flanders, Ghent, Ypres, and Bruges."[39] Even as rebellion shook England, the wool towns of Flanders, commercial allies of England, were at war with the Count of Flanders, Louis de Mâle, and his lord, Charles VI, the King of France. To the political and economic dimensions of this enmity were added the religious tensions occasioned by the schism at the summit of the Catholic Church, with two rivals, Urban VI and Clement VII, claiming the papacy, and states and cities declaring allegiance to one of the other claim-

36 Baswell, "Aeneas in 1381," 11.

37 See Baswell, "Aeneas in 1381," 9–13, for analysis, including translation of Walsingham's account; Davies, however, contends that the incident "should not be attributed solely to Despenser's belligerence," given that the feud between the Bishopric and the town was of long standing and often "violent and bitter" (ODNB, 911).

38 Baswell, "Aeneas in 1381," 48–49.

39 Baswell, "Aeneas in 1381," 40.

ant, in accord with their respective political needs and alignments. As the French supported Clement, so England passed into Urban's camp.

England was multiply threatened by France in the 1380s, fearing not only the collapse of its wool trade with Flemish cloth towns but also actual invasion by French forces. Parliamentary debate in the early years of the decade centered on the choice to be made between attacking France via the Iberian peninsula—the so-called *chemin de Portyngale* [road to Portugal], favored by John of Gaunt, Duke of Lancaster and most powerful uncle of the young King Richard, who claimed through marriage the throne of Castile — or by the *chemin de Flandres*. Thanks to the papal schism, Urban was willing to call England's campaigns against its, and his, enemies crusades; in 1381 and again in 1382 he issued decrees (called "bulls" from the *bullae* [papal seals] authenticating them) to Bishop Despenser authorizing him to preach a crusade against the French. While the lords in Parliament tended to favor Gaunt, the Commons—concerned that financing Gaunt's Spanish venture would arouse further rebellions such as 1381's, in which Gaunt was a major target of the rebels' ire—preferred to finance Despenser's proposal to invade Flanders, saving the cloth towns for English trade and defeating the Clementist French king and his vassal the Count of Flanders. (As another incentive, by labeling Despenser's expedition a crusade, Parliament could expect the Church to help pay for it.)

Although Urban's bulls had given him permission only to preach a crusade, Despenser saw himself as an *episcopus bellicosus*—perhaps in the model of Arch-Bishop Turpin, Charlemagne's legendary warrior bishop in the *chansons de geste*, or of Amphiaraus, the high priest of king Adrastus of Argos in Statius's *Thebaid* who is presented as an archbishop in the *Roman de Thèbes*—and undertook to lead the expedition himself, "taking the cross" as a crusader at St. Paul's Cathedral, London, in December 1382. He had already instituted an extremely successful nationwide appeal for funds to support his expedition, offering papal indulgence to all those who either agreed to serve in his army (if qualified) or to pay for others to do so. (John Wyclif, the reformist theologian later declared a heretic, denounced the crusade and its recourse to indulgences; Henry Knighton, a contemporary chronicler, claims that women responded to Despenser's corps of crusade preachers and collections with special enthusiasm, so that, in his words, "that hidden treasure of the kingdom which is in the hands of women was put at risk").[40] Amid popular excitement at his initiative, and with royal and parliamentary approval but no secular lord as his lieutenant (as Parliament would have preferred), the bishop sailed across the channel in May 1383 and arrived in Cal-

---

[40] See Norman Housley, ed., *Documents of the Later Crusades, 1274–1580* (Basingstoke and London: Macmillan, 1996), 98–100, for Wyclif's attack (and further Herbert B. Workman, *John Wyclif* [Oxford: Clarendon Press, 1926, repr. Eugene OR: Wipf and Stock, 2001], Vol. 2, 64–74); Henry Knighton, *Chronicle, 1337–1396*, ed. and trans. G. H. Martin (Oxford: Clarendon Press, 1995), 324–33, at 325.

ais on 17 May leading an army of perhaps 4000, including several middle-status professional soldiers who would serve as his captains.

After early success capturing Gravelines and Dunkirk as well as several smaller coastal towns—success, according to Thomas Walsingham, that led London apprentices to lay down tools and race off to join the crusade where, however, as an undisciplined mob, they did Despenser and his army no good—the campaign went awry, via a failed siege of Ypres (controlled by the Count of Flanders but with a population entirely Urbanist), a retreat before a much larger French army led by King Charles VI, the selling of the captured town of Bourbourg to the French by its English commander for 2000 francs, and, as a final act, the sack of Gravelines, the taking of which had inaugurated the crusade. While most English historians have offered commercial reasons for Despenser's attack on Flemish Urbanist centers, instead of French Clementist ones, and explained its failure as the result of inept leadership, a recent essay by Kelly DeVries, based on Flemish sources, including Froissart's famous *Chronicles*, argues that the crusade's strategy was shaped by appeals from Ghent—a city long allied to England and in rebellion against France and Phillip the Bold, Duke of Burgundy—for Despenser's forces to attack towns inimical to Ghent's militancy.[41]

Despenser led the remains of his army back to England in early October and later that month, in Parliament, the Chancellor of the Realm, Michael de la Pole, impeached him on four counts: not raising as large an army as he had promised for the expedition; returning from the Continent before the year he had agreed to serve; forestalling by his promises of success a continental expedition to be led by Lancaster or one of the other "royal uncles"; and bringing about the crusade's disastrous failure by refusing to share command with a secular lord who would be in de facto control of the campaign. The proceedings were often harsh, and perhaps motivated in part by Gaunt's frustration at having had his *chemin* deferred (he finally got his crusade in 1386, which ended in his renouncing his claim to the throne of Castile in return for deals "that did something for him but little for the English national interest or for the ambitions of the pope").[42] Despenser defended himself vigorously but was found guilty on all counts in a contentious proceeding and was denied the temporalities (or sources of revenue) of his office, which were only restored after he accompanied the king on the latter's invasion of Scotland in 1385, and through the intercession of Bishop Arundel of Ely.

When Henry of Lancaster (John of Gaunt's son and heir) deposed Richard in 1399, Despenser was one of few nobles who remained loyal to the ousted monarch; imprisoned by Henry (now Henry IV) in July 1399, he was released in November, again through the intervention of both Arundel (soon to be re-

[41] Kelly DeVries, "The Reasons for the Bishop of Norwich's Attack of Flanders in 1383," in *Fourteenth-Century England III*, ed. W. Mark Omrod (Woodbridge: Boydell, 2004), 155–65.

[42] Rogers, "The C-Revisions and the Crusades," 147.

turned to the position of Archbishop of Canterbury from which Richard had banished him in 1397) and Queen Philippa of Portugal, Henry's older sister, whose warm relations with Despenser are manifest in extant letters between the queen and the bishop, recently studied by Tiago Viúla de Faria. In a letter of 1402, Despenser thanks Philippa for interceding with Henry. As Viúla de Faria asks, "could not pressure from Philippa of Portugal on Henry IV and her petition to Archbishop Arundel have influenced the way Despenser was treated?"—i.e., with unlikely leniency, despite the bishop's resistance to Henry.[43] Viúla de Faria also hypothesizes that Despenser was the conduit by which the *Confessio amantis*, the major English work by Chaucer's contemporary, John Gower, came to Portugal, where it was translated into Portuguese by Roberto Paym (Robert Payn), "an English-born canon of Lisbon Cathedral"; the bishop sent several gifts (possibly including the manuscript of the *Confessio*) to Philippa in 1402 through the offices of her treasurer, Thomas Payn, probably a relative—even the father—of the translator.[44]

After having spent nearly a year, apparently at Henry IV's order, in the company, or custody, of Archbishop Arundel, Despenser only obtained royal pardon in the Parliament of July 1401; his relationship with the king remained rocky, however, and he refused to appear before the monarch and his council in June of that year, in connection with yet another dispute between the bishop and the town of Lynn. An angry letter from Henry to Despenser accuses the latter of ignoring the king's commands (July 1404). During the last years of his life, he stayed put in Norfolk for the most part, until his death, 23 August 1406. He died intestate.

[43] Tiago Viúla de Faria, "From Norwich to Lisbon: Factionalism, Personal Association, and Conveying the *Confessio Amantis*," in *John Gower in England and Iberia: Manuscripts, Influences, Reception*, ed. R. F. Yeager and A. Sáez-Hidalgo (Cambridge: D. S. Brewer, 2014), 131–38, at 135.

[44] Viúla de Faria, "From Norwich to Lisbon," 131, 136. Several letters to and from Despenser during the reign of Henry IV—none concerning the abortive Crusade, but several attesting to his friendly relationship with Queen Philippa of Portugal, and many witnessing his combative personality and predilection for quarrels—can be found in All Souls MS 182, edited by M. Dominica Legge, *Anglo-Norman Letters and Petitions from All Souls Ms 182* (Oxford: Blackwell, for the Anglo-Norman Text Society, 1941).

F. Conjectures as to Despenser's Attraction to the *Roman de Thèbes*

1. Mythic History of Self, Family.

As to the question of what may have induced Henry Despenser to have London, BL Add. 34114 (henceforth MS S) made for him, Baswell offers persuasive answers, and in what follows we shall be much indebted to his research and analysis. In his reckoning, the manuscript containing the version of the *Roman de Thèbes* here translated was produced some years after the failure of the 1383 crusade; it is one of three commissioned by Despenser that provided him with, in effect, compensatory myths of lineage and heroism—narratives placing the battling bishop in a larger, positively resonant historical context. Specifically, MS S functions as "a book of martial belligerence (even in the cause of crusade) set in a distinctly international context, exploring aristocratic style and imperial ambitions, both secular and religious. . .. Despenser's arms feature at the opening of the three poems of battle and empire, the crusade story, *Eneas*, and *Thèbes*. . .. [MS S] can be seen as part of a complex pattern, throughout his career, of asserting aristocratic ideology, even recuperating its perquisites and modes of power. . . the texts [it] contains can be seen as a kind of prehistory not just of his class generally, but even specifically of his noble family"; in sum, to Baswell, its selection of crusade and *roman antique* narratives makes the manuscript "a myth book of the Despensers."[45]

Despenser also had two manuscripts of Latin histories produced for him: BL Cotton Claudius E.VIII, containing the *Flores historiarum* and the *Continuatio chronicarum* of Adam Murimuth—the latter offering a history of English royalty and favorably representing Henry Despenser's ancestors who served and supported Edward II—and BL Arundel 74, a copy of Bede's *Historia ecclesiastica gentis anglorum*. As Baswell states, "Together, these three mauscripts situate Despenser's commissions within a long tradition of dynastic narrative that underwrites British imperial ambitions with connections to ancient empire." Baswell further believes, "If Additional MS 34114 served [Despenser], in part, as an icon of royal English prehistory in the Mediterranean, Bede's *History* provided an analogous British and Saxon prehistory; and the two antiquities issue in the sequence of royal narratives in MS Cotton Claudius E.VIII, in which Despenser's own family arms are so conspicuously displayed."[46] Baswell dates the three manuscripts produced for Despenser to the years after the crusade of 1383 based on decorative elements referring directly to the battling bishop: "it is Despenser's

[45] Baswell, "Aeneas in 1381," 42–44.

[46] See further Baswell, "Aeneas in 1381," 44–46, on the decorative features linking these manuscripts as the products of "a group of manuscript decorators at Norwich," functioning as "something more like an atelier" (44).

personal role in leading the crusade of 1383 that seems to have given rise to the small cross that features in the first quarter of his arms, as it appears on the first page of Additional 34114, and repeatedly in MS Cotton Claudius E.VIII. He inserted himself as a crusader within his books of classical empire, antique crusade, and English royal history."[47] The Despenser arms also appear in the frame of the so-called Despenser retable, a sequence of images depicting the Passion, Crucifixion, Resurrection, and Ascension of Christ, painted on five connected wooden panels originally mounted above the high altar of Norwich Cathedral. (Sarah Stanbury has recently analyzed the sequence of images as a commentary on the disruption of social order and hierarchy during the Rising of 1381 and the subsequent recovery of control by the threatened elites, thanks to the prompt martial response of Despenser and other Norfolk nobles.)[48]

Following Baswell, one can argue that MS S, even more than the other two Despenser-commissioned manuscripts, served the bishop as an exercise in compensatory nostalgia, recuperating disappointment and disaster through the filter of narratives of chivalric and crusading glory, tales of idealized values and mythicized, almost superhuman struggles that look back to the First Crusade, and to the deeds of antique heroes as "the good old days" for the warrior nobility.

On the other hand, England's fear of French invasion, palpable throughout the 1380s, may also have prompted comparisons between an endangered London and besieged Thebes. At about the same time as MS S is being produced for Despenser—or perhaps earlier—Chaucer's *Troilus and Criseyde*, Book 2, depicts Criseyde and her maidens entertaining themselves reading the story of Thebes in the "paved parlour" (l. 82) of Criseyde's palace in Troy. This "geste of the siege of Thebes… romaunce of Thebes" (ll. 83-4, 100) would seem to be a version of the *Roman de Thèbes*; Pandarus counters (ll. 106-8) by saying that he knows the story in twelve books, i.e., Statius's *Thebaid*. (Thus Chaucer suggests that Criseyde will be reading about Thebes in French as a *geste* and *romaunce* before Pandarus counterposes the Latin version.) Then, in Book 5, Cassandra interprets the disconsolate Troilus's dream by recounting the story of Statius's *Thebaid*, in the midst of which (after v. 1498) most manuscripts of the Chaucerian poem introduce a twelve-line Latin summary of the epic, allotting one line to each of its books.[49] (Lee Patterson stresses the importance of "the recursive shape of Theban history" for Chaucer's representation of Troy and its inhabitants in his poem, and as a

[47] Baswell, "Aeneas in 1381," 52.

[48] See Sarah Stanbury, "The Despenser Retable and 1381," in *The Visual Object of Desire in Late Medieval England* (Philadelphia: University of Pennsylvania Press, 2008), 76–94.

[49] Geoffrey Chaucer, *Troilus and Criseyde*, ed. B. A. Windeatt (London and New York: Longman, 1984).

subversive counter to the myth of linear succession which encouraged the poet's contemporaries to think of London as a "new Troy" (Trinovantum).[50]

2. Chivalry after 1383

To the extent that Despenser was a warrior noble, he might well have found in the *Roman de Thèbes* an old but still relevant meditation on chivalry as a way of life for people of his class and desires. The fragment of *L'ordène de chevalerie* at the end of MS S would seem to support the idea of Despenser's interest in chivalry. His older brother, Edward Lord Despenser, was eulogized by Froissart, who knew him well, as the most handsome, courteous, and honorable knight of his time in England.[51] A strong concern with chivalry as a way of life and system of values and ideals percolated through European civilization in the fourteenth century, even as the realities of state-formation, politics, and warfare placed it under great strains. Nostalgia, idealism, and conviction mingle in a number of manifestations, including: the idealization of the one professional soldier on the fictional Canterbury pilgrimage by its Chaucerian narrator, in the so-called General Prologue to the *Canterbury Tales*; somewhat earlier, Edward III's Arthurian revivalism, culminating in his creation of the Order of the Garter as an homage to the knights of Arthur's Round Table;[52] and the encomium to knighthood and the values of chivalry in *Le livre de chevalerie* by the French knight, Geoffroi de Charny, who died as the French king's standard bearer in the battle of Poitiers (1356), the high point of English success in the Hundred Years' War.

As a concept combining the arts of mounted combat and the supposed ideals of a warrior elite, late medieval European chivalry invited condemnation as well as exaltation; its actual exemplars were frequently mercenaries (*condottieri*) who fought for anyone who paid them, and famous knights such as Sir John Hawkwood spread terror by their violence and their mafia-like intimidation and extortion (It has been argued effectively that Chaucer's Knight was such a mercenary.)[53] The great fourteenth-century alliterative poem, *Sir Gawain and the*

---

[50] Lee Patterson, *Chaucer and the Subject of History* (Madison: University of Wisconsin Press, 1991), at 136 and see esp. 129–36. On the popularity of this idea, influenced by Geoffrey of Monmouth's *Historia regum Britanniae,* see further Sylvia Federico, *New Troy. Fantasies of Empire in the Late Middle Ages*. Medieval Cultures 36 (Minneapolis: University of Minnesota Press, 2003), 13–15.

[51] T. B. Pugh, "Edward, Lord Despenser," *Oxford Dictionary of National Biography*, Vol. 15, 909–10, and www.oxforddnb.com/view/article/7550, accessed 16 July 2016. See above, p. 34, for the probable depiction of Edward as a Garter knight.

[52] Francis Ingledew, Sir Gawain and the Green Knight *and the Order of the Garter* (Notre Dame, IN: University of Notre Dame Press, 2006).

[53] On Hawkwood, see William Caferro, *John Hawkwood. An English Mercenary in Fourteenth-Century Italy* (Baltimore: Johns Hopkins University Press, 2006). The case for

Green Knight explores chivalry as an ideal tested by the desire to survive, an inevitable human imperfection (and has been argued to have some connection with the Despenser family).[54] A quite different perspective on chivalry is provided by the Scrope-Grosvenor trial, London 1386, a dispute over which of two knights had proper title to a particular coat of arms (heraldic symbols establishing identity on the battle field). As Paul Strohm puts it, "the trial created an occasion for chivalry to perform itself and to reiterate and reconfirm its values"—this at a time when the notion of chivalry was increasingly archaic and, at least in London, thoroughly challenged by commercial elites.[55]

Perhaps Bishop Despenser found in the *Roman de Thèbes* a pleasing representation of chivalric values in the face of overwhelming power and malevolent fortune. The failure of Polynices and his Greek allies to take Thebes could have resonated with Despenser's failure at Ypres, and indeed with his whole crusade. A further parallel could link Dares's surrender of his tower to the besiegers with Elmham's giving up Bourbourg to the besieging French army for 2000 francs—a deed for which Parliament impeached him and other Despenser captains. The subsequent trial of Dares for treason dramatized the tensions between a king given to obstinate rage (Eteocles) and his barons seeking to protect their rights and liberties. On the other hand, the *roman* offered an idealization of chivalry as a spur to performing great deeds. Also attractive to Despenser would be the power of the myth of lineage; on living up to your lineage, see MS S vv. 1851–54, where the leader of Tydeus's ambushers tells those fleeing Tydeus to remember the "geste fiere, / des estors et des vasselages / que touz jours fist vostre lignages" [fierce deeds of battles and vassalage that your lineage has always accomplished]. Despenser's lineage included the two Despensers killed for their loyalty to (or being favored by) Edward II.

All of this is conjecture, of course. The fact remains that the only version of the *Roman de Thèbes* extant in an insular manuscript owes its existence to a pugnacious, high-ranking churchman who saw himself as a crusader and embraced a tradition of chivalric bellicosity, which is also evoked in this twelfth-century retelling of a classical epic. That the story of Thebes recounts the tragic failure of a foreign campaign centered on the siege of an enemy city may have offered some

---

Chaucer's Knight as a mercenary has been made most famously by Terry Jones, *Chaucer's Knight: The Portrait of a Medieval Mercenary*, rev. ed. (London: Methuen, 1994.)

[54] Ann R. Meyer, "The Despensers and the *Gawain* poet: A Gloucestershire Link to the Alliterative Master of the Northwest Midlands," *Chaucer Review* 35.4 (2001): 413–29, has argued for a supposed link between the Despenser family, though not specifically Bishop Henry, and the *Gawain* poet.

[55] Paul Strohm, *Theory and the Premodern Text*, Medieval Cultures, 26 (Minneapolis and London: Minnesota University Press, 2000), 11. See Maurice Keen, *Chivalry* (New Haven: Yale University Press, 1984) for a realistic assessment of chivalry and its defenders in writing: idealizations of warrior lives, full of violence and pragmatism.

comfort (albeit of the cold variety) to the battling Bishop of Norwich, Henry Despenser.

III. Further Divergences between MSS C and S of the *Roman de Thèbes*

1. Young Oedipus goes to the temple of Apollo to find out who his father is. In MS C vv. 175–206 (not in MS S), the temple is identified as Delphi, a description of it is offered and a reason given why people go there, and the obscurity of the god's replies is noted. MS C is showing off its tradition's classical knowledge.

2. MS S vv. 231–42, 249–54 identify the Devil, here named Carcodet, as the force behind Oedipus's unintended killing of his father. These lines are not in MS C, which does not mention the Devil.

3. MS S and MS C report the meeting between Oedipus and Jocasta differently: MS S is less analytical about Jocasta's response to the young man who's killed the Sphinx when he comes to Thebes; MS C vv. 385ff stress his attractiveness and virtues, and have townsfolk suggest he'd be a good new husband for their needy queen, while MS S vv. 430ff recount the seduction of the queen that night after much drinking.

4. MS S vv. 482–537 offer a proleptic account of the brothers, their evil deed in stomping on Oedipus's eyes, and the rest of the story of their destruction and Thebes's, which is not in MS C.

5. MS S vv. 1030–81 offer an elaborate description of the King Adrastus's daughters, fuller than in MS C, and adding the spicy detail of the pleasure of holding the girls *nu a nu* (v. 1075).

6. After MS S v. 1297, MS C adds 36 verses on Polynices's impatience to go to Eteocles's court to claim his turn as ruler, and Tydeus's dissuasion of his doing so. The passage makes Polynices young and impetuous, but Tydeus knows better; he sees the danger Polynices faces if he goes in person to claim his place from Eteocles.

7. MS C vv. 1905–20 add to the message given Eteocles by the survivor of the ambush an explanation of how messengers should be treated; the passage shows concern with the rules and norms of the aristocratic warrior lifestyle—however theoretical and idealized they may be. (In the long version of the *roman*, Tydeus

has a romantic interlude with the daughter of King Lycurgus on his way back to Argos from ambush.)

8. MS S vv. 2780–980. The encounter with the old devil and second Sphinx riddle: again divergent MS traditions between MS S and MS C; MS S's ecphrasis of the devil's fortress and of the old woman/devil are much extended vis-à-vis MS C. Also added is the byplay between Tydeus and Polynices over who will answer the riddle, and the destruction of the devil. This episode much expanded in MS S vis-à-vis MS C.

9. MS S adds a passage to a battle outside Thebes (vv. 5800–40) not in MS C stressing the damage done to the horses of knights by lower-class infantry and archers. MS S vv. 5910–15 recount the elimination of the infantry/archers from the battle, lines not in MS C.

10. MS S vv. 5970–6105, 6155–205 are battle passages of fierce combat not in MS C: passages that expand and intensify the bloodiness and murderousness of the battle outside the city, perhaps inspired by analogous scenes in the *chansons de geste*, tradition-based feudal epics.

11. MS S vv. 6260–95: Menoesceus of Thebes finds the two dead brothers who've killed each other; they're his nephews. He has them brought into the city, bleeding onto the white horses that carry them; no one can see them without crying. The MS S passage heightens the pathos of the scene.

12. Regarding the death of Parthenopeus at the hands of Dryas, whom Eteocles told to keep out of his joust with Parthenopeus, the texts of MS S and MS C have many small divergences. Then at vv. 11157–95, 11205–22, occur passages not in MS C, which has a different text from a different transmission containing the grand episode of Capaneus's storming Thebes, defying the gods, and being struck down by Jupiter's thunderbolt (see above).

13. Regarding the assault on Thebes to avenge Parthenopeus, Polynices meets and kills Eteocles, who sneakily kills his brother as the latter dismounts to mourn Eteocles's death. The text of MS S varies greatly from MS C here, reflecting different traditions/transmissions.

14. In the last assault on Thebes (during which, in MS S, all the Greek host are killed but Adrastus, Capaneus, and a third Greek who goes to bring news of the disaster to Argos) in MS C, Capaneus is already dead, so a different Greek survives, named Acrastus.

IV. Suggested Further Reading

A. *The Romance of Thebes*

Le roman de Thèbes, ed. Léopold Constans. SATF 30. Paris: Firmin Didot, 1890, 2 vols.

Le roman de Thèbes, ed. Francine Mora-Lebrun. Lettres Gothiques. Paris: Le livre de poche, 1995. (Edition of MS S)

Le roman de Thèbes, ed. Guy Raynaud de Lage. 2 Vols: Classiques français du Moyen Age, 94, 98. Paris: Champion, 1966. 1968. (Edition of MS C)

Le roman de Thèbes. Edition bilingue. Publication, traduction, présentation et notes par Aimé Petit. Champion Classiques. Paris: Champion, 2008. Based on the edition of Raynaud de Lage.

Le Roman de Thèbes, Manuscrit A (BnF, fr. 375), ed. Luca di Sabatino. Textes littéraires du Moyen Âge, 42. Paris: Classiques Garnier, 2016.

*Le Roman de Thèbes. The Story of Thebes.*Translated by John Smartt Coley. New York, Garland Library of Medieval Literature, Series B, 44, New York: Garland, 1986.

B. Romance and the *Romans d'Antiquité*

Baswell, Christopher, "Marvels of Translation and Crises of Transition in the Romances of Antiquity." In *The Cambridge Companion to Medieval Romance*, ed. Roberta Krueger, 29–44. Cambridge: Cambridge University Press, 2000.

———, "England's Antiquities: Middle English Literature and the Classical Past, c. 1350–1500." In *A Companion to Middle English Literature and Culture c. 1350 - c. 1500*, ed. Peter Brown, 231–46. Maldon, MA: Blackwell, 2007.

———, "Fearful Histories: The Past Contained in the Romances of Antiquity." In *Romance and History: Imagining Time from the Medieval to the Early Modern Period*, ed. Jon Whitman, 23–39. Cambridge: Cambridge University Press, 2015.

Battles, Dominique. *The Medieval Tradition of Thebes*. London: Routledge, 2004.

Blumenfeld-Kosinski, Renate, "Old French Narrative Genres. Towards the Def inition of *roman antique*." *Romance Philology*, 34 (1980): 143–59.

———, "The Gods as Metaphor in the *Roman de Thèbes*." *Modern Philology*, 83.1 (1985): 1–11. DOI: 10.1086/391425.

Donovan, L. G. *Recherches sur le* Roman de Thèbes. Paris: SEDES, 1975.

Federico, Sylvia. *New Troy: Fantasies of Empire in the Late Middle Ages*. Medieval Cultures 36. Minneapolis: University of Minnesota Press, 2003.

Ferrante, Joan M. *To the Glory of Her Sex. Women's Roles in the Composition of Medieval Texts*. Bloomington: Indiana University Press, 1997.

Fuchs, Barbara. *Romance*. Routledge, New Critical Idiom, 2004.

Green, D. H. *The Beginnings of Medieval Romance: Fact and Fiction 1150–1220.* Cambridge: Cambridge University Press, 2007.

Hanning, Robert, W. "The Social Significance of Twelfth-Century Chivalric Romance." *Medievalia et Humanistica*, n. s., 3 (1972): 3–29.

———, *The Individual in Twelfth-Century Romance.* New Haven: Yale University Press, 1977.

Harf-Lancner, Laurence, "L'élaboration d'un cycle romanesque antique au XIIe siècle et sa mise en images: *Le roman de Thèbes*, *Le roman de Troie* et le *Roman d'Énéas* dans le manuscrit BN français 60." In *Le monde du roman grec. Actes du colloque international tenu à l'École normale supérieure, Paris 17–19 décembre 1987*, éd. Marie-Françoise Baslez, Philippe Hoffmann et Monique Trédé, Études de littérature ancienne, 4, 291–306. Paris, Presses de l'École normale supérieure, 1992.

Hubble, Elizabeth. "*Par fiance bien tenir*: Medieval Same-Sex Kinship and Sworn Brotherhood in *Le Roman de Thèbes.*" *Medieval Feminist Forum*, 49.1 (2013): 5–29.

Huot, Sylvia. "The Manuscript Context of Medieval Romance." In *The Cambridge Companion to Medieval Romance*, ed. Roberta Krueger, 60–77. Cambridge: Cambridge University Press, 2000.

Johnston, Ronald C. "Sound-Related Couplets in Old French." *Forum for Modern Language Studies*, 12 (1976): 194–205. DOI: 10.1093/fmls/XII.3.194.

Kay, Sarah. *Courtly Contradictions: The Emergence of the Literary Object in the Twelfth Century.* Figurae. Stanford: Stanford University Press, 2001.

Kelly, Douglas. *Medieval French Romance.* Twayne's World Authors Series, 838. New York: Twayne, 1993.

Krueger, Roberta, ed. *The Cambridge Companion to Medieval Romance.* Cambridge: Cambridge University Press, 2000.

Nolan, Barbara. *Chaucer and the Tradition of the* "Roman Antique." Cambridge Studies in Medieval Literature, 15. Cambridge: Cambridge University Press, 1992.

Patterson, Lee. "Virgil and the Historical Consciousness of the Twelfth Century: The *Roman d'Eneas* and *Erec et Enide.*" In *Negotiating the Past: The Historical Understanding of Medieval Literature*, 157–95. Madison: University of Wisconsin Press, 1987.

Petit, Aimé, "Le premier portrait féminin dans le roman du Moyen Âge. Les filles d'Adraste dans le *Roman de Thèbes.*" In *Convergences médiévales. Épopée, lyrique, roman. Mélanges offerts à Madeleine Tyssens*, ed. Nadine Henrard, Paola Moreno et Martine Thiry-Stassin, 377–88. Bibliothèque du Moyen Âge, 19. Bruxelles: De Boeck Université, 2001.

———, *L'anachronisme dans les romans antiques du XIIe siècle: le "Roman de Thèbes, le Roman d'Enéas, le "Roman de Troie, le "Roman d'Alexandre.* Nouvelle bibliothèque du Moyen Âge, 65. Paris: Champion, 2002.

———, *Aux origines du roman: le Roman de Thèbes*. Paris: Champion; Genève: Slatkine, 2010.

Ribémont, Bernard, ed. *Études sur le "Roman de Thèbes, qui des sept arz set rien entendre"... Introduction, bibliographie, choix de textes*. Medievalia, 43. Orléans: Paradigme, 2002.

Roberts, Anna. "The 'homicidal women' Stories in the *Roman de Thèbes*, the *Brut Chronicles*, and Deschamps's 'Ballade 285.'" In *Domestic Violence in Medieval Texts*, ed. Eve Salisbury *et al.*, 205–22. Gainesville: University Press of Florida, 2002.

Sanok, Catherine. "Almoravides at Thebes: Islam and European Identity in the *Roman de Thèbes*." *Modern Language Quarterly* 64.3 (2003): 277–98. DOI: 10.1215/00267929–64–3-277.

Stahuljak, Zrinka. "Sexuality, Shame, and the Genesis of Romance." *The Cambridge History of French Literature*, ed. William Burgwinkle, Nicholas Hammond and Emma Wilson, 57–66. Cambridge: Cambridge University Press, 2011.

C. Henry Despenser, Bishop of Norwich (d. 1406) and Historical/Literary Studies

Allington-Smith, Richard. *Henry Despenser the Battling Bishop*. Dereham, Norfolk: Larks Press, 2003.

Aston, Margaret. "The Impeachment of Henry Despenser." *Bulletin of the Institute of Historical Research* 38 (1965): 127–48. DOI: 10.1111/j.1468–2281.1945.tb01345.x.

Baswell, Christopher. "Aeneas in 1381." *New Medieval Literatures* 5 (2002): 7–58.

Charny, Geoffroi de, *Livre de chevalerie. The Book of Chivalry of Geoffroi de Charny. Text, Context, and Translation*, ed. Richard W. Kaeuper and Elspeth Kennedy. Philadelphia: University of Pennsylvania Press, 1996.

Davies, R. G. "Henry Despenser." *Oxford Dictionary of National Biography*, Vol. 15, 910–12 and online at www.oxforddnb.com.

Devlin, Sister Mary Aquinas. "An English Knight of the Garter in the Spanish Chapel in Florence." *Speculum* 4 (1929): 270–78. DOI: 10.2307/2849550.

DeVries, Kelly. "The Reasons for the Bishop of Norwich's Attack on Flanders in 1383." *Fourteenth-Century England* III, ed. W. Mark Omrod, 155–65. Woodbridge: Boydell, 2004.

Ferrante, Joan M., ed. and trans., *Epistolae* (http://epistolae.ccnmtl.columbia.edu)

Housley, Norman, ed. *Documents of the Later Crusades, 1274–1580*. Basingstoke and London: Macmillan, 1996.

Ingledew, Francis. *Sir Gawain and the Green Knight and the Order of the Garter*. Notre Dame, IN: University of Notre Dame Press, 2006.

Kaeuper, Richard W. *War, Justice and Public Order: England and France in the Later Middle Ages.* Oxford: University Press, 1988.

Keen, Maurice. *Chivalry.* New Haven: Yale University Press, 1984.

Knighton, Henry. *Chronicle, 1337–1396*, ed. and trans. G. H. Martin. Oxford: Clarendon Press, 1995.

Legge, M. Dominica. *Anglo-Norman Letters and Petitions from All Souls Ms 182.* Oxford: Blackwell, for the Anglo-Norman Text Society, 1941.

McKisack, May. *The Fourteenth Century, 1307–1399.* Oxford History of England, Vol. 5. Oxford: Clarendon Press, 1959.

Meyer, Ann R. "The Despensers and the *Gawain* poet: A Gloucestershire Link to the Alliterative Master of the Northwest Midlands." *Chaucer Review* 35.4 (2001): 413–29. DOI: 10.1353/cr.2001.0004.

Poole, Reginald Lane. "Henry Despencer." *Dictionary of National Biography*, Vol. V, 860–62 and online.

Pugh, T. B. "Edward, Lord Despenser." *Oxford Dictionary of National Biography*, Vol. 15, 909–10 and online.

Riley-Smith, Jonathan, ed. *Oxford Illustrated History of the Crusades.* Oxford: University Press, 1997.

Rogers, William E. "The C-Revisions and the Crusades in *Piers Plowman*." In *The Medieval Crusade*, ed. Susan J. Ridyard, 145–56. Woodbridge: Boydell, 2004.

Saul, Nigel. *Richard II.* New Haven: Yale University Press, 1997.

Stanbury, Sarah. "The Despenser Retable and 1381." In *The Visual Object of Desire in Late Medieval England*, 76–94. Philadelphia: University of Pennsylvania Press, 2008.

Strohm, Paul. *Theory and the Premodern Text.* Medieval Cultures 26. Minneapolis: University of Minnesota Press, 2000.

Tyerman, Christopher. *England and the Crusades, 1095–1588.* Chicago: University of Chicago Press, 1988.

Viúla de Faria, Tiago. "From Norwich to Lisbon: Factionlism, Personal Association, and Conveying the *Confessio Amantis*." In *John Gower in England and Iberia: Manuscripts, Influences, Reception*, ed. R. F. Yeager and A. Sáez-Hidalgo, 131–38. Cambridge: D. S. Brewer, 2014.

D. The French of England

Ailes, Marianne, and Ad Putter. "The French of Medieval England." In *European Francophonie: The Social, Political and Cultural History of a Prestige Language*, ed. V. Rjéoutski, G. Argent, D. Offord, 51–78. Bern: Peter Lang, 2014.

Busby K. and C. Kleinhenz, eds. *Medieval Multilingualism: The Francophone World and its Neighbours.* Turnhout, 2010.

Gaunt, Simon. "French Literature Abroad: Towards an Alternative History of French Literature." *Interfaces: A Journal of Medieval European Literatures* 1 (2015): 25–62: http://riviste.unimi.it/interfaces/issue/view/569/.

Wogan-Browne, Jocelyn [with Carolyn Collette, Maryanne Kowaleski, Linne Mooney, Ad Putter, David Trotter], ed. *Language and Culture in Medieval Britain: The French of England c. 1100–c.1500.* Woodbridge and York: York Medieval Press, 2009, 2013.

Wogan-Browne, Jocelyn, Thelma Fenster and Delbert W. Russell, eds., trans. and intro. *Vernacular Literary Theory from the French of Medieval England: Texts and Translations, c. 1120–c.1450.* Cambridge: D. S. Brewer, 2016.

V. Note on the Treatment of Text: The Nature and Aims of this Translation

In making this translation, we have aimed to stay as close as possible to the French, while hoping to avoid "woodenness" and communicating some of the variety and excitement of the original, and have therefore chosen to render it line by line, rather than in prose. Old French tenses within narrative vary frequently, fluidly changing the reader's perspective on events and creating a sense of greater or lesser immediacy: we have followed these variations when it seemed rhetorically effective to do so, and also on occasion have introduced tense variations into the original for an equivalent effect. We have gratefully used Francine Mora-Lebrun's valuable edition and modern French translation of the text, *Le roman de Thèbes*, Lettres Gothiques (Paris: Le livre de poche, 1995), which uses London, BL Add. 34114 as its base, and have also had recourse to a microfilm of the manuscript kindly lent by Professor Christopher Baswell. For convenience citations from the original text are to Mora-Lebrun's edition. Paragraphing is ours.

Images from London, BL Add. 34114 are now available in the British Library's digitization: see its Catalogue of Digital Manuscripts at www.bl.uk/catalogues/illuminatedmanuscripts/record.asp?MSID=8701.

The Romance of Thebes

Anyone who is wise should not hide it
but should reveal his wisdom
so that when he departs from the world
he will always be remembered.
If Sir Homer and Sir Plato
and Virgil and Cicero
had hidden their wisdom
we would not know about them now.
That is why I will not keep my wisdom hidden
or suppress my learning,
but I will take pleasure in telling
something worth remembering.
Let them be silent, those who work at this craft;
unless they are clerics or knights,
they can listen just as well
as asses can harp.
I shall not speak of tanners,
of peasants or of shepherds,
but I shall tell you about two brothers
and relate their deeds.
One of them was named Eteocles,
the other Polynices.
Oedipus begat them
on Queen Jocasta.
He wrongfully conceived them with his mother
after he had killed his father the king.
The sin that created them
made them evil and mad.
They destroyed Thebes, their city,
and then the whole kingdom;
their war destroyed their neighbors
and both of them as well in the end.

I shall not speak further
about the two brothers now.

I want to begin my discussion
by telling about one of their grandfathers.
The grandfather's name was Laius;
he was King and Duke of Thebes.
He went to the gods to ask
what they had destined for him.
Sir Apollo let him know
by the answer he gave
that Laius would soon beget
an evil son who would kill him.
And before a year had passed,
Oedipus was conceived,
who later sinfully killed his father
as had been prophesied.
The king was terrified
by the answer he had been given;
he commanded that the child be killed,
that he live no longer.
The mother weeps and cries out and rants,
wrings her hands, tears her hair,
falls in a faint over her child,
and gives vent to great grief:
"Poor sad creature, what shall I do?
Unhappy woman, what will become of me?
Miserable thing, why was I born?
Sinner, why did I live?
How can I be the murderer
of the baby I bore?
Little babe, why were you born?
Why were you ever conceived?
For what crime, for what wrong,
little one, will you be killed?
You are not the son of a whore,
of a monk or a nun!
Ah, sweet thing, for ill I bore you,
for ill I nourished you, for ill I nursed you!
It was for ill that your father begot you
since he has ordered you to be killed.
We will all be blamed for your death,
your father rightly, I wrongly.
He commanded you to be killed,
my dearest son, against my will.
He wants to challenge the gods

and prove their answer wrong.
But they speak truth, I believe,
it will be as they said."
The queen weeps and grieves
so over her son,
that no one can listen
to her sorrow.

The king was quite frightened;
he called three of his servants.
He promised them gold and silver
and commanded them secretly
to take his son from his wife
and cut off his head.
Now they go off with the child,
leaving his mother weeping;
she strikes her face, wrings her hands,
and prays to the gods for death.
When she has lamented and wept at length,
when she has beaten and exhausted her body,
her sighs are less frequent
and she begins to sleep.
The mother, exhausted, sleeps,
as her son goes to be killed.
But now we will see who has greater power,
Apollo or Laius:
if the infant is decapitated
then the god is proved false;
but if he escapes from the hands of those servants,
the king will be right to fear him.
The servants go off secretly
as the king had asked them to.
When they were far from the city
they entered a great forest;
they stripped the king's son,
of the linen that covered him.
He was small; he did not know his fate,
he was not aware that death was coming.
He stretched out his hands and smiled at them
as he had done to his nurse.
But they are moved to pity
by the smile he gave them
and they say: "We will be committing a sin

if we kill him when he is smiling at us."
They pierced both his feet
and hung him from a tall oak;
they did that so he would not be devoured
or eaten by bears or lions.
Now the three servants return,
leaving the king's son hanging.
They tell the king: "You may be sure
you will never see your son.
If you can protect yourself from the living
you need have no fear of the dead."
They have reassured their king
but they have betrayed and deceived him,
for the child who hangs on high
will soon be rescued.

The King of the city of Orces
has entered the forest to hunt;
he brought a pack of dogs with him,
and he has already taken a deer.
When he heard the child crying
it is no wonder that he was afraid.
He looked up at the oak,
saw that a child
was hanging there;
he was astonished.
He drew his sword, cut it down,
and wrapped it in his cloak:
he saw that the child was beautiful for his age.
He returned to the hunters
and showed them what
he had found by chance.
They all advised him to carry the child away,
to nourish him and educate him.
And so he did with King Laius's son;
sir Polybus took the child with him;
he had him brought up, he cherished him
as if he had been born of his own wife.
He fostered him
until he could wield a lance and a sword,
hunt in the woods and on the shore,
carry a goshawk and a sparrowhawk.
And when the child was fifteen,

he was noble and valiant, wise and big.
The king so cherished him
that he made him his special friend, his confidant;
and because he so cherished him,
he made him a knight.
He gave his land to him
and turned his knights over to him.
He was big and wise and valiant,
a worthy knight;
he jousted in tournaments
and led great attacks,
so the word spread
through the whole country of Orcestre
about the foundling,
who was such a good knight.
His companions were envious,
they insulted him in their talk,
more than a hundred times they called him
son of a whore, bastard:
"You have climbed high in your arrogance,
but you don't even know who your father was;
only the whore who hung you in the oak
can tell you."

The young man was quite upset
by the accusations and insults;
he was so distressed and angry,
he left his lord without taking leave.
He was so angry when he went off
that he never asked leave to go.
He goes to talk to Apollo,
he wants to ask whose son he is;
he goes straight to Apollo
to ask who his father was.
The god says: "Why would you want to know that?
You will never satisfy your desire to know him.
There will come a day, this is the truth,
when you will say: "Why did I ever see him?"
And you may be certain of one thing,
you will never satisfy your desire.
And yet, if you go towards Thebes,
you will have news of your father."
He leaves the temple as quickly as he can

taking no notice of the answer,
for it was told to him obliquely;
that is why he takes no notice of the answer.
He makes his way straight to Thebes
because of his father, whom he wants to see.
Close to the city of Phoce,
in a great plain, beside a cliff,
there was a beautiful, noble temple,
and I tell you, as far as I know
that day there was a great assemblage
of many people from the country
for they were celebrating a feast
of one of the gods they worshipped;
they were playing noble and lovely games.
The youth came there in his wandering;
he had a desire to stay,
he wanted to watch the players.
Why should I make a long story of it?
It was not long before
a fight broke out
because of a lead disk
that two young men were throwing,
and striving hard as they threw.
The conflict grew worse
from the attack of the barons,
the lords got so involved
that great harm was done that day.
The young man who, being there,
should have found his father,
in fact learned nothing about him,
for he decided to go to Thebes.
Then a boy struck him with the lead disk,
and that is how Oedipus got into the melee,
just as it was destined—
it could not have been otherwise.
For the infernal Devil
had meddled with them that day;
he got the lord involved
from which great damage was done that day.

Many men were hurt,
King Laius was killed;
his head was cut off that day

by no other sword
than that of his son,
who later suffered great torment from it.
For Carcodet, who conquers the world,
encouraged him to kill the king.
He has forgotten the god's answer
and so has cut off the king's head:
thus was fulfilled
what the gods had destined for them.
When the King of Thebes died
there was great and fierce distress.
Beside the temple, beneath a tree,
they placed him in a marble casket.
When they had put the body in the earth,
each went his way without hostility;
the king's people went off in sorrow
for the lord they had lost.
When the queen heard the news
you can imagine she was not pleased;
instead she laments loudly,
weeps and sighs tenderly:
"Alas, poor me, what shall I do
about my lord whom I have lost?
Now I am a widow without a lord,
I have no one to guard my honor.
If battle or war arises
I shall not be able to hold my land."

Oedipus does not delay
but moves swiftly towards Thebes
and says he will not stop
until he finds his father.
Beside Thebes, on a mountain
high and bare and very round,
lived a devil,
very cruel and mad.
They called him the Sphinx in that country;

---

249 **Carcodet who conquers the world** *Carcodet qui veint li mont*: Carcodet appears to be a name for the Devil.
281 **They called him the Sphinx** *Spin l'apeloent el païs*: The Sphinx is usually presented as female in the head and bosom, but the French text makes it a male figure.

he killed many good men.
He had made up a riddle
which no one could solve by any means;
but nonetheless he insisted
that if someone could solve it,
he could take vengeance on the Sphinx,
who would lose his head immediately.
If he could not solve it,
he in turn was certain to lose his life.
The young man knew nothing about that,
he came rushing right past
and when the monster saw him from afar,
he rushed down the cliff to meet him.
Seeing that the monster was large and well-built and strong,
Oedipus was afraid for his life.
He was in great fear, but nonetheless,
whether he liked it or not, there he was.
The Sphinx spoke first:
"Friend," he said, "this road of mine
has a law I will tell you.
If you don't know it, I will teach it to you.
Those who come and those who go
by this road beside the mountain
hear a riddle from me;
it is well for you to know its rules:
whoever cannot solve it
must die immediately
and if anyone is so clever
that he can tell me the answer
[he may do the same to me,
cut off my head, I grant that]."
Oedipus was wise and valiant:
"Friend," he said, "since you apply
this rule about the riddle to everyone,
I do not want you to make an exception for me.
Since I have come here
one of us will die today.
But tell me the riddle now, I will hear it
and then I shall answer."

311–12 **[he may do the same. . .I grant that]** [*Tot ensement face de mei:. . . bien l'otrei*]: These two lines, absent from MS S but necessary for the comprehension of the passage, are supplied by Mora-Lebrun from Constans' edition.

"Friend," he said, "now listen well
to the riddle, and remember it.
You have heard tell of a beast:
at first when it wants to move on the ground
it goes on four feet, like a bear;
and then comes the day
that it no longer needs all four,
it goes quite swiftly with two;
but later it will need three
and then four. Friend, tell me
if you have ever seen such a beast.
If you don't know it, you will lose your head."

Oedipus had deep wisdom,
he took counsel with himself
and answered elegantly:
"Fool, you have condemned yourself;
now let me tell you
this riddle was made for me.
When I was little and nursing,
I went on the ground on four feet
and when I was two,
I was given a stick
to give me some support
to go around the house,
and when I had greater strength
and was a little bigger,
I no longer needed a support.
I could stand on my two feet.
To move better, I shall need
the stick when I am old,
and when I am very old
and weakened by age,
then if I want to walk around
I shall have to find two sticks.
I shall walk about with two sticks;
those are the four feet I shall have.
Now you have heard the answer to the riddle:
you must lose your life."
Oedipus has drawn his sword from its sheath
and cut the Sphinx's head from its trunk;
then he dismembered the whole body,
and the red blood flowed out.

The news reached the city,
you may be sure that it was welcome to those inside.
Among them they have a great discussion,
asking who did it:
"By what trick can he be dead,
that devil that was so strong?"
From the city many people come out
who go to see the Sphinx where he lies.
On one side they find the youth
armed on his swift horse;
on the other they see the devil
lying, hideous and huge.
Big and small rejoice
and praise the youth's prowess.

Then they lead him to the city
and take great pains to keep him there.
They have led him to the hall
and commended him to the lady;
she makes every effort to serve him,
to treat him well and flatter him.
That night the supper was rich,
I don't know how to tell you
how richly they provided him
with the wealth of the city.
When the meal had been served
and the eating was finished,
they went away that night,
but the youth was delighted to stay behind.
Jocasta looks at the youth,
she sees that he is courtly and wise and handsome;
"Friend," she says, "tell me
in faith, I charge you,
were you at the games the other day
where I lost my lord?"
"Lady," he says, "since you insist,
I will not lie to you about it.
I was at the games and at the celebration
where your lord lost his head.
If you are seeking the name of the one
through whom he died, I know it well;
but if you want to know his name,
I need to have a pact and an assurance

that he will not incur your hatred."
"So be it, friend," says the queen.
"I pledge my faith to you
that he will never have my hatred.
What good would it do me to hate him?
The man who died can not be cured."
"Lady," he says, "with that sword
that cut off the Sphinx's head,
that was so bold and strong,
your lord the king was killed.
Know that truly I killed him,
I know that I did wrong;
I would very willingly make it up to you."
He folds the hem of his tunic
knotted in his fist and extends the gage to her.
Jocasta takes it willingly.
Sir Oedipus was very happy
that he had given the gage to her.
Then he begins to speak with her
and to comfort the queen:
"Lady queen, do not weep,
do not destroy your body;
you know well that sighs
never restore the dead to life.
If I have killed your husband,
you have my pledge for it, by your mercy."
Now he has so pleaded his case
that both are in agreement;
for a woman is easily led to where
a man can do his will with her.
The beds were prepared,
they went to bed in the hall.
As they retired they had a lot of wine,
both honey-water and honeyed-wine;
they have quite a lot of both—
that night they enjoyed themselves.
In the morning at break of day
they all gather in the tower;
the princes and the vassals

418–19 **He folds the hem. . .the gage to her** *Le pan de son bliaut a laz/ pleie. . . le droit li tent*: Knotting the tunic is a gesture of atonement (see *plicare* in Ducange, *Glossarium mediae et infimae latinitatis*).

and the townsmen of the city.
They go to speak to the queen
to seek and ask counsel:
"Great and small, we all advise
that Oedipus be our lord;
there is no opposition,
that Oedipus be our lord.
All want to choose him as king;
all want him to have the kingdom
and to have you as his wife
for we can find no one better
who could hold the honor so well."
When the queen hears this,
she rejoices in her heart;
without further counsel she makes them a promise
and sends for the youth
in the chamber where he was lying.
When he hears that she wants him,
he rises as quickly as he can;
when he hears that she sent for him,
he goes straight to the queen
in her royal hall.
More than a hundred dukes and counts are there;
they make him their lord
and give the honor over to him.
They have given the queen to him
and he has swiftly married her.
The wedding was celebrated with great happiness:
there you might have seen many minstrels
singing with their viols
and their rotes and their harps;
before the day had ended, I think
more than a hundred bears were killed;
there were great poetry contests;
there were many does and stags,
many swans and peacocks,
geese and cranes and herons.
The assembly lasted a whole month;
it certainly cost more than a thousand pounds.

---

455 **who could hold the honor** *qui si bien [tienge] l'onor*: Honor is the technical term for dominion over the land. The bracketed word, absent from MS S, is supplied by Mora-Lebrun from Constans's edition.

Now the lady has taken her son as her husband—
what could she do worse?
And he who had killed his father
in great sin and great wrong
has taken his mother to wife;
he has badly wronged the gods.
But they were ignorant of their destiny,
that was so rough and harsh.
They lived twenty years without finding out
while they did whatever suited them.
They were together for twenty years,
they had four beautiful children,
two boys and two girls:
no king or queen ever had any more beautiful.
But let us leave the women aside.
We should not speak more of them now,
there will be enough place and time
to take them up again.
We have to speak of the brothers
and tell their deeds:
how they were evil beyond measure,
how they acted against nature.
And by that destiny
they destroyed Thebes and the country,
and twenty thousand men died
without a friend to comfort them,
nor a relative to weep for them
to see them dead or buried.
The brothers were very evil:
their dispute led to such a conflict
that it could not be put right
until their whole kingdom was destroyed
and other neighboring kingdoms
were hurt by their conflict.
The King of the city of Argos
so laid waste to his kingdom
that after the men were gone, the women
took up the war and destroyed Thebes
and laid it waste,
so no man or woman remained.
None of the men came back
except Adrastus, who had led them;
he alone, he and the women,

returned to their kingdom,
after they had destroyed the city of Thebes
and laid the whole country waste,
and mourned their friends
whom they had put in the earth.

Now we should let this be;
we must speak of the two brothers,
that Oedipus had brought up
to be valiant knights:
the first was Eteocles,
the other Polynices.
Oedipus has been king more than twenty years;
he never knew his parentage
until once when he was in a bath
and the queen was serving him,
she saw his feet, that had been pierced
when he was little and was hung in the woods.
She asked him: "Don't keep it from me,
how were your feet wounded?"
She asked and pressed him and entreated him
so much that he told her:
"Lady Queen, all I know is
what King Polybus told me:
he said that he brought me back
from the middle of a wood where he found me,
hanging high up in an oak
where I suffered these wounds.
I don't know who hung me there
nor who pierced my feet,
but I do know that that is what
Polybus, who brought me up, told me."
The queen suspected
that this was her son whom she had born,
and the three men took from her
on the king's orders.
She has the men traced and brought in,
makes them swear an oath
to tell her the truth
about what they had done with her child.
They do not lie
but tell her what they did.
Now Jocasta knows from the three men

that the king is definitely her son;
she weeps and says to him:
"We should not have been born
for we shall both be damned!
Your father is the man you killed,
I am your mother, whom you have wrongfully had."
The king feels he is cursed
when he learns what he has done;
for the horror of his act
he says he will mutilate his body.
He tears out his eyes
and throws himself into a ditch;
he swears that he will never come out again
because of the sin for which he must grieve.
His villainous sons, now grown,
mock him,
and when they find his two eyes,
they trample them underfoot.
For the sin and the wrong his sons have committed
the king laments strongly to the gods
and prays them piteously
to take revenge for it:
"Powerful king of the heavens, Jupiter,
Tisiphone, Fury of Hell,
destroy for me the proud ones
who trampled my eyes under their feet.
Sow such terrible discord between them,
fatal for both,
that they will not be able to govern
the kingdom they hold."
He invoked the gods so directly
that they granted all he asked for.

Now we shall leave the king,
for we must speak of the sons.
Between them there was much discord
and fighting over the kingdom,
just as Jupiter and Tisiphone
incited them.
They found an unusual solution
that would turn out badly for them:
that is, when one of them reigned,
the other would go into exile

and after a year had passed
the exile would return and be crowned.
By such an arrangement
they would reign quite equally;
whereas if each took his share
the realm would be diminished.
So they agree that without war
each would hold the land one year.
Both of them want to hold it the first year;
the elder makes his claim,
but the other says he will have it
or he will make war.
The elder seeks a judgment
and asserts by oath
that whatever the court decides
for the first year, he will abide by it.
The brothers had sworn beforehand
on their idols and by their laws
that if discord arose between them
they would submit to the judgment
and mediation of the barons,
they would be reconciled without a fight.
All the barons come together,
each says what he thinks;
no one prevents the court
making the right judgment.
They award the honor to the elder first,
the next year to the younger.
Meanwhile, let the younger look around
for a king to serve;
let him serve, this first year,
the King of Greece or Persia,
or go even further to Babylonia
or to his relatives in Sidon.
When the judgements are made,
the younger leaves the palace weeping.
Eteocles holds the kingdom,
Polynices goes into exile;
whether he likes it or not,
he can not avoid it.
There is no choice: so he equips himself
and makes his way to the King of Greece.
There is not much preparation

for he takes no one with him,
no squire or companion,
only his horse.

It was in May, in the morning
that Polynices went away.
Polynices rode alone,
deep in thought and afraid,
for he does not know for certain
where he can go safely.
He fears that his brother will, like a thief,
set an ambush for him along the way
for there will never be perfect love
between two who share such an honor.
From now on he commends himself
to Fortune,
and he prays hard to the gods
to guide him safely.
Polynices says he will go
to the King of Greece who was nearby;
many wanted to go with him
but he did not want to take them.
He tells them that he will go all alone,
he will not even take a squire.
He rode so long through the mountains,
the valleys and the plains,
by roads and paths,
he rode seven days altogether.
He rode along beside a sea,
but the sea was so stormy
that no one could tell
or imagine what it was.
All night it rained and froze,
hail fell and snow flew,
and the twelve winds coursed
through the world as they pleased.
Aeolus, their lord and ruler,
could not hold them back,
they make a tumult in the air,
they fight each other and raise a racket.
On all sides there is fierce thunder,
lightning flashes furiously;
the firmament staggers

and the earth within it.
Great trees are uprooted,
little ones broken up;
the rivers all overrun their banks
and flood the fields.
Polynices does not stop riding
because of the storm,
but he expects to die
because the storm is so bad.
He rides through a wood
where he meets fierce beasts:
gryphons, serpents, vipers, lions,
leopards, tigers and dragons.
But the storm has frightened them
and beat them down and whipped them,
so not one of those he encountered
ever touched him.
He rests his horse
on a very high hill that he has climbed,
from which he sees a light shining
on the tower of a city, Argos.
He sees the castle of the city,
and the carbuncle that shines on its summit;
the carbuncle shines brightly there,
to show the harbor to sailors
who sail the sea at night
and do not know where to dock.
That is why Phoroneus put it there,
an ancestor of Adrastus,
who is now king of the city;
he holds power over the Greeks.
Polynices rides directly
to the shining carbuncle.
He has reached Argos
where the old Adrastus reigned;
there that good king was
who was Prince of the Greeks.
He entered the city deep in thought,
he met no one
who might tell him anything
or lodge him in his home.
All were sleeping in their beds
because it was almost midnight.
He has come to the royal steps,

dismounted from his horse;
beneath the tower he descends to the portico
where there is not a stick of wood,
nothing there was made from a tree—
it was all of marble.
He was very tired from riding
and began to fall asleep.

But then Tydeus arrived,
the Duke of Calydon;
he had left his land
and come here to the king seeking to make conquests.
He comes right there,
fleeing the storm that is chasing him.
The valiant Tydeus,
the son of Oeneus,
was exiled and fleeing,
doing penance
because of a brother he had killed
in his own country, Calydon.
He was riding with the moon
as Fortune guided him,
without a companion or squire
only himself and his mount.
At the olive tree beneath the tower
he ties up his valuable steed;
he advances and enters the vault.
Polynices thinks he is crazy;
he gets to his feet
and accosts him fiercely:
"Who are you who thrust yourself on me?
By all the gods I believe in,
before you lodge here
one of us will get into a rage.
Go find lodging further on,
you can't dismount here.
Since I have made my dwelling here,
it would distress me to abandon it to you
Tydeus answers frankly
without any distress:
"You are foolish to get upset,
I am only asking for a few feet.
Give my body a place inside
and let my horse stay out.

Between the two of us there is a large space,
I do not know what harm I do you,
784 this dwelling is big enough;
if you have me as a companion
it can only be good for you;
let my horse stay on the stone."
788 Polynices pays no attention
but asserts and swears
that neither Tydeus nor his horse
will have a place there.
792 Hearing him, Tydeus understands
that begging will get him nowhere.
He draws the sword at his side
and holds his shield before his chest.
796 He is well placed,
he will not ask permission any more:
"The more I beg you, he says,
the less it will advance me, I know.
800 One can beg a villain forever,
it brings nothing but trouble.
Now whether you like it or not
I am here, in this place.
804 Whether it bothers you or not,
you will have my company."
Polynices leaps up at him
holding his sword in his fist;
808 they have begun a battle,
a combat of madness.
In the portico the two barons
are fighting like dragons;
812 the one who was there first
swears he will chase the other out.
They have great hearts and fierce desires,
neither would give as much as a glove for the other.
816 They are both worthy and valiant knights,
but their bodies are quite different;
if they had known each other
I do not think they would have fought together.
820 Polynices is noble and big
with blond curly hair;
his face is bright with good color,
his shoulders broad, his feet wide,
824 his sides long, his flanks thin,

his hips large and manly,
his crotch straight and big;
there was nothing unattractive about him.
He was young, not yet twenty;
he was a worthy and valiant knight.
Tydeus is older in years,
smaller in body but greater in strength;
his hair, beard, and moustache are black,
his face fierce as a lion's.
His body is small but his heart great;
he is like Roland in prowess.
And the two barons fight
for such a petty reason.
If they had sworn to kill each other,
they would not have fought harder.
Both are of fierce character,
very bold and combative.
Their swords are large and quite sharp,
their shields are from fierce beasts:
the exiled Polynices
had a great hide of a lion
that covered his whole chest,
which Oedipus had given him.
And Tydeus had a boar
that used to devastate his country,
which the goddess gave him;
she bestowed it on him for revenge.
Together the barons joust,
attacking each other like lions.
Both strike very hard,
sparing each other not at all.
They strike with such fury
they make red sparks leap up.
They exchange such great blows
that the whole vault resounds.

---

835 **Roland** *Rolant*: The most famous warrior hero of the traditions that recounted the battles fought by Charlemagne and his army against their enemies.
848–50 **And Tydeus had a boar. . .the goddess gave him** *Et Tydeus l'ot d'un senglier. . . que la deuesse li dona*: This is probably a confused reference to the story of the boar Diana unleashed on Calydon after she had been slighted by its king, Oeneus (Ovid, *Metamorphosis*, Book 8); the boar was slain by Meleager, a son of Oeneus and brother of Tydeus.

There you might have seen such a great series of blows
to the helmets from the polished swords
that the whole tower resounded
and the vault reverberated.
I know it would not have been long
before one killed the other,
but King Adrastus awakes,
alarmed by the racket.
The king is roused by the noise;
he sends a chamberlain down
to find out what is making the noise
and return immediately to tell him.
The chamberlain goes into the courtyard,
he sees the knights fighting there;
he comes quickly back to the king,
tells him about the fierce battle
going on in the portico below
where the vassals are fighting.
The king gets up swiftly,
taking no robe or equipment,
except for a gray fur
he put on over his tunic.
He is so anxious to get down there,
he does not remember to take a cloak;
but a youth comes down the steps,
running through the hall,
and before the king reaches the courtyard
he wraps him in marten fur.
The king comes out into the night,
holding a candle in his hand.
He had burning candles brought
to where he found the fighters;
when he sees them fighting there
he puts himself between them, threatening them
that if they do any more wrong today,
tomorrow he will have them hanged on that hill.
Then, looking at their armor,
he begins to think
that they are the ones
the goddess promised him when she said
that a boar and a fierce lion
would marry his daughters.
He asks them who they are,

where they come from and where they are going:
904 "Who are you and where are you from?
What are you fighting over?
Why are you fighting at such an hour?
What sin has taken hold of you?
908 If you were from my realm,
you would not be fighting here;
I know you were born elsewhere
if you fight at this hour
912 when other creatures sleep;
you seek each other's death."
They answer him: "Go to sleep,
we have nothing to do with you;
916 we have no leisure to chat with you now,
we want to talk of other things."
The king does not get angry,
but begs them very gently
920 to tell him the truth
of what he had asked them.
Sir Tydeus answers first:
"I came from Calydon the other day;
924 I am the son of Oeneus the king,
I came here to be with you."
Adrastus turns to the other one
for he sees that he is the more upset.
928 He asks him: "Sweet friend
where are you from, what country?"
Polynices does not tell the name of his father
because he was his own brother's son;
932 rather he tells him that he was born in Thebes
like all his relatives.
"Come now!" he says, "why do you hide it from me?
We know the wonders well enough,
936 what Oedipus did to his father
when he killed him and took his mother.
You seem like a good knight to me,
I will not cherish you the less for that,
940 for if you are of that lineage
you are of very high birth."
The vassals recognize the king;
each answers for himself
944 from what people and what land they come
and who they are and what they are looking for there.

The king knows their lineage well,
that they are of high birth.
He has their horses well cared for
and commands them to disarm.
And then he kisses them both heartily
and makes peace between the knights;
he brings them to an agreement and separates them
and sweetly welcomes them both.
He is very happy in his heart
that he is hosting these sons of kings.
Then he makes them swear and guarantee
and give their word
that as long as they live
they will henceforth be friends and companions.
No friends, not Pirithous and Theseus.
not Pylades and Orestes,
nor Patrocles and Achilles
loved each other more.

At the stone beneath the olive tree
the knights disarm.
As they disarm, there were enough people
to take and receive their arms.
They had neither baggage nor equipment;
though they are uncovered before the king
their bodies are so noble and well-made,
they look like counts of the palace.
They were simply dressed,
one in silk samite, the other in silk with gold threads,
and they are well hosed, the young men,
each in Alexandrine cloth.
The rich king dressed them in
two motley cloaks, wide and new,
and received them very richly
up in the master apartment.
Into his own chamber
the king brings the knights.
It was very noble, that chamber:
the pavement paneled,
encrusted with crystal;
on the front wall there was a border
of emeralds and jacinths,
there were more than a thousand ounces of gold.

A curtain was hung there
that a queen had sent him.
Semiramis, as I heard she was called,
had sent it by sea from Egypt.
The curtain was wondrous:
no one had ever seen one so precious,
one so well woven
nor of such fine work.
The one who wove it was hanged for it
by the goddess she had conquered.
The supper was prepared;
lighthearted and happy they were
as they served the knights.
There were many kinds of food—
there is no more to say.
The king has water brought,
two youths going to fetch it,
and the knights go to wash;
in two basins of purest gold
they wash and then go to eat.
At the high table sits King Adrastus,
on the other side Tydeus;
and a bench was placed there
for Polynices to sit.
I shall not go on about the courses,
but many are brought to the table,
served by more than ten youths,
each one a person of worth.
For love of his guests the king washed
and ate a cold haunch with them.
When they had eaten enough
and drunk several different wines,
the servants removed the cloths
and raised the silver chandeliers.
Inside the chamber the light was as strong
as a summer day.

996–97 **The one who wove it. . . the goddess she had conquered** *cele la fist. . . por la deuesse qu'ot vencue*: This is a reference to Arachne who boasted that her skill at weaving was greater than the goddess Minerva's and owed nothing to the goddess. In a contest, Arachne depicted the loves of the gods, and further angered Minerva, who, though impressed by her skill, turned her into a spider.

1024 The king sends for his daughters,
ordering their governess to get them ready,
to prepare them nobly
and send them into the chamber.
1028 The king has his daughters roused,
dressed and prepared
to be shown to the knights,
whom he wants them to marry.
1032 They came, heads bowed,
gold threads woven through their hair;
their tunics were of silk,
the furs over them ermine.
1036 Barefoot, hair hanging loose,
the nymphs came into the chamber,
ready to show their bodies
to the foreign knights.
1040 When the daughters saw the barons
whom they did not expect to see,
it is no wonder they were ashamed;
their faces turned red.
1044 They do not know who they are;
when they see them they are quite ashamed
and begin to blush
and to look at their father;
1048 they come right up to the king
who sits them beside him.
The girls were very noble,
there was no one so beautiful in their country;
1052 Pallas and Diana could never
surpass them in beauty.
Listen to what I know of them
and do not blame me for not knowing more.
1056 They are neither small nor too big,
but wise and attractive,
of the same size and appearance
in which there was nothing unattractive.

1038–42 **ready to show their bodies. . .no wonder they were ashamed** . . .*monstrer voloient lor cors. . .vergoine orent, n'en est merveille*: The passage in MS S is self-contradictory: the girls wished to show their bodies to the knights, but they do not know that the two men are there. The line in the Raynaud de Lage edition makes more sense in the context: "Li rois vouloit moutrer lor cors," "the king wanted to show their bodies."

1060 Their hair is blond, long and fine,
falling to their feet,
their foreheads are open, well-formed, and white,
their sides elegant,
1064 their eyes clear and loving—
no one has seen any so wondrous—
their noses straight and becoming to them,
not too small nor too big.
1068 Their mouths are straight and regal,
with small white teeth all the same size;
their smiles and their kisses are worth more
than those of a hundred thousand others.
1072 Their faces are clear and of high color,
white and red and well formed,
their chins are closed, well formed and long;
one could not describe them properly.
1076 The rest of their body is quite noble,
slim and soft and attractive;
the man who, naked, could hold them naked
would be well provisioned and retained.
1080 When Nature adorned them,
she gave them such softness
that I could not describe it;
I will let it go now.
1084 The king was not a peasant,
he did not prevent his daughters
speaking with the youths;
it does not bother him, indeed he welcomes it.
1088 They speak courteously
but not too long;
they were afraid to annoy their father
for the night was passing.

1092 The king spoke to the knights
whom he saw to be courteous, worthy, and lively:
"You appear to be very worthy men,
you are valiant knights.
1096 To see you exiled
gives me great pain and pity;
but you should not be troubled,
for God might well help you.
1100 Since you have turned to me,
your worries are over:

I shall give you my daughters
and turn my land over to you."
The knights see they are well provided for
and answer: "Thank you very much!
This gift pleases us and we agree to it
and offer you good will and gratitude."
The king has asked for wine,
which is brought in fine gold chalices.
When the knights have drunk,
the beds are made, and they go to sleep,
tired out from their fighting;
the maidens cover them
and they sleep quite soundly
for they are exhausted and sore.
The girls retire,
return to their chambers
and speak privately,
just as they wish, of their friends,
who are very handsome and charming
and worthy and valiant knights.
They reveal their desire to each other
with hearts happy and joyous.
Others might sleep, but Adrastus is awake
taking counsel with himself,
to marry his daughters;
he will give them to these two princes.
He is crafty, he considers
that he can marry them without expense.
He has no need to look for husbands elsewhere
when he has found them in his own land.
He desires marriages with them
because they seem to be of very high birth.
In the morning the soldiers get up,
go to the temple to pray to the gods.
When they come out of the chapel
the king summons them courteously;
there is no one else, just the three of them,
the two young men and the king.
"Lords," he says, "they are my heirs,
the girls you saw here last night;
I shall leave my domain to my daughters
when I die.
If it pleases you, I shall give it to you,

dividing my kingdom between the two of you.
Be lords here while I am alive,
I grant you my whole domain;
I am an old man, I want to rest;
I have endured so long I am exhausted,
I can no longer ride out
or suffer harm or stress.
You are young knights,
you can easily endure pain
and govern my kingdom
which is broad and abundant.
You who can suffer torment
take my kingdom into your care
and make great efforts,
and decide rights and wrongs.
I who am old and broken,
let me go and live in peace;
all my delight will be in riverbanks
and forests, which I have in plenty.
There I can lead my life in joy
for I know well there is little of it left."
Tydeus answers first:
"This pact," he says, "I do not refuse,
I willingly take one of them,
but to avoid any rancor,
let my companion choose before me,
let him take the elder, I agree to it."
Polynices agrees
that the elder be given to him
and Tydeus concedes her to him
But he is not acting the fool,
for if, as most people say,
the elder is nobler,
I shall say and I do not lie,
the other is no less noble.
The king sends for his vassals,
his friends and his intimates;
he has his barons summoned
and all his men assembled.
When they are all gathered,
the court and the baronage is sizeable;
there are many dukes and counts of high rank
and lords and lesser vassals.

On their counsel the king gives his daughters
to the knights as their wives.
With great honor he gives his daughters,
the whole city roars and resounds with it,
and minstrels rejoice;
they sing so much they are all hoarse.
Polynices will receive
the one whose name is Argia;
Tydeus and Deipyle
are united as well.
The court that the king held
lasts fully fifteen days,
the weddings
do not have an end.

The word goes through the lands
that the girls are married.
There are some for whom the news is not good:
when the news came to Thebes
that Polynices has taken a wife
and will want the kingdom afterwards,
Eteocles was not at all happy.
He had never been so angry;
indeed he hates this marriage
because he sees harm will come to him from it.
He knows his brother has such strong friends
that he will not be able to wrong him
and if he does, Polynices will take revenge
and challenge him for his land.
He has sent for his confidants,
leading them into his orchard;
he asks their counsel in the matter
which his brother has brought against him,
for he knows well that it is to oppose him
that his brother has taken the king's daughter,
that with the force of the Greeks
he expects to take back the kingdom here.
But Eteocles is not about to give it up,
he would rather be hanged;
he will hang rather than relinquish it
or let his brother seize it.
They advise him: "Then take action;
seek help against this,

make peace with your enemies,
ask help from your friends.
Reinforce this city,
restore the towers and the walls,
for there is no tower in the city
that is not falling down from age.
And take particular care
that all your men love you well;
love the greater and the lesser,
that is how you will hold your realm.
Maintain justice in your land,
exert yourself to uphold the right;
and do not allow the stronger
to harm the weaker.
Be generous to everyone
and do not hoard gold or silver;
give gold to your men
for there is no greater treasure under the sky;
give it to them when you have it
and promise to give it when you get it,
and when you have nothing to give
laugh and joke with them.
If you do not do this, you will lose,
and we shall see you undone."
The king answers: "I shall do it,
I will not neglect this advice."
The king was very wise and worthy,
he allies himself with all his neighbors;
there is no neighbor, however poor,
that the king does not beg him to make a pact.
With all he makes truces and treaties,
alliances against his brother.
He had a large household—none has a better,
no king or emperor;
all are noble men by birth.
You might have seen a thousand, all the same age,
worthy bachelors and youths,
the oldest of them not yet thirty.
Each one desires to win renown
through chivalry for his beloved;
they curse long truces
and they all say it is bad
to bring so many good knights together

just to sleep and eat.
Most of them want to leave
because it is hard for them to wait so long.
When some do leave, Eteocles
rides after them, spurring hard,
and makes them all return,
whether for love or entreaty.
What shall I say? He holds them until
his brother's term ends.
When the time approaches, one day before,
the King of Thebes has his court assemble
and takes counsel in closed session
to plan an astonishing treason:
he plots a great betrayal
if his brother should return.
Either secretly or openly
he will kill him, if he can get help.

The noble brother was in another land,
knowing nothing of this planned war,
not protecting himself from the felon
who plots treachery.
Polynices wants very much to return to Thebes
to have the agreement fulfilled.
He does not suspect his brother at all,
he wants to go to claim his right.
He asks leave of the king
who grants it to him.
In bitterness and fierce anger
Tydeus begins to laugh.
"By God," he says, "if you go there,
you will never return.
Your brother is evil, he will kill you
for your wealth which he covets.
You stay here and I will go
and deliver your message,
for it seems to me that you should first
find out what is in his heart through your messenger,
before you ride off without protection.
For I have heard and I believe it,
that he would rather suffer a long war
than yield the land to you."
Polynices agrees

and Tydeus sets out.
So Polynices remains
and Tydeus leaves the chamber.
He descends the steps,
saddles his horse,
takes his arms, mounts the steed,
and commends his wife to God.
He is equipped and well armed,
he has set out on the road.
He goes riding on his way
while Deipyle remains weeping.
His wife weeps, cries out, groans,
for her lord who is going,
but Tydeus pays no attention to that,
he leaves the city riding hard.
Now God help him and his claims,
his valor and his faith,
for if Eteocles has his way
he will never see Polynices again.
When Tydeus had gone so far
that he was approaching the city,
he rode day and night
despite hunger, thirst, and hard beds,
so that before the week passed
he came to Thebes, not without pain.
He took in his hand a branch
from an olive tree that he found;
he carried the olive branch
as a sign of peace
when he went to claim the kingdom
and deliver his message.
As he enters the city
he asks for the palace;
he rides through the street
greeting knights, as he meets them:
"Lords," he says, "instruct me
where I might find the king."
One of the knights answers:
"In the palace up there on the mountain;
he intends to hold a meeting
but he is still at his dinner.
If you want to speak to him
you have only to wait."

The messenger goes straight
to the great court filled with knights.
He rides swiftly
and with confidence.
Tydeus comes to the entry,
climbs up the steps;
wearing his hauberk and his sword,
he enters the painted hall.
Tydeus was brave and courteous;
he rides on his horse before the high table,
salutes the king and his barons,
then delivers his message.
He has stopped in front of the king
and speaks aloud: "Now listen to me!"
The king is silent and Tydeus speaks,
hiding nothing out of fear;
he does not hesitate from cowardice
to deliver his whole message.
"King," he says, "I come as a messenger to you;
it is right that you know
why I have been sent.
I shall tell you, pay attention to me.
After your father's misfortune
you made a pact with your brother
that you would hold the realm in alternate years;
he has many guarantors for this.
Now your brother sends me to you
and asks you through me
that you abandon this city
and cede its rule to him.
You have held the realm for a year,
now he asks you out of love
to keep your accord with him,
as you gave him your word.
One year will pass quickly,
the rule will come back to you.
He prays you to leave his land to him
and go to seek conquest elsewhere.
You swore it to him, you know that well,
you will perjure yourself if you renege.
You should not betray your loyalty
because you lose your inheritance for one year;
but if you want to belie it,

these men will not be able to allow
so many worthy men to betray their faith,
for you alone,
for every one of your men of good birth
is a guarantor of your brother.
It is far more appropriate
that you keep your agreement with him
and that you act properly towards him
for your faith more than for any other's."
Eteocles does not react hastily,
though he has changed color;
he was very angry in his heart,
but he responds to the messenger:
"I send this to my brother," he says, "through you,
that he is a rich man—I am happy for him.
Never could his ancestors have had such wealth.
If I left him this country
he would not stay here,
he has such great affairs there
he would have no interest in these.
You can tell him one thing:
he would do well to let me be.
It would be well for that lord
that I continue to hold this realm;
for if I had no realm here
I would go to him there.
He is my brother, it would be a shame to him
if I were poor and he rich.
Let him rest there in great pleasure,
let him lie in his bed with his wife,
and I, here, will content myself
with poverty, as best I can.
How could he bring such a rich wife
as his to this kingdom?
In her country she has great wealth,
here she would have great poverty;
she would regret her wealth
and curse us every day.
She would fight with my father,
my sisters and my mother.
It would be a great wrong if his wife
brought her arrogance to us here."
Tydeus understands the trick:

"By God," he says, "he will not
leave his land to you this year;
instead he will start a great war against you.
You should know that you will
soon see a great host come;
as you watch they will take booty
with engines and machines of war.
We will get so close to the walls
no one inside will be safe.
This is the truth, I am astonished
that you do not follow better advice.
Where do you expect to get help?
When your land is destroyed
and many barons lie dead,
you will have to redress this wrong.
After the great disaster,
you will yield his claim, I know;
you will yield his whole share to him,
but know this, by then it will be too late.
It would be better that the vassal,
now, without harm, hold his inheritance."
The king says: "You are learned in the law,
you are quite skilled in speaking,
you know well how to arrange your words,
but I would not abandon my reign
for anything you might say,
as long as I can hold it.
I shall not abandon it for any threat
that king or duke or count might make!"
And Tydeus answers the king:
"I warn you, by your faith,
the term has passed
that he should have been crowned.
You are treating him badly—
he is wrongfully king who belies his faith."
Eteocles gets very angry,
he turns red with fury,
he is enraged at the messenger
and addresses him fiercely:
"If you do not leave, you will come to harm,
nothing will protect you."
When Tydeus hears himself threatened,
he thinks he will go mad with rage,

he turns black with fury
and says to the King of Thebes:
"If you do not yield his claim
I tell you, on his part,
that before the year is over
we will show you a hundred thousand armed men.
If the walls of this city
were of iron or steel,
not one would remain standing
unless you keep your agreement with him."
Eteocles listened
as the messenger spoke;
he takes it badly
and answers quite fiercely:
"You know too well how to speak madness,
to insult and abuse me.
Whoever made you his messenger
did not wish to succeed.
Now tell him from me
that he should hold on to what he has.
I do not want him, from now on,
to send to me about the agreement;
let him know that whatever I have,
I will not let him have a glove's worth of it.
Now I shall see who will attack me
and who will destroy my walls."
Tydeus says: "You have made a mistake;
whether you like it or not, you will yield it to him.
You have broken the word of the covenant,
I challenge you on behalf of his share.
Now have your palisades built and your ditches dug
and your roads repaired;
it will be too late to restore
the old walls of this city."
Tydeus turns to the barons;
there is not one who is not distressed
for they know well that without any doubt
the country will be altogether laid waste.
But they do not dare contradict the king
because they know his great wrath.
Tydeus berates them on their loyalty
and repeats what the king has said:
"Lords," he says, "listen to me.

You have heard from your king
that he will not maintain what is right,
1532 he is clearly perjuring himself.
Polynices, through me, charges
those who are pledged to him in faith
to come quickly to him in Greece
1536 and support him in this war.
If anyone abandons his land or his loyalty for Polynices,
I pledge to him that I will make it good.
Let him not worry about possession,
1540 for you can be sure of one thing:
Polynices has a lot of silver and more gold,
there is no such noble treasure under heaven,
and he will give it to his retainers,
1544 he will not keep it for anything else."
Not one single baron, however powerful,
replied to him, not yes or no.
All the barons are of one mind,
1548 the most powerful say not a word.

When he sees that he will accomplish nothing,
Tydeus turns the head of his horse;
the king has not offered to lodge him
1552 and he departs without taking leave.
Through the hall everyone talks about it
and strongly praises the messenger.
One whispers to another:
1556 "He speaks well, this one, by my faith;
he has lost nothing by speaking,
if only his right had been acknowledged."
The messenger rides off, spurring angrily
1560 and brandishing his sword.
This is a sign of war
and total devastation.
The king committed great treason,
1564 but gained nothing by it.
He has risen from the table,
called for his constable
and secretly he called
1568 also for his intimates.
They came quickly
and the king told them his desire.
He said: "You are not my friends,

if the messenger gets away alive."
He has promised them gold and silver,
mules and horses to their desire;
he will declare free of all obligation
the man who will pursue Tydeus.
They return to their lodgings,
have their horses saddled;
they were fifty, the knights
who went after the messenger.
Those he chose are the liveliest,
the strongest and the most fierce.
Agilely and secretly
they leave the city
by a drawn gate
that was down towards northwest;
their shields hang loose at their necks
so they can ride lightly.
There were fifty in the company
without a squire or servant;
each of the fifty by himself
was as good as a king for courage.
They move along another path,
but Tydeus does not go as quickly;
he is afraid his horse is exhausted,
while theirs are fresh and full of rage.
He will soon value his good sharp sword.
Help will come too late
if his own prowess does not protect him;
his friends are far from him,
his enemies too close.
The traitors that are following him
are now in front of him,
hidden at the edge of the woods,
leaning on their lances.
They have gone to meet him
where the Sphinx used to be, the monster
who would kill and wound
men as they tried to pass.
It was a very dangerous passage,
where many men lost their heads.
At nightfall on that path
the knights set their ambush.
Whether I want it or not, Tydeus

has to come to that pass;
to that pass he has to come
because there is no other way through.
The fifty have seized the pass
and Tydeus is riding into it.
The sun is already hidden
and the day has turned to night;
the moon rises, it shines bright
and he hastens on his way.
He has plunged into their ambush
but he does not see them
until he hears their horses neigh
and sees their shields shining.
From under his shield he looks to the left,
and spots them; he would rather not be there,
nonetheless in his heart
he finds great bravery.
He perceived them from fairly far
because the moon was shining brightly.
He knows very well that he is betrayed,
but he is not frightened;
he has great prowess and courage,
so he speaks with confidence.
He crosses the middle of the plain,
he speaks and asks them:
"What people are you who wait there,
who lie in ambush in these woods?
You are thieves or evil men, I think.
But you are hiding for no purpose
for I am all alone, as you see well.
I have nothing with me for this encounter
but my arms and my horse.
If you want to joust with me
you have only to stay there:
I await you on this road,
where I shall joust with you."
They have not said a word
but they are all equipped and prepared.
They rush from their ambush,
staying closely together;
they attack him from all sides,
shouting and advancing.
They expected to seize him quickly

but he defended himself well,
he defended himself against them all
like a bold and valiant warrior.
Tydeus defends himself very hard
and fights with courage.
Chthonius attacks him first,
as their lord and leader,
but God protected and defended Tydeus,
so he did not reach him.
All of them thrust themselves en masse
and assail him quite fiercely;
they wage a great and powerful battle—
he might well fear for his life.
He draws his sword which Oeneus
gave him when he knighted him;
no knight ever had one so good,
neither iron nor steel can stop it.
Galant the blacksmith forged it
and Vulcan smelted it;
there were three goddesses at the tempering
and three fairies at the engraving.
It will not yield to any blow
no rust will attach to it,
and no man who is struck by it
can be healed of the wound.
The knight has struck with it
and split straight down to the belt
the man who first attacked him.
To the others he says:
"Hold back there,
my sword cuts very well!
I challenge all of you to death.
He will get help too late
whom I shall strike in anger."
The traitors are enraged
because of the companion they have lost;
they make every effort to avenge him.
The fighting is fierce with no holds barred.
They have struck him with such force

1675 **Galant the blacksmith forged it** *Galanz li fevres la forgea*: This is probably a reference to the legendary Germanic smith, Wieland, who appears in the epic *Waltharius*.

that they have knocked him from his horse.
They tell him: "You are down,
now Chthonius is avenged."
Then they cry: "Strike, barons!"
He defends himself like a lion
but he is alone and getting tired
and they keep pressing him hard.
He sees a high cliff beside him
that would be good for fighting;
they watch as he climbs up.
Now you will hear a great battle.
The cliff is strong and defensible,
it was once a devil's nest.
The Sphinx, who made many good men miserable,
was there in ancient times.
Tydeus climbs up to the opening
that will give the vassal a strong defense;
if any of them attacks him
he will be able to defend himself without fail.
They pursue him, spurring,
then they attack him on foot,
they assail him on all sides
and throw sharpened darts at him.
They cry out: "He can't save himself
on the cliff or anywhere else."
But the cliff does protect him,
he fears nothing except from the front.
Then a great adventure occurred,
good for him but hard on them.
There was a dark rock above,
sitting on the others,
but perched so precariously
that it was ready to fall.
The stone was so large
two oxen could not have pulled it.
But Tydeus pushes it down,
making the whole hillside tremble;
anyone it met on its way,
you can be sure, was killed!
It struck worthy barons,
I do not know if it was nine or ten;
these will not press him anymore,
they can not do anything to enrage him.

They had been among the best of the country:
Theron and Halys,
Dorylas and Phaidimus.
Tydeus will no longer fear them;
the stone struck them in such a way
that it killed and destroyed them.
The others are disconcerted
and say to each other:
"This one is truly a devil
who can defend himself even with stones."
When he sees them trembling so
he begins to taunt them:
"A fever seems to have
seized you in your boldness.
But just wait a little
and you can be cured of this ill;
the sword will cure you,
for it has good relics in it."
He leaps swiftly to the ground
and attacks them boldly.
Anyone he reaches does not go further,
he has no protection from death.
Tydeus leaps up and then down,
attacking them like a worthy vassal;
on all sides he strikes them dead
with his valor and his power.
Then the others pull themselves together
and make an effort, forcing him up the hill;
they think they can take him up there
but he knows how to defend himself
and therefore he does not fear them;
he drives them back and throws them down.
He puts up a very good battle
because of the cliff which he was defending.
Tydeus is in a very strong place,
not fearing a war engine or iron or fire
or anything else except at the opening.
And that he defends with his sword;
the first one to come in
will pay dearly for it.
No door was sold so dear
nor defended so well by a porter.
At the well-made entrance

that was cut into the strong stone
they all attack in one line,
climbing up as best they can.
And Tydeus defends himself strongly:
anyone he accosts, he cuts through.
His blows are wondrous and great;
Roland never struck better.
He has killed so many of the first line
that he strikes the living with the dead:
the dead, who fall from above,
fall down on the living below.
Whoever falls there does not get up,
he has to die; he ends there.
The attackers know they are getting weak,
they would willingly have gone back
if it had not been for Galeran of Sypont
who rouses them on the king's behalf:
"Vile cowards, what will we say
when my lord asks us
what we have done with the messenger
who insulted him at his own board?
He called him a perjurer in front of us;
that should distress all of us.
We will have a bad reception in our country
if we do not bring him back dead or captive.
Worthless men, what will we say to the king?
How shall we dare appear before him?
Our shame will be terrible
if Tydeus gets himself out of this situation.
It will be an outrage if one shield
conquers so many knights.
Especially since the king chose us
from his whole empire today."
At these words they turn back;
they will wage a fierce battle now,
together from all sides
they throw their sharpened darts.
His hauberk and his shield,
which was cut from one side to the other, fail.
He loses a lot of blood, he changes color,
but he keeps on fighting;
he defends himself with his steel blade
which has killed so many knights.

He defends himself with great force
for he finds no mercy in them.
They make an enormous effort to capture him
and he to defend himself against them.
He has killed the constable
and his nephew, Vougrin of Naples;
when the others see these two dead
their strength ebbs.
They begin to flee
and to abandon their horses,
but the brave Galeran holds them back
though he would suffer for it later.
He calls them all by their names:
"Stop," he says, "sons of barons!
Noble knights, the king's retinue,
why do you flee in such disarray?
Where are the great knightly deeds
you boast of to your friends?
Where are the great blows
you brag about at the hearth?
Where are the proud words and the threats
you used to make there?
You are facing a crisis,
now we shall see what your prowess is.
Stop," he says, "come back!
Remember the fierce deeds
of battles and vassalage
that your lineage has always accomplished
who even in fear for their lives
never committed a cowardly act.
Avenge your brothers, your friends,
that this vassal has killed.
If you do not fail me
I shall make him leap from that height,
he will have to choose a bad route
if he does not want to give himself up to us.
If any ever loved the king,
let him show it now, let him come with me."
Whether for fear or for shame,
they returned to their duty.
Galeran goes ahead and leads them,
swearing by the arm of his love,
that if Tydeus should escape alive,

he will henceforth consider himself dead.
He makes his way ahead of the others,
but Tydeus is not afraid of him;
he covers himself well, draws his sword
and awaits him at the entrance.
What shall I say about it? Between the two
they exchanged wondrous blows.
Galeran strikes Tydeus,
cutting off a piece of his shield;
he deals him such a blow with his sword
that Tydeus is stunned by it,
but the blow fell outside
and did not touch his body.
Tydeus knows how to strike with a sword:
he deals Galeran such a blow
that he buries the blade
in his skull.
As he pulls it out, the other falls to the ground;
for him the war is over.
The others would willingly have left
if they had been able,
but Tydeus is so close to them
that he put them all to death without confession.

Not one of that company
escaped with his life,
except for the one that he made swear
to tell everything to their king.
Then Tydeus mounted his chestnut horse
that was worth a thousand gold pounds.
He made his way through the mountain,
but he was weak, bleeding badly.
He was so wounded through his body
that his innards poured out;
the noble man is fatally wounded
and has no one to carry his arms.
He rides hard in great pain
until he can not ride any further.
But he has ridden so far
on the great road and the path
through the country he knows best
that he reaches Greece as best he can.
In Greece he came straight to Argos

where Adrastus was holding his court.
The king was in his palace
hearing cases with his barons.
Tydeus entered the palace exhausted;
his varnished hauberk was torn
and he was wounded throughout his body.
The hauberk on his back was altogether ripped
and the tunic beneath it bloody.
His shield seems like a wooden buckler,
for it was pierced from one side to the other;
it had just been bought for a thousand sous
but now it was worth little.
Not a handswidth of it was still whole—
he was not a coward who had carried it in battle.
With such equipment, as I said,
Tydeus came before the king.
He shouted: "Arm yourselves quickly,
let the king summon his army!
Take up arms, knights!
This messenger is badly wounded."
When the king sees him, he leaps to his feet,
you can be sure he was very angry;
he takes Tydeus gently in his arms,
covering his fur cloak with blood.
Very gently and softly
he sets him down on the ground.
Swiftly the king takes off his hauberk
and asks for unguent for the wounds.
On his chest there is a large wound;
when Adrastus sees it, he is very upset;
when he sees what the lance's blow did
he has no hope for Tydeus's life.
He asks who did it to him
and Tydeus tells him everything.
Then his wife, disheveled and pale,
comes running through the hall;
through the hall, disheveled,
she runs like a mad woman.
Polynices weeps so hard
that nothing can comfort him;
he almost goes mad from grief
when he sees his messenger so wounded.
But the king sends for an Armenian

who knew a lot about medicine;
he worked so hard, night and day,
that by the end of a month he had healed Tydeus.

I should tell you now about the Thebans,
what grief and pain they suffered.
The messenger descended before the king,
the one Tydeus had bound by oath.
He stopped before the king
and said aloud: “You should never have been born!”
Then his grief overcame him and he fainted;
when he revived, he spoke.
He told of the disaster
and the great misadventure,
how they were all killed by one man,
and no one else escaped.
He accuses and berates the king;
and no one contradicts him:
“You have committed such a betrayal
that your reward will be
to lose your heritage
and be thrown out of your kingdom.
I come from the mission you sent,
where you have suffered great harm;
you will never see it repaired
for all the gold of your kingdom.
You have lost your knights,
the messenger has killed them all.
No one but me has escaped,
and it distresses me that he did not kill me too.
You can find them under the cliff
of the devil Sphinx—this is no fable.
Evil king, why did you do it?
Why did you betray a vassal
like Count Tydeus,
who came here to speak to you?
You will not be able to repent;
it would have been better for you to flee that day.
Ah, Tydeus, what a fine baron you are!
How well you can strike great blows!
Blessed be your strength,
you have every right to bear a shield.
If you do not come soon to Thebes

and attack it with a great army,
may it never please Apollo
that you live three more days!"
The king lowers his head, enflamed with anger,
he commands the messenger to be killed immediately.
When he hears himself condemned to death
the messenger draws his steel sword from its sheath.
He drops his cloak before the king,
and points the sword against himself;
then he speaks
like one who has no care for himself:
"It would be a great disgrace to me
if I were murdered by you
when such a knight let me live
and did not want to kill me.
I will never die by your sword
for my own is more appropriate."
He places the pommel on the ground,
through the middle of his body he pierces himself;
he pierces himself through the middle of his body,
the iron comes out half a foot.
He struck himself with such force
that no lament could escape;
the blood spurts with such violence
that it completely covers the king
and the barons who are with him,
so their tunics are all bloody.
When the word spreads,
everyone in the street talks about it;
once word has reached the street,
it can no longer be hidden.
There is great grief throughout the city.
There is no such villain under heaven,
no matter if his heart is as hard
as the stones of that wall,
that he would not weep for sorrow
at the tears the Thebans shed for their men.
The women run through the streets,
crying and weeping for their loved ones;
mothers weep for their children,
sisters weep for their brothers,
girls lament their lovers
when they hear the chilling news.

If the city were attacked now
or ruined or captured,
I do not think they would have wept any more
or shown greater grief.
The knights and the courtiers
and the peasants and the townsmen
accuse the king of treason;
they say they should not be beholden to him.
All of them go together to the king,
they ask him in great alarm
what he has done with their friends,
where they will find them, in what country,
where they should go to look for their friends,
to bring them back to bury them.
The king told them about the valley
where the vassals lie dead
and the people go in great sorrow
with great cries and weeping.
Huge are the crowds that go to the valley
and great the sorrow they show.
No one remains in the city,
more than three hundred thousand go.
When they have wept enough
and mourned their friends,
they bury them, because they know well
there is no recourse against death.
The king of Thebes was very distressed
over what he had done, for now he knows
that a war has begun,
which will devastate his land.

Wherever he has a friend, he sends for him
and prepares himself well for the coming siege.
His soothsayers discover by their divinations
that a Greek army is approaching at full gallop;
they are really on the march!
Adrastus sends for his people;
he warns whoever holds a fief or land from him,
or wishes to profit by fighting for him,
against using any kind of excuse
to avoid helping him in his hour of need.
He orders his army, drawn from his far-flung lands,
to assemble at Argos:

it's a formidable force he's collected—
you never saw a larger one.
Indeed, such an army could only be matched
by those of Caesar and Pompey;
even the Trojan host, famed in story,
couldn't boast so many princes and counts.
Here's the Duke of Auphrigenia,
there's Cader of Archemenia
and the African of Mycenes;
with the sole exception of the Duke of Athens,
there wasn't a baron missing
who held land from Adrastus.
From Arcadia came Parthenopeus,
leading twenty thousand Greeks;
nature never created anyone finer
anywhere, anytime.
Then came Hypomedon,
who was a close relative of the king;
he brought with him a company
lacking neither wealth nor good breeding.
And Capaneus came too,
a huge man descended from the race of giants:
with him came a troop
of experts in making war.
Tydeus had it proclaimed in Calydon
that every warrior there should come at once—no excuses.
And Polynices could supply from his own lands
a thousand knights who would fight for him;
most were his pledges
whom he had ordered, by messenger, to come;
Eteocles had wronged some of them
so they had mortal hatred for him,
detesting his lordship so much
that they abandoned their inherited lands because of it.

When all these troops had gathered together
they made up such a massive army, it seems to me,
that it would take an entire day to traverse
the ground they occupied along the riverbank.

2083–84 **Indeed, such an army. . .Caesar and Pompey** *onc ne fu mais tiel aüné. . . Cesar et la Pompeè*; A reference to Lucan's epic poem, *Pharsalia*, left incomplete at his death in 65 CE.

The king sent for Amphiaraus,
a very eminent archbishop
who presided over their religious law
and knew all of heaven's secrets;
[He answered the gods' riddles and cast lots to read the future,]
and brought dead men back to life;
he even understood the languages of birds.
There wasn't a better divine in the whole world.
The king asked him to foretell
the future of the army, holding back nothing.
Amphiaraus sighed heavily,
bowed his head, didn't want to reply;
but the king strongly insisted
that he tell him the truth about the augury.

"Sire," he said, "I'll tell the truth,
the whole truth, and nothing but the truth:
if I know anything about the future,
it's that if you insist on leading to Thebes
all these people you see before you,
very few of them will ever come back,

For you will lose Capaneus,
Polynices and Tydeus;
Hypomedon will die there
and so will Parthenopeus,
and so many others
that I can't begin to tell you.
And I will die, if you lead me there—
I won't even live for two weeks.
Not that any man will kill me;
instead the earth will swallow me up,
me and my horse,
down, down into the depths of the abyss."

Capaneus leapt to his feet
and spoke angrily:
"Sire," he said, "you ought not to believe
whatever you hear from this priest.

2123a **[He answered the gods' riddles and cast lots to read the future,]** *[il prent respons et giete sors]*: verse missing in MS S, translated from MS C v. 2059.

He really can't tell you
anything about the future.
What he is, is a coward; his goal is to make up stories
that will keep this army from moving.
How can we let Polynices be disinherited
and thrown out of his kingdom—
the man who married your daughter
and was wrongfully exiled by his brother?
Once we get there with this great host
we'll attack them and quickly capture the city.
It will bring you great honor if you can beat them all
and win back your son in law's domain for him.

Then get going, your majesty! Don't believe such predictions;
your day of reckoning will certainly come,
and when it does, no priest will protect you from it—
but it won't happen until then."

Everyone concurred in these words,
and refused to believe the archbishop.
The king had the call to battle sounded,
a flourish of trumpets and drums:
the criers of the *ban* raced through the army,
telling everyone to get under way—at once!
In the meadows outside the town
a good three hundred thousand men assembled
and set a course straight for Thebes,
hardly caring who saw them.
They crossed the deserts of Nemea,
finding it a very difficult stretch indeed.
By the time they entered the realm of King Lycurgus,
they were sure they would die of thirst;
panic-stricken, the barons
searched for water, their only hope of survival,
and suffered mightily
from their thirst and the heat.
It was May, in those long days
when the sun is hot,
the weather is clear and serene,
and birds sing in the morning.

2174 **the criers of the *ban* raced through the army** *li banier vont criant par l'ost*: The *ban* is the public proclamation of the king's orders.

At the time when the army got underway,
it hadn't rained in three months:
the earth, without rain,
was burnt and parched.
So dry had it become
that its every creature was equally emaciated.
Despite looking all day,
no one in the Greek army, from vanguard to rearguard,
found any place, on mountain or in valley,
where they or their horses could drink.
This made the Greeks extremely anxious;
they repeatedly implored their god
to send rain down on them,
since they didn't know where else to find water.
On the one hand heat tormented them,
while on the other they burned with thirst.
All the horses—warhorses, packhorses, palfreys—
were also suffering so badly from thirst
that they couldn't go even go a step further,
that's how woebegone and exhausted they were.
As for the infantry, most of them
were just about completely worn out.

The Greeks couldn't take any more of this;
they were right on the verge of dying
when their leaders decided jointly
to scour the forests
of the entire surrounding countryside
seeking any stream,
wherever it might be,
at which the army could halt.
The Greek council,
fully alert to the problem,
determined that no obstacle should prevent them
—no matter how far away such a river might be—
from searching the countryside
until they had found some water.

As soon as they arrived at this decision,
they got underway.
Tydeus rode in front
as the Greeks' standard bearer;
he took the lead with his company.

At the foot of a mountain,
they entered a marvelous valley,
very hideous and dark,
hemmed in on both sides
by great forests and thick woodlands.

Count Capaneus followed them
with a full thirteen thousand of his own men,
pushing on in search of a stream
and leaving the rest of the army behind.
Beginning in the morning,
the entire Greek army traversed woods and plains
without ever reining in their mounts
until the afternoon.
The sun was already setting
and the Greeks were extremely tired.
They rode on, enduring great discomfort,
until chance led them to a really lovely orchard;
there was neither herb nor spice
that you could think of or name
lacking in this orchard.

The garden was beautiful and well enclosed
on every side by a strong fence,
except that an entrance in front
had a door, wide open,
through which King Lycurgus was accustomed to pass
in order to enjoy himself.
As soon as the Greeks had arrived there,
even before reining in their steeds
they looked way down into the garden.
Off to one side, under a laurel tree,
they saw a maiden,
as noble as she was beautiful.
She had a child with her
who was the son of King Lycurgus;
his name was Archemorus
and the damsel loved him as much as she possibly could.
There they were in the shade,
she and the emir's son.
She looked around and saw the army lined up;
the sight almost made her lose her senses.
She was terrified, in a panic;

she grabbed the child and tried to get away,
but bold Tydeus rushed after her,
leaned down over his horse's neck
and grabbed her by the sleeve,
laughing as he said to her,
"Damsel, you're my captive!
Be so kind as to tell us
—don't be afraid, speak to me, now,
and tell me the truth,
for we are very desperate knights—
if you know any place
in these woods, before or behind us,
where we can find a river.
For God's sake I beg you, my dear friend,
save the lives of all these people.
Take pity on us, help us;
our situation couldn't be worse!
I'm telling you the truth: it's now four days
since our warhorses have had anything to drink.
We've come directly from Greece;
most of our men
are so upset and discouraged, so exhausted,
that they can't go one step further."

The maiden was very well bred;
when she heard all this she was deeply moved,
so she answered the knight:
"My lord, I won't hide from you
The fact that this entire land is so dry
There's not a spring or a marsh
that isn't completely parched and dried up.
Thanks to our pride and our sins,
God has sent down on us from heaven
bitter hatred and great war.
Nonetheless it would be shameful
if all of you and your lords
weren't able to get some relief right now.
If I weren't carrying this child,
I'd lead you to a little stream
that's as pure as it is clear:
it's the stream of Langia
which will, I think, restore you.
I don't dare be so bold as to abandon him;

but you seem to me such a noble person
that, whether he lives or dies,
I won't refuse to lead you right to the stream's bank;
but if you want to come with me,
make sure that you treat me honorably."

At that moment the king,
who had been following the barons, arrived.
When he heard the news,
which certainly seemed good to him,
he said straightaway to the young woman:
"By Apollo, whom I cherish greatly,
I'll appoint an escort for you
That I'm sure will guard you well.
Where are you, Capaneus,
Polynices, and Tydeus?
I commend this woman to you:
guard her for me from now on."
"Sire," they say, "we'll do it well:
if it's in our power, no harm will come to her.

When the maiden heard that,
she was completely overjoyed.
She set the little child down on the ground,
making a bed of grass and flowers for him.
She left him as soon as she could
and took the path that she knew well.
"My lords," she said, "follow me;
I'll lead you to that stream."

When she had reached a point
the length of four bowshots from the garden,
she pointed out the water to them;
When bold Tydeus saw it,
boy! was he pleased: as rapidly as he could,
he sent his messengers back to the army
with orders to shout it out to the four winds,
for all the horsemen and foot soldiers to hear:
"Your troubles are over!
get yourselves to the water right away;
whoever is thirsty, go get that water!"
Great joy coursed through the army,
where before there had been great distress.

Those on horseback raced ahead,
not bothering to look for roads or paths;
no trees or hedges could block their way,
since, in a pack, they created a trail as they went.
They galloped ahead at full speed
and those on foot followed after them.
Each one in his own way
hastened pell mell to the water
as soon as they saw the shore
no one alive could have held them back:
they didn't look up and down for a ford;
instead they threw themselves into the deepest water.
Then you would have seen exhausted horses
filling their stomachs and entrails;
they drank so much because of their burning thirst
that, willy nilly, their hearts burst.
As for the infantry, you would have seen them jump,
clothes, shoes, and all,
into the stream up to their necks;
neither a fool nor a wise man could keep them
from jumping into the deepest water,
so afraid were they that it might run out.
What can I tell you? There was such a crowd
Going in and out of the water
that as a result the stream lost its course,
and began to run backwards—yes, in reverse.

Adrastus, the lord of Greece,
with Archbishop Amphiaraus
and all the princes and dukes,
drew back beyond the rest of the army,
and Tydeus the brave led them
to that well-bred damsel
who had gone to so much trouble
in order to point out to them where the water was.
Adrastus, himself no churl,
spoke to her first:
"My dear," he says, "what's your name?
I thank you, and so do my barons,
very, very much, indeed.
You've been helpful to my people
and I'm absolutely convinced
that you are nobly born.

She responded elegantly:
"My lord, I am an exile;
My name is Hypsipyle.
Through sinful treason
I was banished from my kingdom,
Lemnos, the island where I was born.
Something amazing happened in Lemnos,
completely unheard of by anyone, man or woman:
the women there, by embracing villainy,
planned among themselves a horrible crime:
in a tremendous betrayal,
each woman killed her spouse;
those with no husband killed their father,
son or nephew, cousin or brother.
My father was king of that city;
my mother had died a little while before,
so he no longer had a spouse,
and I was still quite young.
I could not find it in my heart
to commit such a crime
as killing my father,
no matter how much they urged me to.
That night, while all the world slept,
Every male in Lemnos was slain.
Knives in hand,
The murderers came straight to my father's palace;
they climbed up with a ladder
and entered through the window of the great hall:
neither a strong bolt nor a lock could keep them out.
They went looking for the king in his chamber,
and kept searching everywhere
until finally finding him there, asleep, they killed him.
I was terrified, and didn't intend to wait for them;
I knew very well that, if they found me,
I wouldn't have escaped even if I had a hundred lives.
I fled, following the moon;
and for two whole days I never stopped fleeing,

2404 **Something amazing happened in Lemnos** *Une merveille avint en Lenne*: The story of Hypsipyle and the murderous women of Lemnos that follows is told in great detail in the *Thebaid*, Book 5; it occurs in the *Argonautica* of Apollonius of Rhodes (mid-third c. BCE) and is alluded to in the sixth letter of Ovid's *Heroides*, "Hypsipyle to Jason" (before 8 CE).

along roads and paths,
at great speed,
just as chance led me.
I came upon a lord
who has taken me into his household, with great honor;
he is the lord and king of this land.,
but I don't know if you have heard tell of him.
He had one son by his wife;
I take care of the child, whom he loves dearly, for him;
Nature never formed a more handsome boy."

But listen to the terrible misfortune
that happened only a few hours later:
while she remained with the Greeks,
a powerful, evil serpent appears,
coming out of the forest and entering the garden.
From his nostrils shoot forth
the fiery flames stoked within his body;
whatever he encounters, he burns to a crisp.
He finds the child all alone, with no guardian;
he hisses, and sticks out his stinger
as long as a staff,
and pricks the child under the breast.
Then he sucks out the heart from under his armpit
and drinks his blood through the wound:
the child, who was beautiful and fair,
turns black all over, moans, cries out, and howls in pain;
his body dies as his soul flees from it,
and the serpent remains there,
falling asleep next to the child.

The damsel, who was far from the orchard,
heard the cries, and asked leave to go.
As soon as she could she left the army,
but to no avail, because she arrived too late;
she came back as soon as she could,
but destiny was too strong for her.

As soon as she arrived, in haste,
she saw the sleeping serpent
who had killed her child:
there he was, lying right beside his victim.
She was scared of the huge monster,

and turned back in flight,
loudly bewailing her child,
killed by such a devil:
"Aaay! You beautiful, fair child—
what a terrible mistake to leave you alone today!
Now you're dead, my beautiful darling,
and I can't stay in this land.
Aaaay! Miserable wretch, cursed with bad luck,
see how dishonored I am now!
I'll truly have to die—
I can't bear to live any longer."
The poor creature cried out so loudly
that everyone at the riverbank heard her.

Capaneus hears her cries
and shouts, "Curse my luck!
I hear that damsel's cries;
I have to find out
who has attacked her—
he certainly won't get away with his life!"
As quickly as he could he ran to where she was,
carrying his great spear in his hand.
He found her all disheveled,
looking like a madwoman.
He implored her, "My dear, my dear,
who did this to you? Don't hide it!
You can be sure that I'll avenge you:
I'll kill him with this spear
and dispatch him through the gate
by which all the dead leave this world.
You can count on it that this very day
he'll take the place reserved for him in the middle of Hell."
She hears him, looks at him,
and finally answers him:
"Sire, what's the point of my telling you?
I can't get any help from you."
"Tell me, sweetheart, and trust me;
if I can, I'll avenge you."
The maid replied at once,
"Sire, I've lost my child."
"My dear, how have you lost him?"
"Sire, a serpent has taken him from me."
"A serpent?" "Exactly, Sire, I promise you.

I'll point it right out to you:
it's bigger than an elephant ,
and it's lying over there, right next to the child."

Capaneus went over there,
holding his spear in his right hand;
as he approached, infuriated,
he struck the serpent with it.
The spear sprang back, up into the air;
You can't kill a serpent that way!
Now Tydeus approached at a gallop;
he hurls his spear, striking the serpent right in the chest,
but the beast doesn't flinch
because the spear rebounds off him.
Then Polynices aimed his spear at him—
the iron point bounces off without wounding.
Now everyone bombards the serpent with iron and steel,
but they cannot even pierce his hide.
Capaneus presses in closer,
and the serpent hurls himself at him,
failing to strike the warrior
but not missing his steed:
he slashes the horse's throat
quicker than a razor cutting a fine hair.
Having finished off the horse,
the beast encountered another noble warrior,
a valiant and elegant knight
who had no chance to escape:
all of him above his saddle,
including his entrails, the serpent tore away.

By now, Capaneus was furious;
he wrenched a young oak tree out of the ground
and threw it, striking the serpent right on the back,
and piercing him near the broader end.
It burst right through him, from side to side,
so that the tree was buried two feet into the ground.
The serpent realized it had been wounded,
pinned though his middle by a stake;
so that he's entangled around it.
The Greeks, hopping mad,
have now surrounded him;
they keep striking him until they've killed him.

They were a happy cohort
once they had killed the serpent;
they returned to their camp
and celebrated with great joy.
Then they played games, appropriate to each,
in a formal competition.
But she, left as she was with a dead child,
could not partake in the festivities.
She went running straight to the tree
under which she found the child, cold as marble.
He was dead, had been for a long time;
"O God," she said, "what a thing to have happened,
for my child to have perished like this!"
She lifts him up to her breast,
kisses him more than thirty times;
it's no use; he's cold all over.
She feels with her hands around his body;
when she can feel neither pulse nor breathing,
She faints twice on top of the child.
Coming to, she reproaches herself bitterly:
"Ah," she says, "why was I born?
I've exposed myself to such great shame!
Why did I escape alive from Lemnos
only to die such a wretched death here?
This I know well, I have to die;
nothing can save me from it.
I've certainly been put in a terrible situation
by depriving the king of his son;
my death will be excruciating—
there will never have been one like it.
And if I die, it won't be an injustice,
since I'm the one who killed my young lord;
he lost his life because of me,
when I left him alone, unguarded.
Once the king learns of this disaster
it will be amazing if he doesn't fly into a terrible rage."

2562–2563 **Then they played... a formal competition** *pois joerent . . . a la palestre*: In the *Thebaid*, Book 6, these games are described in great detail, in accord with epic traditions; MS S is the only extant version of the *Roman de Thèbes* that excludes such a description.

At that moment she turns away, leaving him,
and quickly quitting the garden
she runs like a madwoman
to the water where she had left the army;
awash in the tears that expressed her great sorrow
she went right to Tydeus.
He said to her, "What's wrong, my dear?"
"Sire, I am completely ruined;
and you are wrong to be celebrating;
the serpent has killed my child,
my little lord, the king's son;
I found him dead; I'm so upset!
I'm not so daring or brave
that I can go to the king and tell him this;
he'll kill me, I'm sure of it,
for having left the child alone.
The queen is so ferocious
that when she sees her son,
whom she loved more than anything, on his bier,
she'll kill me too, I'm certain of it."

Having said this much, the maiden became quiet,
and Tydeus, when he had listened to her,
went to the Greek king and said to him,
"My lord, listen to me for a minute.
We've done this woman a great wrong,
because, thanks to us, her child is dead,
and he died in such a way
that she'll never dare to go back to the king;
by God, he would destroy her;
he'd never have mercy on her.
Sire," he says, "listen to me:
it's through you and your army
that this terrible thing has happened;
it's only right that you and your barons
should now have to suffer in turn on her behalf.
Take the maiden, lead her to the king;
we'll all go together with you.
In my opinion, and this I believe,
the king can't be so strong or cruel
that, if you beg him to pardon her,
in the end he won't grant it to you,
either out of friendship or under compulsion,

nor will the queen be so fierce
that she won't listen to your plea."

Adrastus accepted this advice;
he summoned his men, got underway,
and the entire army set out with him,
making the kind of racket you don't hear every day!
They headed straight toward the city
where King Lycurgus dwelt.
At a bowshot's distance from the walls
the whole army set up quarters on the plains.
Adrastus left his soldiers there, outside,
and proceeded, mournfully, toward the city;
with him went princes and dukes
as many as forty, but no more.
King Lycurgus mounted up,
together with a few of his inner circle;
he wished to go meet Adrastus
when the latter entered the city gate.
He spurred toward him with great joy:
"My lord," he said, "welcome!
I'm very pleased and much obliged
that you have come to see me.
There's no point in your going further;
rather, you'll put up for the night in here.
Send word to your main vassals,
your princes and captains,
that they should seek lodging here tonight,
until the city is all filled up.
The others should settle down for the night outside
and set up their tents;
then they should look around everywhere for rations;
they'll surely find plenty of them."

Adrastus thanks the king heartily,
and pledges to serve him.
"My lord," he says, "this is a generous gift,
making your city
available to me and my people
so freely at this moment.
Now I beg and admonish you,
if you have ever had any concern for me—

if you've ever cared for me at all—
please grant me the favor I'm about to ask of you."

Lycurgus looked down to the ground
and replied, "I don't want to make a big thing of this:
however dear your request may cost me,
I won't hold back from trying to get it for you,
always excepting
my son, my wife, and my own person."
They were just entering the palace
when a messenger came at a gallop
and announced to Lycurgus the bad news
that he would find his son dead,
killed by a serpent
in his garden, where he had been left alone.
When the king realized the truth,
he changed colors, turned all black;
what he had just heard completely stupified him,
so that he almost collapsed to the ground.
"Oh my God!" he exclaimed, "I'm going mad!
I'll never be happy again—
not now, not ever—
until I have killed with my own two hands
the woman who has robbed me of my child,
who was like an April flower."

The queen had awakened;
she'd been asleep that afternoon.
Now she came out quickly,
wearing a fine, close-fitting dress,
but the clamor that greeted her in the great hall
made her ghostly pale,
and when she heard the news
she fainted and fell to the ground;
then she went to pieces, in terrible sorrow.
She fell backwards, and when she got up

2682–83 **always excepting my son, my wife, and my own person** *ne mais que tant en met defors mon filz et ma femme et mon cors*: Mora-Lebrun notes that this is the first instance in vernacular literature [or at least an early instance; chronology is uncertain] of the motif of the "don contraignant" (coerced gift) which will become a regular feature of Arthurian and other chivalric romances.

she beat her hands together and continued lamenting,
full of grief and exhausted by it.
Everyone who ran to investigate the noise
wept when they heard the news.

King Lycurgus behaved very prudently,
since all his barons were there looking on:
he had no choice but to be comforted by them.
He ordered his son, dead through mischance,
to be brought to him.
One hundred servants raced there, all on foot;
but when they saw the serpent,
so hideous and stinking,
they were so terrified that they all shrank back,
and only with great trepidation approached the child.

They carried back the king's son,
giving vent to immeasurable grief.
When the king saw his dead child,
it was a moment of great misery for him;
the queen showed her great sorrow
for her child, now dead.
They cried and wailed over his body
until the barons drew them away.
Amidst much crying and bemoaning,
he was placed in a shroud, there in the hall;
and they sewed him into a green winding-sheet,
brought there from Thessaly.
They had a marble sarcophagus searched out,
and within it they placed the body in the ground.
Above the noble lad
they constructed a marvelous tomb;
I believe you'd never see one any more elegant
unless it was all of silver and gold.

The considerate King of Greece,
Who didn't want this matter to be drawn out,
Came up with a really good idea:
he would reconcile the maiden to the king.
He quickly sent for one of his private retainers,
whom he ordered to go find the maiden for him,
and who sped right off, bringing her back with him.
Just when the great hall was most full of people,

she came before the king, pleading for mercy;
she fell at his feet, groveling.
Adrastus and all his barons
offered to render homage to Lycurgus for her sake.
What more is there to say? They kept at it so long,
praying and pleading,
that her lord spared her completely
from his ill will, his great anger.
To the best of my knowledge,
the Greeks remained there for three more days.

The entire army was overjoyed,
both the horsemen and the foot soldiers,
when a messenger approached the king,
addressing him thus, with great vigor:
"Adrastus, noble and wise king,
why are you delaying by staying here?
The Thebans have come out from their city,
A good forty thousand shields.
They're riding furiously toward you
to prevent you from advancing."
When the king heard this
he was happy—he rejoiced.
He realized, if this news were true,
that the Thebans were finished.
He spread the news via his princes:
and what a sight, to see the entire army now on the move!
They sound their horns and trumpets
and the great valleys resound with the noise;
the advance guard extends
a whole league across the front of the army.
The hills and mountains are steep,
the valleys and plains broad.
Long was their journey that day,
until evening came
and the sun went to rest.
They came to a halt next to a hill
and lay down there until the next morning,
when they got back on the road,
riding through mountains
very lofty and formidable.
Tydeus went in front, guiding them,
holding a large white battle flag.

As they went, they came to a passage
carved out once by a giant;
when Polynices saw it,
he spurred his horse on and galloped into it.
The passage seemed to them very forbidding,
but they couldn't avoid it.
Above it was entirely enclosed by walls,
beneath which they passed through a gateway:
and there was a tower, tall and broad,
formerly belonging to Morgan la Fee;
no one ever saw a tower so high,
excepting only the Tower of Babel.
Over the gate was a fortress;
no one ever saw its like,
for a child of fourteen years
could defend it against one thousand giants;
and the pavement below is
all encrusted with fine silver.
Thirty pillars of enamel and clear beryl
surround the door;
the main wall, which was in front,
contained four diamond-hard stones;
above, in a door frame of fine gold
are the nine stars, as they're called in their language,
and on a gold-colored band
every kind of flower was painted.
All varieties of bird song
could be heard in the vault of the arch above the gate.
The walls are high, strong, and menacing;
they have no fear of steel pickaxe,
siege engine, battering ram, or mace,
catapult or mangonel.
High platforms and great ditches
extended for a league in front of the tower,
enclosed with great effort
within well-made palisades and high walls;
the high walls and deep ditches
were a full league in breadth.
In order not to be surprised by a sneak attack,

2814–2815 **Above. . .are the nine stars** *sus. . . sont li novascle*: The translation of these verses is conjectural.

2823 **mangonel** *mangonel*: A siege engine: another form of catapult.

the tower was entirely surrounded
by a wide and deep lake,
so deep that no one had ever reached its bottom.
This was, then, how the tower was situated;
it could never be taken by force—
and the army has to pass by it
or go all the way back.

A devil was guarding the passage;
No one had ever seen anything so satanic.
Astarot was this devil's name,
and he was a High Constable of Hell.
He had come to take up his post there
in order to lay waste to that region:
he had rediscovered the riddle
once invented by the Sphinx,
and by means of that magic
he was killing everybody there.
He disguised himself as an old woman,
and was as green as an ivy leaf.
Her face was hideous, her expression frightful;
her nose was a cubit long,
and her large, curved teeth
twisted all the way back behind her neck;
the tooth that came out of her mouth
indeed touched the back of her neck.
Her eyes were red, like a leopard's;
you never saw such an ugly look.
The brows above them
could have filled your whole door.
But here's an even greater marvel:
she could completely cover herself with one of her ears;
those ears were big and wide,
shaggy and hideous.
Her arms were as thick as a mast,
her mouth and nose black;
she had a broad hand and long fingers,
with nails like a lion's claws.

2845 **Sphinx** *Spins*: See vv. 277ff. above.

2861 **she could completely. . . ears** *toute se covre de l'oreille*: A feature of various monstrous peoples known to medieval Europe through encyclopedias such as that of Isidore of Seville (sixth to seventh centuries CE).

Whoever she might strike with that hand
would never eat bread again.
She was dressed in a thick brown cloak
made for her by fairies when they were fasting;
from the moment she put it on
no one could ever do her any harm.
She wore a pair of light shoes,
not cordovans,
but stitched from a large camel skin,
using the entire skin.
With four long lengths of cord
she had tightened them all around;
and a white bearskin
was wrapped around her flanks.
This was not a happy old woman,
but rather a disagreeable and bristly one
who was lying face down in the middle of the great hall
when she heard the joyful noise
that the army was making
as it came to the passageway.

When the old woman heard them,
she leapt to her feet with great energy;
she looked around, saw the approaching crowd,
and was inflamed by anger and hatred.
She picked up a mace she had beside her
and put it around her neck with both hands.
Amazing! Even if eight bulls were to grab onto it,
they couldn't move it two steps!
It was made of well honed steel,
and its equal had never been seen;
it was wickedly sharp,
and no one that it struck could survive.

The Greeks made a great racket
as Tydeus, riding ahead, guided them.
They wanted to advance, if they could—
but suddenly the old woman was in their path.
When she came out from the portal,
the royal guard was terrified;
as soon as those in front saw her,
the bravest of them became scared.
On a grey marble boulder

she of the fierce visage sits down.
She looks at the barons, and threatens them:
"Flee," she says, "this place!
Go back, retreat now, barons!
You won't pass without a real fight.
Withdraw now, turn back—
and be careful that I don't strike you down.
See how full these great valleys are
of the graves of men and horses
that I have killed; I can't even count them,
and twenty carts couldn't carry them away.
Whoever wants to get past here
has to either solve my riddle or die:
you must guess or die!
See the answer or take a chance!"
The army has come to a halt,
and everyone is scared;
they see the valleys full of the dead,
more than one hundred cart-loads of them.
Tydeus answers first:
"Old woman, I'm a knight;
I'm better at bearing arms
than at solving riddles."
"By God," she replies, "that's great.
Then I won't lose anything."

Tydeus was very angry
that this old hag was guarding the passageway.
He called Polynices,
who came spurring up to him:
"My fellow warrior, you guess,
if you know anything about solving riddles.
I've been in a lot of tight spots,
but I've never felt so lost.
This devil that you see here
has enchanted us all."
Polynices said, "I don't know anything about it;
I've never paid any attention to augury.
I know something about other subjects,
but I don't get involved in such things.

2922–23 **you must. . . take a chance!** *A deviner . . . ou a chosir*: The meaning of vv. 2922–23 is unclear, the translation accordingly conjectural.

"Old woman," said young Tydeus,
"how will I be better off if I solve the riddle?"
"If you figure it out, you'll kill me,
and afterwards you can pass through here."
"All right, tell it to me: I'm listening;
and if I can, I'll solve it."
So the old woman said, "Now listen closely,
and tell me, if you know it
—and if you don't, I'll drive you all crazy—
who is it that first goes on four legs,
then on two, afterwards on three:
guess right, or death awaits you."
"Hag, may you come to a bad end!
I know the answer to this one:
when a man is old, he walks using canes;
when he's little, he crawls on all fours;
and when he reaches the age of fifteen,
he stands on his own two feet, like a grown-up."

The old woman hears him, and faints,
and falls, broken, to the marble floor;
two falling oak trees
wouldn't have made a bigger crash.
From that time on, people could pass by,
without dying, without guessing,
without guessing, without dying;
without having to make a choice.

The Greeks came to the gateway,
and chopped up the old woman;
they all got through the passageway
and got back onto their road.
Then they entered a valley
through which they traveled all day.
They went down into this valley
and set up camp beneath a castle
that sat on a mountain,
its tower high and solitary.
Eteocles had enclosed it,
wishing to make himself its lord.

2983 **its tower high and solitary** *la tor en est haut et soltaigne*: The following episode of the castle of Monflor does not appear in the *Thebaid*.

It now held one thousand knights
highly valued by the king;
Meleages, the constable there,
was closely related to the king,
and the townsmen were in the bailly.
The castle was a brand new structure;
the hill sloped away from it on all sides.
Polynices galloped up to it;
with him were King Adrastus,
Hypomedon, and Tydeus.
Those within the castle saw them coming,
but they had no desire to welcome them;
instead, they raised the drawbridge on its chains.
The garrison stood ready
to defend the castle against all comers;
they took up positions on the battlements.
Laughing at this, Polynices called out,
"Come on out where I can see you!
Tell me whose house this is,
who is its lord—what's his name?"
The first to reply was Meleages,
Eteocles' s cousin:
"My lord," he said, "what do you want?
I'll tell you about us and our lord
peacefully, without anger:
my lord's name is Eteocles,
this domain is called Valflorie
and the castle, Monflor.
My name is Meleages,
and I'm a very close relative of the king.
I'm the constable of this castle,
and that's the truth, not a story.

Now it's your turn: you tell me—and don't hide anything—
who you are and where you're going;
those are very good-looking troops you have there,
to have occupied these mountains.
I see fine knights,
young men, and impressive battle-steeds,
gold-embossed shields with floral decoration

2990 **the bailly** *al baille*: The outer courtyard of a castle, surrounded by a defensive wall.

as well as banners of a thousand colors,
green helmets and white hauberks,
and brand new lances with sharp iron cutting edges.
But I think your entry into Valflorie
will be your big mistake:
if you occupy the outlying area,
you'll not leave without a lot of suffering."

"Oh, come on!" said Polynices,
"If your name really is Meleages,
then you ought to have turned over this castle to me
as soon as I gave you my name.
After all, you're my first cousin,
the son of my aunt.
My father's name was Oedipus,
Eteocles is my brother,
and I'm that Polynices
whose turn it is to govern the realm after him.
He's held the land for his year,
now he should go off to conquer some other place;
I've come to rule the land during my assigned year,
so you really ought to turn Monflor over to me.
If you give it to me peacefully, without conflict,
I'll in turn bestow the entire honor on you;
you hold very little other land,
so I will make you the lord of Monflor.
But if you won't surrender it amicably,
and I can take it from you by force,
I swear by all the gods in whom we believe
and by the faith that we hold
that neither lineage
nor friendship nor kinship
will keep me from hanging all of you by the gates
with nooses and twisted willow-cords.

"My lord," said Meleages,
"if it comes to that, then there's nothing more we can do.
But you won't get anything from me without consultation;
I'd rather lose my life
than commit treason;
so first I'm going to confer with the other barons.
My lord," he added, "wait for me;
I can't do anything like this by myself.

I'm going off to speak with Eteocles's barons,
to try to find out
if they are willing to surrender Monflor to you
and recognize you as their lord."
He turned away, went back up to the keep:
all the barons there were distressed
by the sight of the approaching army;
they feared they couldn't hold out against them.

Once Meleages had rejoined the barons,
he reasoned with them:
"My lords," he said, "what shall we do?
We all know perfectly well that this is the rightful heir.
By law, he is as entitled to the realm
as is Eteocles,
who has had his year ruling the land,
and should now go off and win victories elsewhere.
This one has come for his year of rule,
so I beg you, with all good will,
to surrender this fortress to him
without being angry or being forced to,
since he is the natural heir.
Turn it over to him; I don't see any other solution."

Ogier of Valplenier spoke in reply,
standing up in the front row:
"Meleages, you're a big fool,
and lacking in courage to boot.
It's disgraceful that you want to break your word
and wrongfully betray your lord,
proposing to give yourself up to a vassal
who isn't legitimately our superior."

To whom Meleages answers,
"Shut up, you!
I'm ready to prove,
mounted and in full armor
in single combat with you,
that your judgment is false,
and that this younger brother
is indeed our legitimate lord.
If he comes in peace to this land,
no one should start a war against him.

The peers of the realm swore allegiance to him,
and I was there at the negotiations.
You were among the first to swear
as one of the knights there.
But now you're going back on your word,
like a traitor, as far as I can see.
If you dare to defend your opinion,
go arm yourself right away
and I'll fight you for my own sake,
for my lord and for my loyalty to him;
if I can defeat you,
who want to deny him his land,
then Monflor should be surrendered to him,
and he recognized as its lord."

A mournful silence gripped the assembly;
no one denied it to him, no one granted it,
no one took it away, but no one gave it.
Ogier made no move toward Meleages,
nor did he want to go out on the plain:
he just wanted to hold onto the castle.

A knight from Benevento
then spoke up, reasonably:
"My lords," he said, "listen to me.
We have all been the king's men;
and we all swore allegiance,
each one of us, loyally.
We ought not to perjure ourselves
by surrendering this castle to anyone else.
So let this claimant go in peace to his brother,
to confer with him and with his mother;
if Eteocles hands the land over to him for his year,
we'll hand over Monflor to him in peace as well.
Indeed, we'll be overjoyed to do it—
there'll be little resistance from us!
But before that happens we'll never turn it over to him,
for that would seem like cowardice."
And everyone in the tower cries out,
"That's the best advice!"

The barons went to the top level of the tower,
and had the windows opened;

they stuck their heads out into the daylight
through the openings in the tower.
Then Meleages spoke,
calling out to Polynices:
"My lord," he said, "Hear me out.
These barons are the king's vassals;
they don't want to make of Monflor
a name that redounds to their dishonor,
nor do they want to take my advice
to grant you entrance here.
If you wish, I'll remain here;
or if you prefer, I'll leave."

Achillor spoke next: "Sir knight:
so help me God, there's no other way.
You'll never set foot in here,
nor make a forced entrance.
There are plenty of good knights in here,
along with noble barons of Syria,
and we have enough provisions
that we're not worried they will run out:
Look! Even if you were to besiege us for fourteen months,
we still wouldn't have to put off eating.
We also have enough white wine;
so you can't disturb us at all.
Get out of here!
We're hardly afraid of your threats;
just let your older brother
rule over the whole realm.
Go right back to Greece,
and make war on the Venetians,
who are laying waste your country;
we don't care much for your arrogance."

Polynices stopped under a tree,
and dismounted on a marble block;
with him were King Adrastus,
Hypomedon, and Tydeus.
"My lords," he says, "look at that tower!

3176 **who are laying waste your country** *qui vous guastent vostre contré*: A reference to twelfth-century wars of aggression undertaken by the Venetians in eastern Europe for commercial purposes.

It fears neither siege engines nor frontal assault,
neither arrows nor lances,
and against it siege machines aren't worth a penny;
that tower is impervious to stone-throwing machines,
it fears no catapult that might strike it.
There are plenty of knights at Monflor
who don't add much to my realm;
so advise me on what I should do,
and how I should behave.
Let's just leave Monflor and push on ahead,
and commend the place to the living devil!"
When Tydeus heard that,
he glanced at Adrastus
and then said to Polynices:
"What could we expect to find further on?
Upon my faith," he continues,
"we'll have no chance to win anything else!
You've certainly spoken like a terrible coward,
a rogue, a scoundrel;
and you deserve to be insulted,
given your ability to say stupid things.
You mustn't leave Monflor,
the gateway to your realm,
until we have torn down the walls
and completely wrecked its trenches.
We won't have much chance to win a war
that we might have to fight on someone else's turf
if we don't take this rickety shack
before Eteocles can find out."

Adrastus, the rich king, said,
"Tydeus, you've certainly got it right;
better a gold crown for you
than for King Nabuchodonosor.
Now let those folk in Monflor know
that I'm going to make them tremble in their castle;
I'm going to use Greek fire
to burn out the streets of their town-dwellers,

3218 **Greek fire** *fou grezeis*: A mixture of inflammable materials widely used in siege warfare, first by the armies of the Byzantine empire in the ninth century. See the Introduction, p. 8, and note 14.

to throw down and ravage their strong walls,
and to squelch the pride of those barons."

No more keeping you in suspense:
Polynices mounts his war horse;
the heralds circulate throughout the host, passing on the word
that everyone should make camp right away.
Then you could have seen all those troops settling in,
with so many luxurious tents erected for the barons;
those tents covered the hillsides
and extended down into the plains all around.
The Duke of Calydon's tent
was supervised by his seneschal, Garsadoine,
the legitimate son of a count,
and seneschal of the entire army.
In front of the entrance to the lord's tower
he erected the king's tent,
which was made of multicolored silk,
decorated with animals and flowers;
stories were beautifully painted on it,
telling of old laws and remembered deeds,
tribunals and trials,
judgments and wrongs done;
depicting mountains and valleys,
dances and royal games,
maidens and their lovers,
wives and their husbands,
broad fields and rivers;
and a thousand kinds of animal,
goshawks and sparrowhawks,
palfreys and warhorses;
hoary old men,
both bald and long-haired;
mountains and forests,
the ambushes and traps
that young men set for their beloveds;
jousts and attacks,
castles and cities,

3235 **he erected the king's tent** *tendit al rei son paveillon*: Allegorically decorated, fantastically luxurious tents came to be a feature of the medieval adaptations of classical epics as well as of chivalric romances. See the Introduction, p. 4.

fortresses and strongholds.
The natures of all other creatures
were painted on the tent.
And the golden eagle seated on the globe atop the tent
was so beautiful
that no one ever saw another that shone so brilliantly—
nor could a peasant even dare to look at it;
neither King David nor King Solomon
ever had such an eagle atop their pavillion-tents.
It had so many precious stones—
carbuncles, enamels,
sparkling clear gems,
hyacinths shining brilliantly—
that, when the sun or wind touched it,
flames jetted forth from its mouth.
Around this tent were more than thirty others,
belonging to the counts and dukes
who served the king with devotion;
each one held his fief from him.

The king sits in front of the castle gate,
and with him the Greek barons,
who take up their arms
and go on the attack with the infantry,
which had already begun the assault,
letting fly many a sharp spear.
They hurled spears and shot arrows so fiercely
that no one in the castle dared to leave even his eyes unprotected.
Behind them, Polynices went on the attack,
with his bold, fierce squadron,
numbering twenty thousand young men,
brave and noble, completely loyal.
They attacked boldly,
arriving all together at the castle walls;
each one struck at the wall with his pick,
but they couldn't open a breach in it.
Those inside defended the wall strongly;
look! Now the battle is general and intense.
Tydeus, meanwhile, is up on a hill;
he has a very large, ferocious, and redoubtable army
of Caledonian knights
who attack expertly, without delay;
along with three hundred crossbowmen

and more than four thousand archers,
who let fly arrows and quarrels.
Right up to the walls go the young warriors
whom Tydeus has just dubbed knights
and newly armed;
they have trenchant chisels and strong picks,
but the walls are made of gray-brown marble
which they cannot in any way shatter;
nor could they stay there very long,
for those up above, who were no fools when it came to defense,
kept bombarding them with huge stones.

Hypomedon was in a valley;
there isn't a better vassal in the entire army,
and with him he had fifty knights,
good warriors, brave and bold.
They charged up to the earthen ramparts,
and weakened them in thirty places;
they smashed seven hundred blocks within them,
knocking down some of their posts.
Had they been allowed to remain there,
they could have brought down the wall;
but the defenders within were aware of them,
caught them there and killed them all.
At the sound of the trumpet they threw down boiling water,
burning thirty of Hypomedon's barons;
so he ordered the assault to cease,
and his troops returned to their camp.

That night they lay down and slept
until morning, when they arose.
Tydeus, having risen,
sent for his machine-building engineers
and instructed them to make siege engines
with building wood brought back from the forest.
Then he has them make two stone-launching catapults,
strong, piercing, and nice and light;
before evening comes,
they're all ready to hurl stones.

There's a tower above the gate,
very pretty, but not strong;
the two machines hurl

sharp-edged boulders and huge stones;
they break and destroy its walls,
tear apart its pillars.
There were some knights inside it,
or so I believe, and twenty archers;
they were killed, wiped out,
as the tower crashed to the ground.
Those within felt great sorrow over this,
and mourned profoundly for their relatives;
inside Monflor there was terrible grief,
as the defenders lamented the absence of their lord.
The warriors who are their mortal enemies
are attacking all too well,
hurling Greek fire at them
and destroying the houses of the town-dwellers;
[no vault or cellar is left,
no stone hall nor minster.
The flames enter through the windows;
those in the apartments within flee.
Those on the main floor suffer great heat:
there isn't a baron, no matter how brave,
who doesn't tremble with fear.
They all curse their lord
for not coming to their aid here,
since he was alerted the day before yesterday.
In the tower, they sound the horns
even as their people panic;
King Adrastus orders his army to press in close
and place their ladders against the walls.
Those within don't want to surrender,
so they work hard to defend themselves:
they hurl seven hundred spears and more,
to prevent those outside from climbing up.
The fire dies down. When night comes,
and they see how dark, even black, the night has become,
the royal troops sound the retreat;
they've done a good day's work.
The army returned to its quarters

3354 **[no vault or cellar is left. . .]** [*n'i remaint voute ne celier. . .*]: From here to line 3489 there is a lacuna in MS S's narrative of the attack on Monflor. Following Mora-Lebrun, we fill the gap with readings from Constans's edition of the *Roman de Thèbes*.

very happy that evening.
The chief vassals dismounted
in front of the main, royal tent.

There were four counts from Venice
in front of the King of Greece's tent;
they took the king aside:
"Sire," they said, "neither by brute force,
nor by shooting arrows and throwing spears,
will you be able to capture this tower.
But we are wise in the ways of war,
and know all about conquering castles.
If you'll just have confidence in our expertise,
we're so shrewd and clever
that tomorrow we'll deliver Monflor to you
with everyone in the keep."
To which the king replied, "How can you do that?
I'll give you plenty of gold and silver,
and throw open my treasury to you—
all my silver, all my gold.
If you can take the castle
and turn over to me the knights inside it,
I will grant you my friendship
and give you more possessions
than your heart could imagine
or your tongue could name."
"My lord," they said, "just wait a minute,
and we'll tell you what you must do.
Assign to Sir Polynices
five hundred knights, no more;
they'll set up an ambush by moonlight
in the valley below that brown rock.
When the barons are in the valley,
they will dismount from their horses;
under the leafy olive trees
they will rest on their shields
and each warrior there
will hold his horse by its reins.
Have them lodge their spears in the ground:
tomorrow, God will make them all happy.
Meanwhile, assign to Tydeus
one thousand naturally skillful knights,
sensible and self-controlled:

he'll lead them straight toward Thebes.
A good two leagues from Monflor,
they should dismount at Valcolor;
he'll hide his knights
in the shadows, under the olive trees.
Precisely at daybreak, at the same moment,
one force will leave the woods, the other burst out of the valley;
from the direction of Thebes, amidst the plains,
the armies will come, in serried ranks;
they will have brought with them one thousand horns,
which they will now sound with all their might:
the defenders of Monflor will believe
that all that noise is being made by their allies.
At a gallop, then, they will race out toward those outside,
with all flags flying:
they will head straight for the besieging army,
demanding that we engage them;
when you see them coming toward you,
pretend to flee from them:
along with the troops of your vassals
quickly mount your horses,
and retreat in disarray
at great speed across the fields.
Leave your tents pitched here.
Knights with their shields
should form the rearguard:
they shouldn't move any packs or bags,
but should leave behind all the well-groomed steeds,
the gold and silver, the fine cloths,
all those many types of tents and pavilions
and all sorts of luxury goods,
all alone among the rushes.
The people in the castle, driven by greed,
will come tumbling out to grab all the booty
that they'll see out there in the grass;
you'll see the poor folk and the servants
come to the tents,
while the knights from the castle
follow you with their squadrons;
they'll chase you right across the fields.
Polynices, meanwhile, mustn't let the side down:
he should post a sentinel at the top of a laurel tree;
when he sees that the knights have left the castle,

he should ride pell mell to the castle,
and right through that open front gate
he should get himself into Monflor,
invading both the outer defenses and the keep.
He'll find the castle completely empty,
and he'll make them really sorry
that, seduced by greed,
they left their stronghold unattended.
Since we're not fortune-tellers,
Polynices should have with him a pinewood horn,
and sound it four times from the tower
once he is inside Monflor.
When we hear the horn call,
we must have our army stop in its tracks
and, reversing our course all together,
go on the attack against those from inside,
who will now realize they've been made fools of,
when they see how they've been betrayed,
and will now turn to defending themselves,
since they don't want to be taken prisoner.
You'll see all those lances lowered into position
and banners displayed;
many a strong shield pierced and shattered,
many a noble warrior fall to the ground;
behold all those shattered lances
and fine swords drawn.
Then Tydeus will sound his battle cry,
as he comes racing down from the hill;]
the castle guardians won't be able to withstand him;
they'll have to abandon the battlefield,
and take flight back to the castle—
only to find a battle awaiting them outside it."

"By God," says King Adrastus,
"you don't sound like dumb townies;
you are noble dukes of good lineage,
and you've certainly spoken like real warriors.
My lords," he says, "that's the way we'll do it;
we'll not reject this plan."

3489 **. . .down from the hill;]** *par la montaigne*]: End of lacuna in MS S. Vv. 3490–625 are transferred here from later in MS S to restore the proper narrative sequence.

Polynices mounted first,
[taking five hundred knights with him;]
they hid themselves in thickets
amidst branches, under leaves.
Tydeus did the same in Valcolor,
with a thousand knights altogether,
hiding under trees and flowers;
[the olive trees gave them cover.]
The knights have all ridden off,
six thousand in number.
Great joy spread throughout the host;
the ambushers didn't slack off:
they concentrated on what they were going to do
and how they would comport themselves.

Hypomedon kept the watch:
no one could do it better.
He was an outstanding knight,
excelling in bravery and courage;
he wanted to accomplish something really heroic,
which, however, soon turned out to be a catastrophe.
There was a gap at the foot of the wall
made by his knights
during their strong assault on it,
before its defenders inside had repelled them.
Now Hypomedon, all alone, snuck up to Monflor;
while the sentinels blew their horns up in the tower,
he got down off his horse
and climbed up on the earthen rampart.
The count slipped into the gap;
he had come out the other side, it seems to me,
when a lousy castle servant
struck him so hard with a crossbow bolt
that it passed right through his shield.
His hauberk couldn't prevent it
from piercing his body as well;
a stream of blood burst from the wound.

3501 **[taking five hundred knights with him]** *o lui prent cinc cenz chevaliers*: Line not in MS S, borrowed from Constans's edition.
3507 **[the olive trees gave them cover]** *li olivier lor firent ombre*: Line missing in MS S; supplied from Constans's edition.

Hypomedon realizes that he's been wounded:
those who would be angered by this don't know about it yet.
He climbs down from the earthen rampart,
and climbs back onto his horse.
Stealthily, he goes back to his men,
and dismounts onto the green grass;
his blood runs down below his shield,
so that his men saw it.
A hundred of them faint from sorrow,
and a thousand cry tenderly.
Because of the heat his blood spurts out;
they tear a strip from his over-tunic,
and bind it around the wound
in order to stanch the flow of blood.
When the bleeding stopped,
"Ah, God!" says Hypomedon, "how agile I feel!
This wound doesn't amount to anything!"
Right away he mounts his warhorse;
in order to cheer up his men,
whom he sees crying all around him,
He makes himself ride,
But just remaining conscious causes him a lot of pain.

Hypomedon is suffering,
hurting badly from his wound;
he really wants to protect his people,
to guard them on all sides from attack.
He made a careful circuit of the troops,
inspected the hills and the valleys;

he sets up look-outs in several places,
each with two knights from Alemande
who are natives of his land—
counts not only wise, but good fighters as well.
One knight did a really smart thing;
he was rich and well-born,
the nephew of a count of Venice
and seneschal to the King of Greece.
All by himself he went to the base of Monflor,
and looked inside the tower.
He saw Achillor at the window,
on the left, beside a pillar:
"Hey!," he said, "listen to me!"

I'm a spy; the noble king, Eteocles,
has sent me here,
but I don't know how to communicate
what I was sent here to tell.
So I'll tell you—just listen to me!"
The one inside comes to the rampart, off on one side,
and the one outside says to him, craftily,
"Come on, don't be afraid;
early tomorrow, right at daybreak,
you'll see Eteocles arriving.
He'll bring to you at Monflor
a thousand knights, ready for battle,
from among the very best of his realm.
If you see the Greeks flee
when they see the king coming,
pursue them boldly,
for they are a very evil people."
And Achillor answered him, "We'll do just that;
they'll be sorry they ever led an army against us!
If we can do this job
and bring it off well,
we'll be in the king's good graces
and win lasting renown."
Then Achillor said, "Get out of here now,
before the army discovers you;
I'll go back into the tower
and tell my companions
that the noble, legitimate king
is coming to our aid, as he rightly should."
Achillor then went back up into the tower,
while the other went back to his lord:
the nephew of the Count of Venice
came to the King of Greece;
taking the king aside,
he told him about the fake message he had just delivered.

Adrastus is a king by birth,
wise in thought, sensible in actions;
he brings together his privy barons
and tells them what a wonderful thing
that knight has done for them:
they respond with delighted laughter.
night passed and day came;

the watchmen sound their horns in the tower,
the morning sun rises,
the nightingale sings among the pines.
Once the sun shone brightly,
Tydeus came out of the flowering wood,
from amidst its sheltering branches,
dressed in his hauberk, his sword strapped on,]
[his helmet laced in place, his shield around his neck:
no Lombard merchant or silly fool he,
holding his lance straight out,
with its fine personal banner attached;
on his feet he wore spurs
of fine gold, artfully worked.
His armor became him well.
He had a fine horse, a handsome thoroughbred:
it galloped across hills and mountains
faster than any other horse could move on level ground;
it could swim the length of two broad leagues
without having to be spurred on;
even after two leagues, it wouldn't be tired out;
its flanks wouldn't even be heaving.
The knight who sits in the saddle
is one who likes nothing better than starting a war:
he charges down a slope,
making the whole valley reverberate,
and comes to a halt in the middle of the plain,
looking back at his troop.
Sure enough, he sees them coming after him,
racing out of the woods at top speed;
at the sight his whole being is full of joy:
there'll be little hanging back by them today!
He had climbed atop a high hill,
and those within Monflor saw him;
they pointed him out to one another,
because they thought they were really seeing their king.

3626 **[[his helmet laced. . .** [[*l'eaume lacié. . .*: End of passage misplaced in MS S and transferred to its correct point in the narrative sequence.

3626 Another lacuna in MS S begins here and extends to our v. 3861; we follow Mora-Lebrun in filling it with appropriate lines from Constans's edition.

3627 **no Lombard merchant nor silly fool he** *ne semble pas Lombard ne fol*: Italian merchants, already widely traveled in the twelfth century, were generally identified under the catchall term "Lombards."

They fixed their lances into the ground:
they had very beautiful insignias
attached to those lances;
they fluttered all unfurled in the wind,
crafted of the richest Phrygian cloth of gold:
high up in the wind they waved.
Now five hundred trumpets sounded together,
making the ground heave and tremble.
Tydeus came spurring down a hill,
racing right toward the army:
the Greek host unleashes a great shout,
and the foot soldiers all withdraw in haste.
Adrastus mounts, with his barons,
and they leave their tents,
fleeing across the plain,
with the king at the head of his troops.
All the defenders of Monflor now rushed out,
not leaving behind even a single one of their men:
the foot soldiers and the servants
ran right to the tents;
all the castle's knights
came out with their household troops,
racing at full speed after the king.
Polynices loosens the reins,
and makes a rush across the field;
his knights follow close behind,
the whole troop racing
through the flowering field:
when they came out of the woods onto open, level ground,
they certainly didn't look like a bunch of peasants.
Spurring their steeds, they came right to Monflor,
and one hundred of them entered the tower;
finding no porter there,
they chose one from among their knights.
Once they had entered the castle,
they raised the drawbridge after them:
that made them feel the more secure,
and they mounted the walls on all sides.
Now the pinewood horn sounds in the tower,
making those of Monflor look at each other.
Then they recognized that they had been tricked:
and they let up a little in their pursuit.
Then the King of Greece halted,

and said to the Counts of Venice:
"Noble knights, flee no more,
because they're all too ready to hold you in contempt.
Now we'll see, when we make a quick turn-around,
who will be this army's boldest,
and who will do the best job
of slicing and cutting!"
Then they began their charge
into battle against the defenders of Monflor.
What a sight: lances lowered
and so many pennants unfurled,
shields cracked, hauberks dented,
lances snapped, fragments flying,
many a good strong sword-blow struck,
and many a head severed from its body.
You would have seen many a noble man from a far-off land,
who had come to conquer,
lying dead on the field
where the battle was raging.
The warriors of Monflor were very valorous;
they defended themselves well in the battle:
one half of them, I believe,
were either killed or taken prisoner.
Tydeus races about, screaming his battle cry,
and comes spurring into the middle of the field;
he goes to strike a knight so hard
that he splits and shatters his shield,
cracks his hauberk, piercing the chain mail,
and throws him, dead, from his warhorse:
he seizes the steed by the reins.
Eventually the melee comes to an end;
and, look! The entire army of Monflor is taken captive,
except for those who are dead.

The King of Greece leaves the fracas,
spurring off directly to Monflor,
a naked sword in his hand.
Once the battle was won,
Polynices came to rendezvous with him
at a great stone nearby.
The noble men of Sidon,
the barons of Calydon,
and all the counts of Venice

came there to meet with the King of Greece.
Polynices said, laughing,
"Noble knights, come ahead!"
Hypomedon and Tydeus
called Capaneus;
all three of them sat off to one side
and took counsel with the king.
He asks after his prisoners;
there are five hundred of these barons,
and he has them all brought before him,
then has them all disarmed,
and sends them all inside Monflor,
to the dungeon under the tower,
in a stinking pit
full of dangerous vermin.
The prisoners end up under the tower,
suffering from all those vermin,
except for Meleages,
who was Polynices's cousin:
because he was ready to give himself up,
the king doesn't want to incarcerate him;
instead he retains him in his own service,
and then gives him arms and equipment.
The king then has the booty divided up
among his barons, just as it pleases him;
he has armor and horses
given to his vassals.
That night the king slept at Monflor,
and had himself waited on like the lord of the place;
the next day, early in the morning,
the king went on his way again.
He leaves one hundred knights in Monflor,
wise and bold ones of great valor,
and left food for them as well;
they needn't fear that they will run out.
They folded their tents, sounded their trumpets—
the king takes to the road with his army;
straight to Thebes, through the mountains,
he leads the forces of Greece.
They forged ahead until they came to that city;
no reining in beforehand for them!

The Greeks pitched camp
below the city, in Valflorie.
They had a splendid army,
and an abundance of pavilions and tents.
Those within the city had a panic attack
when they saw such a huge army so close by;
they ran to their quarters to arm themselves,
and King Eteocles had the gates closed;
he took charge of that operation himself,
instead of sending foot soldiers or knights to do it:
he knew that his young fighters, by their nature,
would be completely lacking in self-discipline;
he was therefore worried that they might begin a game
they would be quite incapable of finishing.
The day passed; night came.
The king was well versed in the arts of war:
he posted sentries on the ramparts,
one thousand Acopars and five hundred Turks.
Drums rolled,
flutes, trumpets and pan-pipes resounded;
great was the noise they broadcast
from the battlements atop the city walls.
The king had his towers well manned,
and kept close watch against traitors;
he has some vassals who would gladly betray him,
if only they could.
He didn't sleep at all that night,
nor did he even lie down in his bed;
no, the king didn't sleep, but stayed awake instead,
plotting with his privy council
how he should react to this invading army—
should he try to make a deal with them, or not?

Atys speaks first,
the son of an Eastern king

3790 **his young fighters, by their nature** *des jovenceaus sot la nature*: The youngest warriors, the *jovenceaus* [Latin *juvenes*] were notorious in medieval epic and romance literature for the enthusiastic and undisciplined love of combat. Cf. below, vv. 3859ff, and see the Introduction, p. 21.

3797 **Acopars** *Acoparz*: An Eastern tribe famed in contemporaneous texts for their "Orientalized" ferocity; see the note to v. 3730 in the edition of MS C by Aimé Petit.

and a knight of great valor;
who was serving the king out of love for his sister.
"King," he says, "are you crazy or drunk,
that you want to make a deal while you're still free?
You could find yourself soon enough forced to make a treaty,
but a hundred curses on him who does so
before he absolutely has to,
because he's taken prisoner or close to death.
You've changed completely from the other day,
when I saw you acting so furious, so fierce;
there wasn't a baron brave enough
that he dared even to say a word about peace;
now you're ready to offer it like some cowardly peasant.
But the Greeks won't agree to anything
if you don't forswear your right to the land
and promise never to go to war over it.
Faint-hearted man, what happened to your hopes?
Just the other night you were saying
that as long as you lived
you wouldn't surrender an inch of this land:
now you're willing to give it up
without giving or receiving a single blow.
It would be better for you to die with honor
than to live in dishonor.
Have all your forces in the city arm themselves,
and there'll be a good sixty thousand of us;
before daylight we'll attack them,
and I think that we'll beat them
because we'll find them still asleep,
with their weapons laid aside;
we'll strike suddenly with our swords—
they'll be defenseless against us."

Othon spoke after Atys,
a wise man, Plato' s cousin,
and the possessor of a great fief;
he held the main street of Thebes.
"Sire," he said, "listen to me:

3849 **the main street of Thebes** *la maistre rue*: In classical story, Thebes had seven gates, each commanded by a great lord; medieval understandings of how great lords held their property made it logical that the main street leading to a city gate be part of that lord's fief.

in my opinion, you're not planning on doing something foolish.
So Atys has uttered his nonsense—
but if you believe me, you'll never do what he proposes.
Atys is very bold and brave
and he's spoken like a hothead;
his idea is to do heroic deeds,
which might work out well for him,
but that's the advice of a foolish young man,
who'd like nothing better than to start a war every day,
as long as he can go on the attack,
and get into a good fight with someone on the other side.]
He couldn't care less about how the battle turns out,
as long as he can win praise at court.
The Greeks are brave and strong—don't doubt it—
and battle-hardened, as well;
there are four of them against one of us—
only a fool would advise us to fight them!
Assemble an embassy on the morning,
and offer your brother an agreement to end all this;
of all that your father once possessed,
turn over one half to your brother,
on condition that he swear homage to you and let you be;
you ought to love him more than anyone.
Keep your hands on the fortifications in the cities,
but divide up the rest."
In response, the king gave his opinion:
"Do you take me for a child,
advising me to split up my realm
when I could hold onto it forever?
Because you know very well that having two lords over one realm
makes for big trouble.
It will be mine or his; either I'll have it all,
or I'll lose the whole thing.
Know this for a certainty:
I'll either have it all, or nothing."

Jocasta was the king's mother;
she embraces her son and draws him to her.
She begs him, for the love of God,
to arrange to share with his brother:

3861 End of text inserted by Mora-Lebrun from Constans's edition to fill lacuna in MS S

"My son," she says, "for the mercy of God,
believe these barons that you see here.
They will never offer you bad advice;
do what they advise you to.
Now the Greeks have this city surrounded;
your beard will have turned gray—
if you can defend it that long—
before they turn back without having taken it.
Since you can't hold it all by yourself,
it's better that you share it with another
than to want it all, greedily,
and end up having nothing, losing everything.
Besides all that, you swore to him;
if you care at all about your honor,
don't perjure yourself over land,
in an unseemly rush to have a realm of your own."

The king looks down, burning with rage;
he doesn't want to say anything to his mother,
but he swears to the gods he worships
that nothing at this moment can make him,
no matter what she may say to him,
divide anything up with his brother.
The barons say, "So, do it;
if you don't do it, you'll lose by it.
If you don't make an agreement with him,
or submit the dispute for judgment,
we won't want to get caught up in an unjust war,
nor can we be diverted from doing what is just.
But why are you acting unjustly toward him?
There are only you two;
he does wrong who, out of desire for territory,
would have a war between the two of you.
May God curse a war between brothers,
or between sons and fathers!
For, after they've done much damage,
then they're at peace again;
They're friends, but their country
has meanwhile been destroyed, laid waste."

Two barons, privy counselors to the king,
now stood up in front of the others.
They took the king to one side

and advised him in good faith:
"Sire," they said, "what do you propose to do
about these people, who are very fickle?
You know the disposition of many of them
who seek your harm;
if you don't agree to this division of lands
a disaster will follow for you, and quickly."

Eteocles sighs and weeps
when he sees everyone contradicting him;
he agrees, but against his will,
for he was an evil man, of bad character.
But to his trusted followers he said, in confidence,
"I'm a dead man, if I don't have my revenge
on these traitors who, by their pressure,
are making me give up half of what's mine by right.
O, God! If ever I can see the day
that I have them in my power,
and can throw them all in a tower,
how gladly will I avenge myself on them!"

They plead with him, for God's sake, not to do such a thing:
this is not the time or place to make threats,
but rather to put up with everything and not become angry,
nor otherwise seek to coerce those who oppose him.
No man deserves to rule a land
if he hasn't some capacity for patience,
waiting until he can be ready
And able to avenge himself effectively.
He should sit back and be quiet
until he can see his opportune moment.

The king returns to the full council, and the others with him;
"Alas!" he says, "how wretched I am!
Now that I only have half
of what I once ruled as king all by myself!"
He comes to his barons and his mother;
he grants their wish
that he will divide the land with his brother,
but the lordship of it all will be his.

Othon answers: "Now, that's good;
I don't see that there's anything to add.

Now look to who will go in the morning
to offer the settlement to your brother."
3972 Atys says to him: "You should go,
because you'll deliver the message effectively.
It's best to send a man
who can explain the king's proposal persuasively;
3976 you formulated it originally,
and through your efforts it will be well received."

Othon bowed his head, burning with rage:
"You aren't my lord," he replied,
3980 "nor will I go now to negotiate
on your orders."
Now Atys began to get angry
and replied, his temper flaring:
3984 "So you're not my man," he said,
"who cares? Everybody knows
that I have thirty vassals as brave as you,
equal to you in status, and even better born.
3988 I'm not telling you to go for my sake,
but for the sake of the king;
since you advise him to do this,
you ought to be responsible for making it turn out well."

3992 Now the king takes them both to task:
"Arguing like this," he says, "is an ugly business;
it's not customary, nor will I tolerate
your quarreling in my presence."
3996 The king didn't say this
because this argument meant a damn thing to him;
[indeed, he wished instead that Atys
had hit Othon good and hard:
4000 he certainly would have been happy with that,
as long as it wasn't in his presence.
He was very upset about the arrangement to share his realm
that had been constructed for him by Othon.

3978–91 **Othon bowed his head. . . making it turn out well** *Otes s'enbronche . . . bien et a chief traire*: this angry exchange recalls that between Roland and Ganelon in laisses 20–21 of the *Chanson de Roland* (Oxford, Bodleian Library, MS Digby 23).
3998–4129 Verses inserted by Mora-Lebrun from Constans's edition (vv. 3683–814) to fill a lacuna in MS S.

He'll get his revenge for that as soon as he can;
if he can't, he'll die of grief.
But for now he keeps quiet and restrains himself,
bottling up his anger within;
he knows how to keep his annoyance well hidden
until the time and place come for him to let it out.

The king asks for advice
from his assembled barons
as to whom he should send:
he wants Othon, above all others, to do it.
Everyone advises him that Othon should be the one to go:
no other baron is his equal in worth,
none who can cut such a good figure at a court;
whatever he may say, the mission should fall to him.
But Othon vigorously refuses
to undertake to deliver the king's message.
Atys asks him why:
"You have very little fear of the king,
and place little value on his lordship
in refusing to be his messenger.
But if the king were to see it my way,
you would have to make this trip,
or be considered a complete fool
if you refused to deliver the message."
Othon contradicted him,
like one who knows how:
"Now may God never help me
if I'm in any way afraid of your threats;
I don't hold any fief or land from you,
and I'm not much impressed by your fighting words.
If you want to quarrel with me,
and since you are saying such stupid things before the entire court,
even the king's honor won't prevent me
from coming right back at you;
but, please, leave me alone,
because I don't want to get in a fight with you.
If I've ever done anything to you that I shouldn't have,
I'll willingly make it up to you;
so accept it right here and now;
you'll do no better at law.
I want to contradict you about one thing:
I've just heard you say

I hold my lord in such low esteem
that I'm not willing to do anything for him.
I've done a great deal for my lord,
endured a lot of pain and hardships,
and absorbed many blows,
while striking many for him, as well;
I never had to be begged to go
anywhere that he wanted to send me;
but now—I don't wish to hide the fact—
this time I don't want to go there,
and I can tell you exactly why not
(and may it not displease my lord the king!):
it's not even four months ago
—to my knowledge, not even three—
that the Greeks sent us a messenger
strong and brave, courtly and wise:
the son, he was, of the King of Calydon,
and there's not another such knight as he under the sun.
He came to the court, searched out the king,
spoke to him, and turned back.

He went on his way;
our men had drunk too much wine,
they mounted their horses and followed him.
Bad luck for them, by God, that they did!
For all of them died
and the messenger got away.
If he met the king's messenger now
do you think he would treat him with good faith?
If he found any of us
he would kill him and be right to do it."
Throughout the hall they all take counsel,
saying they are not surprised
that Othon won't go
where he expects so much attention,
and all of them say moreover
that no one will go without safe-conduct.
Jocasta speaks: "I shall go
and escort the messenger.
If my son has a say, I do not think
a man under my protection will be seized.
Polynices will make sure
that no one will harm him."

Not one of them believes her,
or would make the trip because of her.
"Lady," they say, "we shall not go
for they don't take your coat of mail or your clothes,
they take your body and your life.
It would be madness for anyone to go there."
Jocasta was worthy and wise:
"I shall go," she says, "as the messenger;
and take my two daughters with me,
since you all fail the king.
For lack of worthy men,
women will take the message."
"The danger," Othon says, "is great;
your son could not protect us.
But go now to the meeting,
you alone with your daughters alone;
if they accept the truce,
let them approach that pine.
We'll go that far—
I don't think we have anything to fear there."
Then the counsel broke up.

In the morning, when the sun was shining,
the queen got up,
dressed and prepared herself carefully
as did her two daughters,
who will go to the meeting with her.
I should tell you about them,
the clothes and equipment they had:
Antigone was the older,
noble, courtly, and respected.
She had a very noble body and lovely face;
her beauty was pure beyond any other;
never in story nor in song
will you hear of a woman like her.
She was dressed in a purple indigo
right over her naked flesh,
so the white skin appeared beneath it.
The tunic was slashed
by thin cuts
down to the belt.
She was tightly dressed

with a loosely bound belt.]
Her feet were in camel's wool socks
and leather shoes.
Her cloak, it seems to me, was motley
and worn thrown over her;
the garments were open
so her sides were revealed.
Her hair was long and blond,
shining more than silver or gold;
a silver thread was plaited through her hair
which hung down to her belt.
She rode a palfrey
that had just been given to the king.
Well-paced and quite alert,
it had a value of three hundred pounds;
it was all black except for the haunches
and the shoulders which were white,
and the legs of red.
The bridle was noble and precious,
the reins of silver,
the head-piece of fine gold,
the stones in it worth a treasure.
The saddle was of white ivory,
the saddle cover brown silk,
and the stirrups and harness
all of massive gold from Spain.
With this array, Antigone
certainly looked like a king's daughter.
The younger girl was Ismene,
never was a lady less like a peasant.
She was still very young but well brought up,
very courtly and well instructed.
Ismene was the beloved of Atys
and she wore a brocade
whose right sleeve she had cut off
and given to Atys.
On the underside there was ermine fur;
no queen ever wore finer.
The sleeves, bordered in fur,
were so wide they touched the ground.

4129 This is the end of the passage inserted by Mora-Lebrun from the Constans's edition.

Ismene rides without a cloak
on Atys's palfrey;
on her fist she holds a sparrow-hawk
which she feeds with a plover's wing.
Now what shall I say of the mother?
As she makes her way with her two daughters
to carry the message, she is very well dressed,
as befits a lady of her age.
She rides a brown mule;
you have never seen a better one.
Three young men, among the best in Thebes,
accompany the ladies.
A nephew of Atys escorts Ismene;
a child of very high birth
and very closely related to her
leads Antigone;
the third who leads the queen
is the son of Herga, the King of Armenia.
Those six made their way
to the meeting alone,
and when they drew near the host,
they found three Greek knights,
at the cypress fountain.
One of them was Parthenopeus—
he was one of the three,
a very rich man, the King of Arcadia;
he was very wise and quite courtly,
dressed in the French fashion.
He was riding a Spanish mule,
and resembled a king in pure beauty;
no woman under heaven, if she were to see him,
would not be very attracted to him.
Indeed, when she saw him, Antigone
strongly desired him in her heart.
She desired nothing so much as him.
They were very well suited those two,
for they were both the same age,
equal in beauty and in rank.
Parthenopeus sees the girl,
none so beautiful under heaven;
I do not wonder if he desires her,
for there is none so noble under heaven.
He moves swiftly towards her,

greets her courteously
and she greets him very sweetly;
her word is a balm to him.
He speaks nobly with her
and she answers engagingly.
"Lady," he says, "do not conceal
who you are and where you are going."
The young man who leads her answers:
"She is a sister of the king,
she and the other young woman
whose right sleeve is ermine.
They are going to see their brother in this host
and this lady is their mother.
They would very much like to find
a way to end this war."
Parthenopeus returns with her,
leading her to the Greek host.
He leads the lady himself,
and takes great pains to serve her.
He leads her, knowing how,
as nobly as he can;
in that company
a base word was never spoken,
nor a word of great wisdom, of preaching,
but only romance and fun.
Parthenopeus does not forget himself—
he begs her to be his love.
She is very worthy and wise,
and tells the knight what is in her heart:
"By God," the girl answers,
"this love would be too sudden.
I am a maiden, daughter of a king;
I should not love lightly.
I should not love lustfully,
it could lead to foolish gossip.
Shepherdesses can be asked this way,
or other frivolous women.
But I don't know you, I never saw you
before I met you here;
if I were to speak of love with you,
you might well think me a fool.
That does not mean—I won't conceal it—
that I would not cherish you

if you proved to be of such high lineage
that you were of my rank,
and if it were so destined
that I were given to you in marriage.
For you are beautiful beyond all other people—
I have never seen so noble a man."
Parthenopeus has now told her the truth,
that he is a king of great power;
if he takes her in marriage it will be good for her,
for he is a king of vast holdings.
"Speak about it," she says, "with my mother,
and with the counsel of my brother
who knows both our relatives and you,
let an agreement be reached for us.
If they accept it, I promise it;
I shall not reject it."
He spoke with her mother
just as Antigone had instructed him.
He loved her very much, he would not keep silent.
He spoke with Jocasta about the matter,
telling her who he was, naming the land;
so he began to ask her for her daughter.
Jocasta knows his lineage well
and consents to the marriage;
she will very willingly give Antigone to him,
but first she will speak of it with her son.

The young people have spoken so intimately,
they have made an alliance of love.
Meanwhile they have entered the host
but that was not to their liking;
what with laughing, joking,
and speaking intimately,
they would have preferred
a much longer journey to the host.
The girls ride through the host
and everyone says they are very beautiful;
Greeks come out of the tents to see them,
more than fifty thousand of them.
They want to determine which is more beautiful
but that cannot be
because there is no way to measure their beauty,
Nature made them with such skill.

The worthy Parthenopeus leads them
directly to the king's tent.
The tent was wondrous and large,
encrusted with flowers on the cloths.
It was neither hemp nor linen,
but purple silk from beyond the sea.
It was purple, indigo, and red,
with many marvels painted on it.
There was a carefully drawn world map
there in relief, quite round,
minutely worked in beaten gold,
on the front flap over the entrance.
The map extends through five zones,
painted as Nature made them;
the two on the outside
are full of snow and ice
and they are colored blue
because they are rather cold.
The hot zone in the middle
is red for fire;
because of the fire or the snow,
no one lives in these three zones.
Between each of the outer zones
and the hot one in the middle,
there is a temperate one,
which is inhabited towards the northwest.
There are the ancient cities
with their walls, towers, and defenses.
The towers are of beaten gold
as are the gates and drawbridges.
All the kingdoms with their rightful kings,
are there, each as it is,
with their seventy two languages,
and the Frozen Sea and the Wild Sea,
the Red Sea made of black enamel,
and the passage of the sons of Israel,
the four rivers of Paradise,

4298 **the king's tent** *tref le rei*: On marvelous structures such as this tent, ostentatiously flaunting the learning of the clerical poet, see Introduction, p. 4 and Christopher Baswell, "Marvels of Translation and Crises of Transition in the Romances of Antiquity," in Roberta Krueger, ed., *Cambridge Companion to Medieval Romance* (Cambridge: Cambridge University Press, 2000), 29–44.

Etna burning and emitting smoke.
Monsters are there of a thousand kinds,
flying birds and fierce beasts;
and our people are painted there,
those from Ethiopia all dark.
The ocean runs through the burning zone
extending its arms around it.
The *Mappamundi* is such a great thing
that anyone who looks at it cannot rest;
he will look much at the sea, so much at the earth,
taking great pains to find everything.
Emeralds, jaspers, sardonyx,
beryls, sards, and chalcedony,
jacinths and chrysolites,
topazes and amethysts,
so many set in gold
shining brightly in the sun.
On the other side, on the main cloth
are painted the twelve months of the year.
Summer is there with his loves,
with his beauties and his flowers;
summer is painted with all his colors.
Winter makes his tempests there,
wind and rains and snow and hail,
and mixes his storms together.
After the seasons, the king had had painted
the judgments and laws
which his ancestors had instituted;
they were the lords of Greece.
So there is the history of the kings of Greece,
those who are worthy of good memory,
their brave deeds and battles
that each had waged in his day.
On the surrounding curtain
are painted leopards, bears, and lions.
On the ground is a brown silk cloth,
you have never seen a better one;
it is encrusted with small geometric forms,
columns and squares.
There is a dove of ivory
in the middle of the roof, painted red,
holding the eagle and the carbuncle
that his uncle, Flori the old,

had won when he conquered Persia,
when he captured the towers of Tarsus.
As far as the tent extends,
it is completely covered with good rugs.
The stakes that hold up the tent
are all red and blue,
the ropes of enameled silver,
twisted all around.
But five hundred knights with their arms
and one thousand townsmen with their halberds
are positioned all around;
it is a wondrous show of force.
They guard the king when he holds council,
when he sleeps, and when he is awake.
In the tent are Capaneus,
Polynices, and Tydeus,
the three sitting on one side,
holding a council with the king,
they tell him to attack,
that he will take the city without fail.

Meanwhile the ladies have arrived
and dismounted in front of the tent.
The worthy Parthenopeus conducts them,
leading his love by the hand.
Smiling, he says to Polynices:
"Here are some of your relatives, very nearby."
Polynices looks beyond him,
and sees his mother, whom he dearly loves.
His heart is cheered by the sight of his sisters,
but he weeps for pity;
he cannot help but weep
for those he sees there.
He goes quickly towards them
and kisses them very sweetly.
You might have seen quite a press at the kissing:
no one will give way to another;
whoever gets the chance,
mother or sister, kisses him;
as each one gets to him,
she kisses him one hundred times as if it were once;
and yet they weep as hard
as if they had found him dead.

For the joy that the ladies show,
more than a thousand men weep.
Polynices behaves very courteously,
taking his mother by the hand,
he leads her to where the king sits.
The king rises and seats her,
then he kisses her and the girls
and asks for news
of those inside the city, what they are doing.
"Why do they support the traitor
who has forsworn his oath to his brother
and refuses to do what is right?
They may be sure of this:
I shall not turn back for anything,
not if I lose my whole land
until I have finished this war."
The queen answers sensibly:
"They do it because they can't help it;
as the elder he has taken possession
and reinforced all his fortresses;
he keeps his men on a short leash.
With the excuse of a minor claim,
anyone with any valor
can hold a realm by force.
But if one were to ask
how they might divide the land between them,
so that each would have his right,
that would make sense and be reasonable.
I think they would offer you this pact,
that they would divide the land with you
and that both would share it equally
except inasmuch as this brother hold his part from the other."
The barons do not like
the idea that Polynices do homage to his brother;
the king's court does not grant
that he should hold anything from him.
All the vassals discuss it
and consider it a very great wrong;
poor and rich, they discuss it
and take it to be a big trap.
The king begs them to be silent
and let the queen speak,
let her say all she wishes

and he will take counsel what to do.
"Sire," she says, "I have spoken
the best counsel I know;
rather than let other harm be done,
I would have him hold it in peace."
The king goes to one side,
and summons those he wants to consult.
The bachelors, the mercenaries,
remain below, flirting,
and pray God that no pact
be worked out or settled
before saddles are emptied
in the sight of the young women.
Ismene says: "We shall soon see—
we shall not have to wait four days—
if they do not reach an accord today,
I swear to you that one will be able
to strike until morning without fail
with a knife worth half a farthing."
Ismene is a very lovely girl,
though she is quite quarrelsome;
she is courtly, she speaks well,
she has been well schooled.
But her sister is such a good creature
she scarcely dares to speak;
she leans towards the Greeks
because Parthenopeus is one of them.
The knights play and laugh
and banter with Ismene.

The king has come out of his tent
with fifty of his friends;
he sat down under the shade of a linden
to take counsel with his barons.
He asked them about the case they had heard,
to learn what they would say and advise.
There is scarcely any baron there
who does not advise that he accept the offer,
except for the homage that was sought.
They do not approve of that,
but if Eteocles gives up the homage
let them divide the inheritance in half.
And if he has any doubt about it,

let Polynices assure him,
in the name of the barons and the king,
that he will keep his word and keep peace with him.
Tydeus sits on one side,
you can hear what he said:
"Lords," he says, "I am amazed
that you give such advice.
From what I hear you say
you seem not to care if he loses by this;
either you understand nothing
or you care little about his advantage.
Why do you condemn this man to loss
when you do not see the other here?
Eteocles is very devious,
clever and up on the law;
he will easily do
whatever one asks of him.
He doesn't care what pact he makes
as long as this host is disbanded,
for he is well aware of our situation,
he knows that our land is very far away
and that it is not an easy thing
to suddenly bring such an army back.
If he sends us away this time,
he has no fear of seeing us again.
Polynices would be mad to remain here,
while we are back in our lands,
drinking white wines at the hearth
and leading the good life
and doing whatever we desire,
for they can easily kill him.
Eteocles will not make good any
of what he has promised.
I take no heed of his oath,
for someone who perjures himself once
will very easily perjure himself
again and again thereafter.
To change the original agreement
would be quite foolish;
let Polynices pursue his first goal
and not withdraw his people.
Eteocles will be wrong, we will be right;
though it would not be wise to think

that they can't defend themselves against us,
if we do take the city
there will be honor and glory for all of us
and very great victory for King Adrastus.
After our deaths they will say:
'Never was such an effort made!'
Moreover, to bring peace to the land
so no other harm is done,
Adrastus should take the traitor Eteocles captive,
and have him put in a tower.
Let him live there always,
and never be set free."
Capaneus, who was the king's intimate,
says "Sire, listen to me.
Whoever will advise you anything else
or give you other counsel
or say anything different from what I say,
if he is your man he belies his loyalty to you.
It is good advice that Tydeus gives you,
no one on earth has a right to reject it."
The king answers:
"I swear to it.
By my idols and by my law,
I shall not take other advice,
nor will I ever act otherwise."
Most of the others are distressed;
they would have advised Polynices to share the realm,
thinking it is a foolish reason
for them to suffer such distress.
The king goes back to the tent
with a very grim expression.
He swears by the gods of his country
that he has taken his counsel,
that no settlement will be made from now on
that differs from what was originally made.
To the ladies he says the same:
"I shall make no other agreement
than the one that was made
when they divided the domain by the year.
Polynices will take that settlement
if he is allowed to pursue it;
if his brother balks at this,
let him be sure he will hear an uproar.

For by this white head," he says,
"we have not come
to let him seize the city from us
before we have taken it by force.
For all the gold of Frisia,
I would not leave now until it was taken.
Rather I will strike five hundred blows,
lance and sword thrusts
and a thousand knights will die
on the ground under the city."

So it was to be: before night fell
sixty eight of them had died.
For nothing, for a foolish reason
the madness began that day.
There was a viper in the city
who had no equal under heaven.
You shall hear a great wonder about her:
she had completely abandoned her nature,
she was so extraordinarily tame
she would not touch a sheep.
If you offered her flesh or bread
she would eat it from your hand;
she would drink a great cask of wine
then she would be drunk with you all day;
she would leap, she would play,
until she altogether exhausted you.
On her forehead she had
a very brilliant carbuncle;
I do not think you would ever
have seen so noble a head in any beast,
and her whole body
shone brighter than fine gold.
The king would not have parted with her
for three hundred Mans pounds.
When she heard the noise the army was making,
she came out of the city towards them.
Then the squires who were drinking
and jousting in the field

4623 **Mans pounds** *livres de manseis*: monetary units in the currency of Le Mans; the actual value of such units differed from place to place, as currency was highly localized in western Europe at this time.

in front of the city killed her—
they thought she was wild.
But when those who were at the gate
saw their viper lying dead,
they attacked them immediately,
driving them back towards the army.
The squires flee towards the host,
crying "Come out quickly.
People are pouring out of the city,
more than twenty thousand are following us!"
In the host there was great tumult,
everyone ran for his equipment;
in the lodgings they all arm,
the whole host roars and resounds.
They mount their horses as quickly as they can,
they have standards of many kinds;
they spur and drive through the field,
a hundred thousand helmets shine.
Never in the army of the Roman empire
was there such jousting of knights;
Charles did not have as many in his company
when he conquered the Spanish.
When the men from the city saw them
they came out to fight against them,
they came out in great force
along the whole road towards the fields;
sixty-four thousand together
came out, I think.
They spread out through the hunting preserve
and everyone wants to fight.
They thrust themselves before the infantry
and urge the Greeks to fight them.
The Greeks spur and press towards them
and join with them hand to hand.
On both sides each man rushes
to splinter his lance first.
Tydeus drives through the ranks,
the very first blow is his.
When he meets Thenelas of Sidon,
neither his shield nor his hauberk can protect him;
Tydeus strikes him in the chest, under the nipple,
throwing him down dead from the saddle.
Aymon strikes Archivenin

and Periphas Menoeceus.
Hippomedon jousts with Sybaris,
strikes him with his lance
through right side of the body
so it thrusts out a foot.
Parthenopeus has killed Itys;
he takes his steed by the reins.
He strikes him in rage,
tears and rips his hauberk,
thrusts the lance through his body
with the whole banner around it.
No wonder if he is distressed
for he lies dead from the wound!
Parthenopeus leaves the crowd,
giving the steed to a youth:
"Friend," he says, "go quickly for me
to the girls who have come to the camp,
and present it with its bridle and saddle
to the girl
who is dressed in indigo silk,
over her naked skin.
By these signs I send the message to my love
that I have done an act of chivalry for her."
The youth drives and spurs over the sand,
leading the steed with his right hand;
he rides so hard on the road
that he finds the ladies under a pine
where they are taking shade on a hill
and watching the fighting.
He comes towards them, dismounts,
holding the steed
by the silk reins near the bit.
He knows the one he has been sent to
by the indigo silk she is wearing.
He greets all three ladies;
then he takes the girl aside
and tells her something that is agreeable to her:
"The King of Arcadia, your love,
has had me bring this to you," he says.
"Know that he is fighting as he should today,
that he left one opponent cold on the field;
no shield or hauberk was strong enough
to protect him from death.

Parthenopeus sends you his steed."
She answers: "Give my thanks to him,
and let him know that for this gift
I intend to render him a noble reward.
Let him know, without a doubt,
that he has me and my love completely.
When he leaves the tourney
I ask him to speak with me;
let him come this way, so I can see him,
I don't know when I shall have another chance."
The youth takes leave of the girl
handing the steed,
with the reins and the saddle, to a young man
whose name is Estevenel;
then he returns as quickly as he can
to the fracas of lances.
The tourney was wondrous,
no one ever saw one more dangerous,
more thick or crowded.
Many noble men were killed there:
you might have seen so many saddles emptied,
such a great rain of arrows,
so many blows across the body,
so many vassals lying on their backs!
You would have seen so many knights fighting,
spurring and driving among the ranks,
that I have never heard of chivalry
invoked so in any land.
That day the fighting was well begun
and maintained and exalted.
The King of Thebes was very valiant,
moving beyond all his men;
he rides through the field shouting his cry,
meeting no one who does not suffer for it.
He encounters Jordan of Africa,
nephew of the King of Salonica.
Eteocles rides towards him, the other waits;
he strikes him on the shield and cuts it through;
he rips his hauberk and tears the mail,
it is not worth half a cent to him;
he puts his lance through the body,
so it comes out half a foot on the other side.
The other fell dead—no priest

could get there in time.
Garsiavar comes spurring hard,
sitting on his Navarrese grey;
for prowess and for size of body,
there was none like him in the kingdom of King Anfors.
He strikes the king so hard on the side
that if it had not been for his good hauberk,
he would have avenged Jordan well,
and the king would never again have eaten bread.
Atys sees him, drives towards him
and joins battle immediately with Garsy.
He spurs and drives with force,
his lance is rigid, he strikes a great blow.
The horse kneels under him,
Garsy falls, soiled in the mud.
Atys turns away with the horse,
he left the other all dejected in the mud.
Ismene clearly sees this blow land
and the steed that Atys leads away.
She knows very well it is Atys
from the sleeve of silk brocade
he had attached as an emblem
to the nails of his lance.
She points him out to her sister
sweetly whispering to her:
"That is Atys I see there,
look how he drives to the tourney.
I should love him beyond all things
because he is doing all this for me.
I would not be the daughter of a king
if I did not distress myself for love of him.
Whether it is wise or foolish,
I will go to bed with him soon.
For fire does not catch so quickly in reeds
as the love I feel in me."
Polynices joins battle with Eblo,
he strikes him down dead on the ground;
when he sees him lying dead on the earth
he says: "I have made a truce with you.
This is how I make the claim to my land,

4758 **Garsiavar** *Garsiavarre*: The French form, Garsiavarre, may be a fusion of Garsy, as he is called below, and Navarre.

God let me conquer it!"
Riding hard, he turns back through the sand,
leading the grey horse with his right hand.
He gives it to Garsy who mounts;
he is determined to die if he does not avenge his shame.
Garsy has mounted the steed
that was brought from Bearne;
for jousting or any such need
there is none as good in Gascony.
Between the ranks he rides at a slant,
he sees Florin astonished
and strikes him so hard that he and his filly
fall down in one heap.
He strikes him on the shield,
dividing it from one side to the other;
he tears and rips his hauberk,
that protects him no better than a shirt.
He hacks through his breast and his body,
knocks him down dead on the ground.
Florin had a son,
a worthy and valiant knight.
He is a young knight,
and he sees his father dead on the ground;
the youth is deeply grieved
when he sees his father dead;
he faints on his steed
and his knights lift him up.
Statius, a cousin of his,
a rich man and Count of Turin,
says "Sire, let it be;
there is nothing to be gained from grief.
But hasten to take revenge,
to kill him, to cut him apart;
avenge the death of your father
for the loyalty you owe your mother."
When Florin's son recovered from his faint,
he gathered his barons around him,
seven thousand knights
who were bold and fierce,
whom he had brought from the East;
they are all his men.
They will avenge the death of Florin
with their sharp polished swords.

Anthony was Florin's son;
he brandishes his sword, spurs his horse,
and goes in a rage to strike Milo,
a knight of very good birth.
He cuts and splinters his shield,
tears and rips his hauberk;
he puts his standard into the other's body
with the great stump of his spear;
he throws him dead from the saddle
and his companions see it.
Then Anthony says a foolish word to him:
"If you are in pain, don't hide it!
You look like a dancer leaping around,
the way your ancestors used to cavort."
Statius strikes a fighter from Frisia,
cutting his shield to pieces;
he throws him dead from his fawn-colored steed
the full length of his lance.
Anthony draws his steel blade,
and strikes the warrior Garsy
on the left side of his helmet—
Garsy falls off his horse on the other side.
The death of Florin, whom he had killed,
was his misfortune.
All seven thousand men in the army have struck,
each has killed his man.
You might have seen so many blows struck there
and so many good knights dying.
Anthony goes jousting over and over again,
grieving deeply for his father.
He goes to strike a knight
who has only recently become a soldier;
he strikes him such a blow in the midst of his shield
that he throws him dead from the horse.

Capaneus is on the heights
that look towards the gate at the head of the bridge,
where he is jousting with his entourage,
all marked with different emblems.
There are so many good helmets in his company,
so many good shields of Spanish blue,
so many good hauberks intricately mailed,
so many well embroidered emblems,

so many good horses from Castile,
so many bridles, so many good saddles,
so many standards of different kinds
that wave in the wind!
Never in the court of any king
would you have seen such a noble entourage.
They are all of a select company
brought up at the duke's court,
three thousand sons of vavassours
and barons and counts;
none is the son of a peasant
or born of low condition.
That day they showed great courage
in force and in attack.
In one line they passed the palisade—
no bar or grate could hold them back—
so they drove the men from inside
back to their gates;
in a swamp below the city
more than two thousand drowned.
If it had not been for the defenders
hurling Greek fire with torches,
no gate could have held against them;
they would have entered with lances raised.
The count acted very well there,
he galloped ahead of his men,
he was the first to invade,
the last to turn back.
At the gate he killed
Alexander of Mont Cenis,
the son of Boniface the marquis
who held Vercelli and St. Agatha.
He had come from Lombardy
to practice chivalry here.

While the host is fighting
the king arranges his battle corps.
He has come outside the dwellings
onto the plain with a large company;
he had a hundred thousand men on foot,

4890 **vavassours** *vavasour*: Men of lower status than the full nobility but still gently born.

each with a lance or spear
and forty thousand archers
besides the agile bachelors
who went to shoot in the battle
and cause damage to the besieged.
The knights who were old and stout,
who had somewhat lost their luster,
do not ride immediately into the battle,
but remain with the king.
There are ten thousand white-haired men,
with their beards outside their visors,
who had committed great deeds in the past.
These order their troops
and lead them wisely,
moving slowly and in close formation.
The king halts in the midst of the plain,
commands silence from his men,
and makes them listen
as he speaks these brave words:
"Lords," he says, "I am not going to hide
what the young men are doing,
spurring and galloping
among the ranks to join battle, as they should.
When they go back,
people will talk about their deeds;
their deeds will be recounted.
We will all envy them.
Every one of us will be angry
if there is no report of our actions.
No tales will be told of you
and there will be only shame
when we are left out
and they have all the glory.
The bachelors will get the attention
and we will be left speechless.
I would rather," he says, "lose my life
than fail to do chivalry.
We must spur and drive
and renew our prowess.
I will tell you how to do it:
we will open our ventails,
so our white heads can be seen
and our great long beards.

It will look like a violent assembly of barons
when we gallop along the shore,
for there has never been, it seems to me,
fierce jousting by people like us.
Make sure the fighting is done
intensely by the gray-beards,
that there is no cowardice
among us.
Wherever we see great distress,
let us all drive towards it in tight formation;
see that no one holds back
until the wall stops him.
Don't be afraid of those boys,
not one will remain in his saddle;
let them know with certainty
that the king is making the attack.
Our infantry will follow us
slowly along the shore
so that if we are in distress
they will give us strength."
What the king says pleases all of them;
they say to each other in Greek
that they will have suffered to no purpose
if they do not follow where he leads them now.
They open their ventails,
point their lances upwards,
and drive directly towards the city,
in tight ranks.
The king has a great gold standard
born before him;
a hundred horns sound in front,
giving courage to the most cowardly.
The sky trembles, the earth trembles,
now it really seems like war.

Atys hears the horses whinny;
he looks around and sees them coming.
"Look, what a great troop
of sheep is coming at us through the plain!"
Othon who was beside him answers:
"It doesn't cost anything to say big words—
they are sheep and you are a wolf—
but by the faith I owe you,

whether you like it or not,
you will cede the place to them
and it will be a wondrous disgrace
that a wolf flees from sheep."
And here come the children,
the youngest of them one hundred years old.
Never did any king
lead such a cohort into battle.
The old are valiant; in their youth
they had often played such games;
now they remember the prowess
they had shown in their earlier days.
Bearing their broad large shields
before their chests,
they sit firmly on their steeds,
and fix their spurs into the horses.
Tightly pressed as they came,
they did not rein in until they reached the walls.
They do not hesitate from fear of death
but go and strike close up,
and with lances and swords
the old men strike great blows.
The Thebans cannot withstand the attack;
they have to abandon the field.
They turn their backs as the enemy strikes,
not stopping until they get to the gates.
Atys rides in front,
on a very fast horse.
Othon berates him:
"Come back, Atys, my good lord!
Frighten these sheep
who are nipping at our flanks."
Atys turns angrily to Othon:
"You are a knave,
leave me alone
or you might regret it."

I should tell you about Amphiaraus,
how he is behaving in this combat.
Amphiaraus is in a chariot

that was made beyond St. Thomas's land.
Vulcan made it with great care,
taking a lot of time with it:
with study and great concentration,
by art and enchantment,
he carved the moon and the sun
and the firmament on one side.
He placed the nine spheres in their order,
in the greatest the signs of the zodiac,
and in the lesser, the other seven,
he set the planets and their courses,
with the ninth in the middle of the world,
that is the earth and the deep sea.
On the earth he painted men and beasts,
in the sea, fish, winds, and storms.
Anyone who understands something of physics
can learn a lot from the paintings.
The giants are on the other side of the chariot,
full of pride and insolence;
they wanted to disinherit the gods
and throw them out of heaven by force.
They made a ladder to climb up—
no one had ever seen its like
for they put one mountain on top of another,
they piled on more than seven,
and the giants climbed them to seize the gods
unless they could defend themselves.
Jupiter is on one side
holding lightning and a dart.
Mars and Pallas follow him,
these two taking on the whole burden.
All the others who reign in heaven
quickly take up their arms;
not one of them seeks an excuse,
they all fight beside the throne.
The giants battle hard,
making lead maces burn;

5045 **beyond St. Thomas's land** *outre Seint Thomas*: St. Thomas was believed to have gone to India to preach Christianity.

5046 **Vulcan made it with great care** *Vulcan le fist par grant porpens*: Another marvelous artifact the elaborate ecphrasis of which shows off the poet's erudition, in this case, classical.

they throw them angrily at the gods
who are denying their claim;
they throw firebrands and burning sticks
and red flames from their mouths,
for their anger against the gods
is more than I could think or tell.
They hurl rocks towards them so heavy
that six oxen or ten or thirteen or fifteen
could not carry the smallest of them;
whatever they hit breaks and shatters.
Against the gods they were terribly angry
because of the throne the gods would not grant them.
The gods rise upwards—
the giants can not control them—
to take counsel together.
The boldest of them trembles in fear,
for they do not have oak shields,
iron spears or ash halberds,
javelins or lances or swords,
iron maces or great lead discs;
only lord Jupiter
has a sharp iron dart.
Mars is beside him on the right,
valiant Pallas on the left;
these two are worth more in the battle
than all the rest of the rabble
and the other wild gods
who live in the woods.
Phoebus is there, a very good archer,
valiant, bold, and fierce,
holding his bow ready to shoot;
he looks at them very fiercely,
then cocks an arrow.
To the giant who is picking up a rock
Phoebus says with great hostility:
"You will soon learn how well I can shoot!"
But the giant answers in great pride:
"I defy you, I wish you harm;
I don't fear you or your darts
for you are a bastard son of Jupiter;
he begot you on a whore,
he filled her belly with you.
You claim heaven as your patrimony,

you have no love for my companions or me."
As the giant finishes his speech,
Phoebus shouts and the arrow flies,
striking him through the spine
so he would never again challenge anyone.
Then Phoebus told him: "Your arrogance,
didn't last very long, it seems to me."
Mars and Pallas are fiercely angry,
they let their sharpened darts fly against the giants;
the other gods throw lightning,
strongly defending their sovereignty.
The gods kill all the giants;
not one of them can withstand the attack.
Jupiter is overjoyed,
any one he strikes does not get up again;
he hits one in the chest—
medicine would do him no good.
I will not make a long story of it:
Jupiter puts all the mountains back down on earth.

This painting was on the chariot,
which Vulcan had carved with great care.
And with stones and enamel
he had depicted the seven arts
behind the frontal:
Grammar was painted with her parts,
Dialectic with arguments,
and Rhetoric with judgments.
Arithmetic holds an abacus,
Music sings by the scales,
painted there are the fourth,
the fifth, and the octave.
Geometry holds one rod,
Astronomy another;
one takes her measure on earth,
the other gives her attention to the stars.
There was much subtle carving on the chariot,
well worked and without fault.
One image cast there,
was the horn sounding the charge,
another always playing the flute
sweeter than a rote or a viol.
The workmanship of the chariot and its material

are worth all of Thebes with its empire,
for the sides are of a fine encrusted gold
and the poles of white ivory;
the wheels are chrysoprase
the color of a burning fire.

Four zebras draw the chariot,
no one can see their hoof prints
in sand or in soft earth,
for they run faster than a bird flies.
Amphiaraus drives them and rushes
to where he sees the greatest press.
He draws his polished sword,
he does not forget to strike well;
all the others are learning from him
how to give great blows.
His sword cut very well that day
and made itself familiar with the Thebans.
Never did Duke Godfrey's sword
inspire such terror in the Turks,
nor did Turpin strike such noble blows
on the Saracens in Spain
as the archbishop did that day
in the battle for Thebes.
He was well equipped with arms,
the best that were made in Parma;
a red shield at his neck
that shone brightly in the sun,
with more than seven gold buckles,
each one weighing ten marks.
His hauberk was strong and light
and shining more than pure silver:
anyone who wore it need not fear a wound.
For his emblem he had a rich cloth
and on his helmet a veil
of white silk beautifully made.
The sun shines brightly as it does in May,
its rays striking the golden chariot

5184 **Duke Godfrey** *duc Godefrei*: Godfrey of Bouillon, a leader of the First Crusade.

5195 . . .**weighing ten marks** *n'i ad cele ou dis mars n'en eit*: A mark was a weight of roughly eight ounces used to measure silver or gold.

and lighting the mountain above
and all the plain below.
All the Thebans are struck with awe
by the chariot and its decorations;
the Thebans are so awestruck,
even the boldest of them flees before it
for they think it must carry some god
fighting for the Greeks.

Amphiaraus knows from his powers of divination
that he will be killed that day;
by auguries the warrior knows
that it is his last day.
Since he knows it with certainty,
he makes the best use of it he can;
he makes great carnage among the Thebans—
no one young nor old can escape him.
Anyone he meets on his way
he sends ahead of him to Hell.
The outer army also has great losses
of their horses and their bodies,
but they would think little of it
if only they could keep him.
Many would be distressed about him,
struck with awe
by the way he died,
his death was so fierce and horrible.
For in the evening, at the hour of nones,
the earth rumbled and the heavens thundered
and just as God had destined
and as Amphiaraus had predicted,
the earth swallowed him without effort,
as it did Abiram and Dathan.
Those who saw this marvel
were frightened and fled,
many fled in great disarray
each one afraid for himself.

Amphiaraus falls into hell,
where the miserable and the unhappy are;

5235 **Abiram and Dathan** *Abiron et Datan*: For their fate, similar to Amphiaraus's, see Numbers 16: 20–35.

he falls into hell, with his sword still drawn
that had done so much killing.
But the way is quite hideous,
the passage hard and dark:
at the gate he finds a porter
a cruel one who begins to bark at him
as horribly as he can
with his three heads.
Everyone who must enter there
has to enter by that gate;
Amphiaraus passes through
that opening and no other.
There he enters a path
where he hears souls tortured;
then on a plank he crosses over
the dark water of Acheron.
This Acheron that rushes swiftly
is ugly and wide, the bank far off,
and it is full of biting serpents.
He crosses with some difficulty,
with his whole company
that Hell had swallowed on the battlefield.
Then he comes to a river
very close to Acheron,
with beasts of a thousand kinds,
that give them horrifying looks.
Acheron was the pilot,
with his companion Charon;
the two of them make the unfortunates
pass between them into a boat.
This river called Cocytus
is more fierce than any flood;
it burns in all ways
more than any Greek fire.
The miserable who remain on this side
are many, sighing hard and lamenting.
Amphiaraus passes over this water
and a great mass of the others with him;
but Amphiaraus goes first,

5268 **Acheron was the pilot** *Notoniers en fut Acheron*: The poet has here given the name of the river to a boatman, whom he adds to the traditional underworld scene.

he is the new standard bearer.
They reach another passage that is a great stinking swamp
large and black and horrifying,
where a thousand dragons move their beaks.
There is a great rushing water there
that cuts sharper than any razor
and runs faster than a hawk flies;
all the authorities, major and minor,
call it the Styx.
There is no plank or bridge over it,
nor anything that can speak.
But Tisiphone bathes there,
combing her serpent hair;
like a wolf she wails and shouts and howls
and moves towards Amphiaraus.
Amphiaraus is terrified
when he hears the Satan approach,
full of bitterness
and crying angrily: "You made a mistake,
coming in here on horseback,
you will only find foul lodging here."
Amphiaraus was very much afraid,
and passed by her in pain.
Then, armed with all his equipment,
he appeared before the king.
King Pluto, holding his trident,
took revenge on Amphiaraus:
from the time he died, Amphiaraus
lost his power to foretell fate.

King Adrastus has fixed
his standard in one place,
a stone's throw from the walls.
He says that he will not draw back,
he is determined to lodge
in front of the gate, in an orchard.
He orders his tent to be pitched there
and the others to take shelter.
He intends to cut off, by force,
the streams that are in the gardens,
so the people in the city
cannot drink the sweet water.
He thinks, if he can surround them,

he can constrain them.
It is an evil plan to deceive them
by keeping them from drinking.
Then suddenly a messenger arrives;
he tells what happened to Amphiaraus,
how mother earth swallowed him
and a thousand others as well.
But you may be sure
that it was not true about the thousand;
the man is exaggerating
to increase the shock.
When the messenger tells him about it,
the king, in fear, makes the sign of the cross:
"Come on," he says, "this is a lie,
you saw this in a dream.
I don't think God would so confound us
that he would open the earth underneath us."
But another messenger follows the first;
it is harder to doubt them when they are two,
and then three and four.
Quickly they remove the standard,
and the king returns to the camp
looking mournful and depressed;
he mourns, weeps, and laments,
and goes mad with grief for Amphiaraus.
I am not surprised that he grieves—
he has lost a large part of his council.
Amphiaraus had taught him how to hold his land
and what was to come in the future;
he knew long before
if things were to fall out badly or well.

In the host there is unmeasured grief;
no one, no matter how hardened,
did not feel sorrow over the death
and fear in his heart.
Then dusk begins to fall
and the sun to hide;
the host has returned to the camp,
they have had a very good day.
But what use is that? They do not boast
of sword or lance blows;
Amphiaraus weighs heavily on them.

No young man laughs or enjoys himself,
no viol or rote is heard,
no one sings or plays;
no hauberk is polished that night,
no steel blade nor helmet cleaned,
no clothes are taken from their chests.
They all have a very bad night;
they retire to their tents,
but no one sleeps well that night.
That night they did not eat, they did not drink,
they did not lie under fine cloths.
They are sad and distressed
because they do not expect to escape alive.
Every one thinks he is finished
because they have lost Amphiaraus;
they grieve for him, they fear for themselves,
and they are anxious to go home.
Now they fear the earth more
than the war.
That night the host was sad and reserved;
in the morning they want to depart.

But inside the city there is great excitement,
that can be heard far off.
In the embrasures up on the walls
they light lanterns, they light torches;
on the battlements they play and laugh.
All of them shout and cry out,
taunting and laughing at the army outside
and shouting insults in derision:
"My lords," say the sentinels,
"you have accomplished many feats today.
You assaulted us fiercely
but you have come out of it badly;
your fortune has taken a bad turn today.
When your master made a great leap,
God was giving you a sign
that you do not deserve our land.
Get out of our land,
don't try to conquer it.
If you don't, pain is waiting for you;
you have started down a bad road."
They are really happy in the city,

they take great pains to enjoy themselves;
they have no respect and even less fear for the outer army
which can not take them unless it can starve them out.
They are confident towards those outside,
and hardened to defend themselves;
they will not, at this point, accept the pact
they offered this morning.
They have tested the enemy today
and know they were greatly dismayed
by the loss they suffered
and the signs they saw.

In the morning, when dawn breaks,
king Adrastus summons his barons.
They come, three hundred or more;
not one is not a count or a duke.
When they are all seated in the tent,
the king asks their advice;
"Lords," he says, "I seek your counsel
on what you saw yesterday.
Let us take counsel, you and I,
for by the faith I owe you,
I will not suppress the truth;
I am paralyzed, I don't know what to do.
The thought of abandoning this siege
distresses me and weighs on me,
but if we stay, I have great fear
that the earth will swallow us all.
It is shameful to go back
but I am more afraid to remain:
one has reason to fear for his own house
when he sees his neighbor's burn.
This death was so cruel
that any other seems trivial in comparison.
Do not think this is cowardice,
for you know well that whatever I say,
I shall not take on the fear
of all the people I see here;
I shall not feel the greatest fear
for I know that every man loves himself
as much as I do myself.
I trust in God, I believe in God,
I shall not be swallowed up sooner,

nor be a greater sinner than all the host.
Do not take me for a coward,
for I submit it all to your judgment.
If you advise it, I shall remain,
or if it pleases you, I shall leave."
The Duke of Mycenes answers:
"Why are we suffering such great pain,
why does such an adventure overtake us
that even the earth harms us?
There is no one who does not see
that God does not want us to pursue the way we have taken.
How do you think you can carry it off?
God does not want this.
I have always heard that if you try to defend yourself
against a needle, you get pricked twice.
As long as we are still free to choose,
it would be better to return to Greece and live
where all our ancestors lived,
than to die here in a great massacre."

Most of the council agrees with the duke;
they advise the king to go back,
but the king is hard to persuade,
he will not turn back unless it is absolutely necessary.
The Count of Amycles has a big heart
and does not care about the good life;
he much prefers chivalry
over hunting on the shore or with bows,
and striking great blows in battle
over lying down and resting.
He was brought up on war from childhood;
there is no better lancer in all the host,
no one who knows better how to look for trouble.
King Adrastus cherishes him
for he counsels him well in time of stress
and is wondrously valiant.
He is a tall man, his visage
dark and sleek and rather fierce;
his hair is flecked with white.
He responds to the Duke of Mycenes,
cautiously at first
because he sees that others are leaning his way
and wanting to go back.

He speaks very measuredly:
"Sire," he says, "in my opinion,
you speak well and truthfully;
given what we have experienced,
it is quite reasonable to go back.
But if it please you, don't say any more,
let me amend it a little.
I will tell you what I suggest:
if you think I am mad,
let him speak who knows how to say it better
and let no anger arise against me.
We are now greatly distressed
because of the way Amphiaraus died;
we could not, I believe, have suffered
greater loss, except for the king.
God has done his will,
there is no turning it back;
he will do the same with us,
whenever it pleases him.
Do you expect to flee from him to Greece?
We can not escape him;
if he does not want to spare us
we will not be safe there any more than here.
If one is the object of God's anger
he cannot hide from it.
If you would take my advice,
we should not turn our backs on this;
instead let us choose from among us a new bishop
with great judgment and reason,
for we should not remain long
without a bishop, without a master.
We should replace our master
and take care to choose someone
who is learned in doctrine,
without love or hate.
Do not be concerned
with wealth or birth or age,
for one should not deny a young man
if he has great wisdom.
And when the bishop is consecrated,
his authority in place,
let him go forward and pray for himself
and for the people and for the king,

showing us how to fast and wear a hairshirt
and give alms through the host.
When the fast is over,
fix a date
for him to lead us in procession
to the abyss; let us be confessed
of our sins at that place
and let him make a great sacrifice.
If the abyss then closes up,
you will know that God hears us."

The holy men, those who fear God,
praise this counsel and approve it,
but they have trouble finding a bishop
from their land who would be a worthy man.
An old and aged poet,
who had spent many days in the woods
following his religious law,
gives them two men to choose from.
He climbs on a stone
and makes a brief speech to them.
He commands them to be silent.
They hold him in such reverence
that when they see him standing,
all, great and small, are silent,
for they know well that there is no evil
or deception in his life.
"Come now," he says, "it is quite right
that God has put us in such straits,
for sin reigns among us
and greed and evil.
God punishes us for our sins
and recalls us with his scourge;
he takes vengeance for our sins.
But if one repents,
God is very merciful,
he will easily make peace.
For our sins, I believe,
the master of the law is dead.
We were not worthy, in my opinion,
to have such a shepherd over us.
Because of our great evil,
God shortened his life,

but he has not so abandoned us
that we do not have branches of his stock:
there remain from his disciples
three or four or five or six.
Though Amphiaraus has died,
we still have Theodamas,
whom the holy man taught from childhood;
we can trust him
to replace his master
if he holds the cross and the scepter.
Melampus is another,
but he is a hundred years old or more.
Between the two, no one can choose
which is better, which is worse;
they are very wise, their way of life is good,
in both of them honor is safe.
But Melampus is already very cold,
it would be more suitable for him to live in peace from now on;
he could not sustain the burden
he would have to carry."
All of the counsel are of one opinion,
that Theodamas should have the pallium;
all together they have agreed to it
because he is of a good age.
But Theodamas demurs strongly,
saying that they are committing a sin and a wrong
to raise a bachelor of his age
to such a position:
"You should install an old man,
wise in the world and in learning."
I will not stretch this out any longer—
the more he tries to put himself down,
the more they desire him;
they all elect him bishop on the spot.

The Greeks in great devotion
held this election;

5592 **cold** *freiz*: an allusion to the medical theory of humors, according to which Melampus, presumably because of his age, suffers from an imbalance toward coldness in his bodily fluids.

5597 **pallium** *l'estole*: The pallium is an ecclesiastical vestment bestowed on a new bishop by the Pope.

against his will, without simony,
Theodamas received the authority.
When he was consecrated, he gathered them all together
and imposed on them a three-day fast.
On the third day after nones
he puts on a black robe
and a hairshirt next to his flesh;
he commands them to form a procession.
In great devotion, the Greeks
form this procession,
with naked feet and dressed in wool they all go
with him in front to lead them.
They get to the abyss, weeping hard;
they lie on the ground, praying humbly.
Before the prayer is done
God gives them a great sign:
heaven thunders, the earth trembles,
it roars three times, then closes and shuts.

The Greeks see the earth shut;
they are very happy, nothing under heaven
did the host want more than that.
They return swiftly to their lodgings
and with the joy they feel
they go to joust before the city.

Those in the inner army come out
vying with each other with great force.
When they see the Greeks near the abyss
they all come out enthusiastically.
They are anxious to fight them
and beat down the pride of Greece.
There were six counts, I believe,
in the city, besides the king,
and there were seven main roads
with seven gates and seven exits.
Each of the six counts and their households
lodged in one of the gates;
each of them had his gate
and each came out from his gate;
and the king's people were lodged
in the main street.
You will now hear the names

of the seven gates and the barons who held them.
Orgive is the first gate,
it was called Orto
for the gardens that the burghers had
in the marshes on that side.
Creon the old, white-haired,
exited from that gate.
with ten thousand men;
he was the most powerful after the king.
The second gate is called Neista;
beneath it there was a deep valley
with wondrous orchards
and woods of pine and laurel.
Through this gate came the king;
with him came more than three,
for when he was outside on the plain
there were twenty thousand in his company.
The third is Homoloia;
there was a pyramid in front of it
that peasants called Pile.
Cadmus, who built the city, lies there.
There are the principal arches
of white marble and enamel.
This is the gate for the shore
where the waters converge;
there you might have seen many good cloths hanging,
many good cloths for sale,
along with Slavs and Turks and Moors.
Count Haemon passed out through this gate,
well reinforced by his men.
The count came out this gate
and once they were outside near the sea
there seemed to be six thousand with him.
The fourth gate is Proetia;
there is a fine field in front of it,
where a ditch was dug and stakes placed
so they could do battle inside the palisade.
Through that gate came Hypseus,
with ten thousand men and more.

5654–55 **Orgive... called Orto** *Orgiz ot non... il la sornoment Ortolaine*: The first gate in Statius (*Thebaid*, Book 8, v. 353) is Ogygiis, Ogygian in English. We have used the French name here because of its play on the gardens.

That is where the fighting began,
and the one who started it died.
Electra is the fifth gate;
it does not impose a great burden on the defenders,
a few people are enough
because it is very hard to get to.
Through that gate came Dryas,
a knight valiant and noble and free,
whose prowess was widely praised;
five thousand followed him.
The sixth gate is called Hypsista;
it lies at the corner of the city,
in a street beside a mountain;
water flows there beneath a bridge
and there is a tower at the foot of the hill.
Eurymedon, who has a great domain,
holds it as a fief.
He came out through that gate;
six thousand came out with him,
sergeants and knights.
The six thousand were fierce in their deeds.
Capaneus made a lot of trouble for them
in the first battle,
when he attacked them.
Culmina is the seventh gate;
with a very strong tower above it.

One passes through that last gate
to get to the fountain of Dirce;
the King of Thebes goes hunting in the forest
there whenever he likes.
Menoeceus came out of the city
through that gate, five thousand with him.
Sixty four thousand all told
have come out, it seems to me.

The Greeks spur, galloping hard,
making sparks fly from the cobblestones.
One might guess at a glance

5716 **Culmina is the seventh gate** *Culmes ot non la septisme porte*: In the phrase *culmina Dircaea*, "Dircean heights," in Statius (Thebaid 8.357), *culmina* seems to have been mistaken for a name.

there were twenty thousand riding at the head.
Behind them comes a great line
that will not end before the marshes;
they are, all together, more than a hundred thousand—
the earth shudders and trembles.
Swearing, they tell each other:
"It will be bad for anyone who holds back;
people will think he's a stable boy
if he comes out with his shield whole!"
All thrust themselves boldly
into the attack.
At each of the gates
you might see heavy fighting.
Melampus was the Duke of Baille;
with his standard of silk
he rides ahead of his company
the length of an arrow-shot through the country.
His horse was dark gray;
he had killed a Turk for it the year before
at the battle of Laliche.
It is of great valor and value,
wondrously fast,
covered with red silk,
and more than a yard
of yellow taffeta over the rump.
Melampus carries his lance on his thigh;
he has an emblem on his hauberk
of two rich colored silks,
cut like a chessboard,
and a shield of ivory half white
and half blood red.
Hypseus is at his gate,
he sees him come but does not move.
The count has a good retinue,
well taught in the ways of war;
there is no confusion among them.
Never was a people so well trained.
When Melampus is quite close,
Hypseus spurs towards him at full speed;

5748 **battle of Laliche** *tornei qui fut a Lalische*: Probably a reference to the battle of Laodicea, where Louis VII fought the Turks in the Second Crusade (1148).

the count rushes ahead of his men,
he joins battle with the duke between the lines.
They are both good knights
but the duke misses and the count strikes him,
hitting him not on the shield
but where he was unprotected on the right side of his chest.
Hypseus thrusts his javelin into his body,
and the hauberk does not protect him.
Melampus has no defense from death;
he is thrown dead from his gray steed.

Aggrieved for the duke, Agreus
rides in anger against a Theban,
and shatters his lance on the shield.
Through the battle he engages as he goes.
He strikes Phegeus with his sword
and severs his arm at the shoulder.
Amyntas, a duke of Persia,
of that foul hostile people,
shoots better than any man alive.
Nothing can escape his shot;
there is no better archer under heaven.
The King of Thebes cherished him.
Distressed about Phegeus,
he immediately looses an arrow,
shot swiftly from the string,
that kills Phedymus in the road.
But the dart was heavily poisoned,
so Phedymus dies a bad death;
from the poison in the wound,
he falls from his horse dead on the road.
Spurring across the field,
Acamus knocks Iphis down;
he strikes him under his right armpit
and knocks him dead from the saddle.
As the count makes his turn around the field,
he encounters Argus in the battle.
holding his naked sword in his fist
because he has lost his lance.
He strikes him with such force
that he makes his head fly from the trunk.
Pheres has made no compact with them:

he strikes Abas so hard with his lance
that he beats him down dead from his horse.
He finds the count and boasts of it to him.

Ion of Pisa is very worthy
and the leader of the next rank.
At the edge of a meadow, beside a cliff,
he encounters Daphneus of Sadocia;
the two rush towards each other,
recklessly pressing their spurs.
Spurring hard,
both strike great blows on the shields;
the lances crash loudly
and the stumps fly up.
Even though Ion is fighting without support,
they both strike great blows, they break their straps;
the laces of the chest harness do not hold
and Daphneus falls from the horse.
As his saddle pack comes loose,
people ride from both sides to help.
Dryas has come out of his gate
ten thousand shields with him.
The combat begins on that side,
and the foot soldiers unleash a great hail
of arrows and darts
killing a lot of horses.
The men of the Greek host are courageous,
they make every effort to drive ahead;
they do not spare their horses,
but spur them into the battle.
Shattering lances and breaking them up,
they lose all their horses there,
but the Greeks do not worry about their horses,
as long as they can join combat as they should.
Near the gate where Dryas is striking,
Parthenopeus is also involved;
he is fighting in that area
and he has many people from Arcadia with him.
He comes riding at full speed,
not holding back at all

5815 **Daphneus of Sadocia** *Dampius. . . de Sadoche*: In Statius (*Thebaid*, Book 8, v. 453), Daphneus comes from Cirrha.

until he joins battle with one of them,
a baron of great valor.
Meleager was his name, I believe,
a near relative of the king.
Parthenopeus strikes him with such strength
that he breaks and shatters his shield,
tears the hauberk, rips the mail,
and thrusts his javelin through his body.
Meleager falls dead to the ground—
that is what the war did to him.
Dryas, sitting on a red horse,
spurs towards them and joins battle with two;
one of them he kills on the field,
the other he leads off captive on his horse.

Alexis, very rich Count of Arcadia
has a dark brown horse,
none better.
He stays far off with all his men,
not letting them go to fight
until he sees a good reason for it.
He knows something about chivalry,
and does not want to lose through foolishness.
But then he sees horses being massacred
by the foot soldiers, who are wreaking havoc;
there is no stopping them
as they go recklessly through the battle.
The Greeks do not want to touch them,
but it begins to trouble Alexis;
He goes wild
that they do such harm and have no care.
Calling his men he tells them:
"Do you see, my lords, how the people on foot
are killing all our horses!
The damage is widespread,
no horse will remain on the field.
How can we endure this?
The shame is great if we let those boys
do this to us with impunity.
Now let us ride towards them
and let there be no talk of chivalrous combat;
do not look for knights
or bother to capture foot soldiers.

Instead, though it may seem villainous behavior,
kill anyone you catch
to make the boys draw back
and stop treating our people so vilely.
From now on, let them stop
killing our horses under us."
With that he spurs forward and, with his men following him,
he turns the weight of his attack on the infantry.
He makes a great massacre of foot soldiers,
killing more than five hundred.
The foot soldiers lose control immediately:
they lose their good lances
and many a peasant breaks his leg
and loses his tunic that day,
for the knights assail them
and the squires despoil them.
The rest of them retreat
for they greatly fear the fierce host;
as long as the fighting continues,
the foot soldiers do not reappear.
From now on there is good tourneying
for there is no more shooting of arrows.
Alexis attacks strongly;
his child will never be shamed
by his bad actions
for he held the place all day
and made light of it,
which was considered great courtesy.
There is a naked knight from inside the city
who has only a lance and a shield,
a shield and a lance alone,
no other equipment.
He throws himself fiercely into the combat
and has everyone talking about him;
the Greeks could easily have killed him
but all of them admire him;
they do not want to touch him
nor to be the butcher who kills him.
Alexis calls on a sergeant
to bring him a stick
and when the other attacks,
Alexis strikes him with the stick.
The other rushes forward between the ranks,

driving hard and Alexis follows.
One goes in front, the other behind,
driving him through the ranks, beating him.
Riding a good horse, he moves swiftly,
and beats him hard on the back and the belly;
he strikes him often on the rump
as one punishes a pupil.
Alexis does not hold back, he shouts
and beats him like a pupil.
Everyone in the battle sees it,
they point it out to one another;
throughout the tourney they laugh at the joke,
on both sides they speak well of it.
Many knights are more envious of it
than of a deed of chivalry.

Agenor, Dryas's nephew,
sits on an iron gray horse.
Young and very noble,
he had just been dubbed that morning.
He joins in the tourney that day
and takes many turns in the press,
doing many valiant deeds
for a youth of his age.
He is the first of the ranks
of seven hundred knights to join battle.
Between the ranks he joins with Alon
and strikes him not on the heel
but on the face so hard
he knocks him back over the rump;
he knocks Alon over the rump,
into a ford, making a soup of him.
But Alon had dealt him a great blow
which broke up Agenor's shield,
broke and shattered it;
he barely missed knocking him dead.
Agenor returns to his men
bringing Alon's sorrel horse with him;
there was no other like it in Spain,
none so prized in the company;
he had killed a Moor for it
on this side of the Gironde, under Blaye.
Dryas rides quickly

to the rescue of his relative
but attacking him with three lances,
the enemy knocks him from his horse.
Agenor turns swiftly towards him
and both defend themselves well,
one on foot, the other astride;
they grapple like wild boars.
Agenor does not stop striking,
he holds off the press on his own
until Dryas mounts the sorrel;
then he draws the sword with its gold pommel.
The nephew and uncle help each other,
they do not forget how to strike well.
The youth won great praise,
as a new bachelor,
and received a noble gift that night,
for his uncle made him his heir,
giving him the gift of his domain
in the presence of the king and his barons.

Eurymedon gathers his people;
if any one of them should break rank,
he was ready to kill his horse.
At the foot of a hill in a valley,
he admonishes his household
not to risk loss by reckless action.
Capaneus departs from the host
and goes to fight in that place;
all his people make a great effort
sounding drums and horns
to create a huge noise at the front.
He comes charging down the mountain,
descending into the valley,
spurring wildly through the meadow.
Capaneus, astride an iron-gray horse,
leads his men forward.
Wanting to crush his enemies,
he makes a plan to trick them:
he would like to draw them far outside the city.
But the Thebans do not fall for it;
they remember the great harm
they incurred earlier for their folly.
They suffered great loss yesterday,

undone by their recklessness
when they went out too far from the city
and lost many men in their flight.
Any one who wanted to do deeds of chivalry
was out of luck there,
unless he joined forces with the infantry,
which caused the great killing of horses.
Lucien charges, spurring hard,
as far as a bow could shoot
but he is surrounded by foot soldiers;
he would have won great praise if he could have returned.
At first he joins battle with Poinson of Meletant,
striking his gray steed on the forehead
and as the horse swerves
Lucien throws himself towards him.
He hurls horse and knight
down onto the path.
The foot soldiers surround him on all sides,
shooting bolts and throwing darts;
they kill his horse under him.
"Curses on him," they cry amongst themselves.
He is now on foot in the press
but he does not let go of his sword;
as long as he can defend himself,
he will not be let himself be captured by servants.
With his good steel blade,
he quickly cut off a limb from one,
a hand from another;
the third he struck so hard
that he embedded the edge
of his blade in his brain.
But the soldiers get angry at him,
they shoot at him from all sides.
It is not good to fall among townspeople:
peasants will show no mercy
to anyone they can overpower.
They do not take the knight alive—
they cut him in pieces.
But his companions will avenge him

Capaneus is very angry
when he sees his knight killed;
in a loud voice he shouts his war cry

and rallies his men to him;
he shouts his war cry in a loud voice
and no one holds back.
The inner army stands firm;
beneath the tower, at the head of the bridge,
they are all closed in narrow ranks.
Every one swears by the god he believes in,
that he will not be a coward
for fear of losing his life.
They have confidence in their strength
for if things go badly
they can regroup inside the palisade
and have nothing more to fear.
Capaneus is deeply committed:
he throws himself among them with no restraint;
the first to move from his ranks,
he will die if he does not avenge his shame.
His household follows him,
three thousand charge at a gallop.
Capaneus does not fear the enemy;
he clears his way with his sword.
Not slow to strike, he cuts
anyone he encounters down the middle.
He cuts him straight through, without a miss;
he punishes them well with his sword.
He cuts through the chest of one, the head of another.
There would have been a lot of mourning that day—
Capaneus would have killed many of the inner army
if he had not fallen in the press.
He is pursuing them with his naked sword
when his horse trips
in a narrow street
and Capaneus falls on his side in the dirt.
He cannot get up, he is stopped there.
Before his men can get him out,
more than forty, wise men and fools,
ride over him.
Before he gets out of the dirt
his arm is badly twisted;
he will give no more blows that day
of his lance or sword.
But his companions do not hold back for that,
they all come on;

an invasion comes through the field.
Nothing can make them abandon
what they had planned,
until they have killed a lot of the enemy.

Menoeceus is at his gate,
he encourages and comforts his men;
admonishing them to strike well,
he reminds them of the fierce race,
the good lineage they come from.
As he exhorts them, he himself
joins battle first before all of them;
he is very bold and valiant.
He sits on an Arab horse
that King Dares gave him:
the two are first cousins,
for Dares was the son of his aunt.
I do not know how to assess the value of the horse:
he moves very swiftly and turns very well;
and his coat is divided down his back,
one side as white as ermine,
the other black as a Moor.
No beast under heaven can run with him;
you may be sure that no bay, no brown,
none is more agile,
there is no brown nor bay
that he would not soon leave in the mud.
One would be a fool to seek a swifter horse.
Menoeceus drives him across the plain,
spurring the horse,
he is the first to join battle, with Pancras.
Pancras, a duke of Russia
and a rich man of some importance,
has a great reputation for chivalry.
He comes spurring on his Pennevaire;
the two spur with great spirit,
and attack each other fiercely.
When they meet,
they strike great blows on the shields;
when the knights encounter each other,
they penetrate shields and hauberks.
The counts strike each other with force,
but they do not pierce the flesh;

they fall back from the horses
onto the plain under the heather
and the men of the inner army and those of the Greek host
spur swiftly to rescue them.
The scuffle over them is huge,
many blows are struck,
but the greater power lies with the Thebans.
Menoeceus moves quickly,
mounts his horse,
seizes the duke by the nose-piece
and returns with him into the city;
the Greek host is left grieving.

Amphyon takes great pains
to strike well, leading his peers.
He has a lot of confidence in his fine horse
that supports his deeds of chivalry.
The two make a very good pair,
Amphyon and his whitish horse,
for the horse goes freely
and he guides him suitably.
He is very courtly in bearing arms,
no Frenchman ever bore them better:
with the lance at his neck and the shield in front,
he goes riding his white horse
and when he gets close to the fighting,
he lets the horse go and it takes the land in great bounds.
On the right he sees a Greek coming,
bearing a great standard;
the Greek is named Porphyrus
and Amphyon turns to meet him.
But the Greek leaps out of the way
and Amphyon misses him;
he misses and the Greek, at a slant,
strikes Amphyon and throws him down.
There is a cross-bowman nearby
who knows what he is doing:
he takes aim, pulls and shoots,
and hits Porphyrus, who lets out a cry
and dies.
It was a mortal blow.

Palemon has lost his lance.

He holds his naked sword in his hand
and rides at the Prince of Aquileia
who has his lance raised.
The prince's body is large and strong;
he fixes his lance in the ground,
because the encounter would not be equal
if he has a lance, the other only a sword.
He draws his sword and runs at him
and they fight.
The prince has great strength;
he strikes Palemon so hard on the shield
that he shatters it over him,
almost throwing him from the saddle.
The other strikes back on his helmet,
cutting off a whole part of it,
cutting his beard and moustache,
and a bit of his chin.
As the prince departs,
he turns to the right.
Palemon has raised his arm intending to strike
but the prince prepares his blow:
he strikes him on the arm, cutting it off at the wrist;
his right hand flies to the ground.

There was great sorrow for two very young brothers
who killed each other.
They were both quite valiant for their age,
and of very high birth;
after the king, there was no more noble
family in the city.
The elder who was very loyal,
was in the company of Polynices
who had sent a messenger
for him and received him
with such hospitality and gifts
that he gave himself into his servce.
The younger brother, still a child without beard
or moustache, had stayed in the royal household;
it was no more than two months
since the king had knighted him.
He had knighted him richly,
his trappings were very valuable;
the king had given him a noble horse,

certainly worth three hundred silver marks;
the horse too had noble equipment.
The young knight has come out to the combat;
he spurs through the stubble
near the woods at the double ditch.
Now see what a misfortune greets him!
For he meets his brother at that place;
they do not recognize each other,
as they ride against each other.
As chance would have it
both attack on the right;
throwing themselves into the joust too furiously,
they strike great blows on the shields,
they ride swiftly and do not fail
to tear the hauberks and dismail them.
The mail is not so dense nor so strong
that it can protect the brothers from death.
They strike each other dead through the body
and knock each other off their horses.
Only on the ground do they recognize each other.
One weeps for the other, lamenting sorely,
each one grieving for the other more than for himself,
for they were of very good faith
and loved one another wondrously.
The grass is red with their blood.
Sudden death presses them,
their flesh turns pale and weak.
They pardon each other and weep for their deaths
and, as long as they can, they pray for each other;
they kiss and embrace.
They die together on that spot.
Menoeceus who has done his turn
and gotten back into the battle,
is riding through the field with his sword drawn
because his lance was broken in the jousting.
At the edge of a wood, beside a medlar,
Menoeceus sees the knights lying dead.
He goes towards them,
and recognizes them immediately—
they were his sister's sons.
His grief is enormous, the greatest he has ever known;
he is very distressed for his nephews,
whom he had gently taken care of

and had always loved.
He almost falls in a faint over them.
But his entourage comforts him:
there is nothing to do but carry the bodies away.
Menoeceus has his two nephews disarmed
and the hauberks taken from their backs.
Two squires on palfreys
carry them over the necks of their horses.
Their bodies are noble and elegant,
dressed in silk cloths;
both are shod in silk.
Their hair is cut short in front;
but behind it flows
long and blond towards the belt;
the locks fall over their shoulders,
but their heads hang down.
They seem quite fine beings
though some red blood drips down;
the sides of the white palfreys
are red with blood.
You might have heard cries and weeping there,
for it is painful to look at them;
anyone who sees the bodies being carried
cannot be consoled;
no one has so hard a heart
that he does not weep for such loss.

Creon, the old and crafty,
sits on a grayish red horse;
he is armed in the French manner,
helmet and hauberk, shield and lance.
He is tall, big, and thin,
bold and impetuous in battle
and has come out with a great host.
The field shines with gold and silver,
with helmets, hauberks, and painted shields,
banners and standards.
The old man would have had a great company
if they had all come out onto the plain.
But he knows how to trick and tonsure fools:
he makes his men hide in the orchards
beneath the leafy olives
so no helmet or shield appears.

He has got seven hundred out in the plain,
not one a fool or a peasant;
they are all trained in chivalry.
They are going to begin the madness
and begin it very quickly;
where they find the men of the Greek host,
they let go the reins of their steeds,
and join battle with the first line.
Those of the inner army are very eager
for chivalry and joyful;
where they find their enemies,
each one unseats his man.
They drive the Greeks back
and throw them down on the meadow;
they are leading them to their undoing
with great speed through the field,
when Polynices comes to help them.
But he will lose men before he leaves.
He has a royal entourage,
many good vassals fighting there;
many knights from many lands
have come to him seeking conquest.
From many lands they came,
none of them old or white-haired.
They serve him in love
and he rewards them generously.
Where he finds his enemies,
he does not fail to provoke every one of them;
he throws him down in the midst of the road,
seizes him and sends him to the host.
The Thebans show their backs in disorder
and return to their hiding place.
If one could have seen the Greeks driving, spurring,
thrusting themselves through hills and valleys!
Striking, striking at their backs,
until they have closed them inside the city.
Then the others come out of the orchards,
and they do not look like shepherds;
you might have seen so many helmets with flowers
and so many shields painted in colors,
so many horses fat and well-groomed,
carrying standards of so many kinds.
The standards float in the wind,

more than a hundred horns sound.
All equipped and in tight formation,
they move quickly out of the orchards.
Immediately they lower their lances
and launch themselves against the host.
When the Greeks see there is nothing else to do,
they turn to meet them like good vassals.
Polynices is the first to turn,
feeling great anger in his heart
against the brother who disinherits him.
He pays one of them so well,
when he finds him in the midst of the rank,
that he destroys his Algerian hauberk
that was supposed to be very strong,
and throws him dead from his horse onto the field.
His companions do not delay
but swiftly return to the madness;
they shatter lances at the first blows,
and break and crack shields;
the Greeks come on with their swords,
and hold the field for a very long time.
They endure three attacks with force,
and the blows are well struck,
but at the fourth, they cannot take it any longer,
they have to abandon the field.
The Greeks flee at a gallop,
but, know this, there is nothing they can do;
for the advantage has gone to the inner army,
which has captured more than three hundred of them.

Polynices rides apart from them,
and goes to one side all by himself;
in a valley, beside a fir tree,
he leaves the route,
for he is very worried about
the great wave coming along the route.
Two brothers who have seen him
catch up to him quickly,
for his horse is worn out from the heat,
and wounded beneath the haunch.
The two brothers capture him,
and it would have been to their advantage
if they had wanted to bring him to the king.

But Eteocles has never kept faith with them,
indeed he disinherited them wrongfully,
seizing a strong castle they had on the sea.
6400 They would never be friends with Eteocles
for before their father died,
he had thrown them out without cause.
After the young men were thrown out,
6404 they lived in the city,
but Eteocles was jealous of them
because of their great chivalry.
The elder says to his younger brother:
6408 "If I bring this man to the king,
he will have no more reason to make war,
he will drive us from his land,
having no more need for us,
6412 for, disturbed as he is, he finds no good in us.
I do not know what harm he will do us,
if he does not drive us out altogether.
If it were not for the opposition of this man,
6416 who is an exile, Eteocles would be so fierce and proud
that he would not value the best man of his kingdom
more than a woman.
If we bring this man to him,
6420 we shall be undoing ourselves and others;
better to let him go
and beg him to keep it secret."
Polynices is afraid,
6424 he does not know what they are thinking.
Sweetly he begins to ask them
for God's sake not to give him up to torture:
"For you must know one thing,
6428 that I shall never be able, not for any amount,
to come to an agreement with my brother,
once he gets hold of me;
he will have no mercy on me.
6432 Let me ransom myself from you;
I shall not be stingy,
I shall give you ten thousand marks;
no one will know it,
6436 except you who receive them."
The elder brother says to the younger:
"I would be committing a dishonorable act
if I took money for ransom

from my natural lord,
who never did me harm.
My heirs would be reproached,
because I was his liegeman,
I received my fief from both of them,
just like the other barons—
land it would take five days to work.
I do not deny that the money would serve me well:
if I had 12 bushels of gold,
I could spend it with great pleasure.
I would give it away in a month;
I would give many sets of arms
to the knights who are with me,
and I would make very large gifts of it;
not a bezant would remain to me.
But, fair brother, may God never let me
do anything for money
that would make my face blush in the court,
nor do such a thing to my lord.
I do not want any foolishness said about it,
so let us set him free.
If the king wants me to explain this,
I shall assert my right in his house;
I shall be well able to defend myself
that I do not have to turn over his brother to him,
for I was his man in good faith,
by the king's own leave.
But if I take money for the prisoner,
then I will have consented to the king's harm
for money, not for vassalage;
he will be able to ask me for the money
and then chase me out of his land.
It is better and much more suitable
that Polynices go free without any accommodation."
That is the end of it; they let Polynices go,
and ride off to fight against two others.

Outside the ranks, in a field quite far away,
beside a beautiful meadow near a pond,
Eteocles has come out
to the fountain at the cypress;
he has twenty thousand men and more.
Riding against them comes King Adrastus,

who tourneys with them in pride;
no old man ever had such a heart.
[The king jousts]
just like a fresh bachelor.
There is a trench by the meadows
where the inner army lines up;
as they move against the host they pass the ditch
and that was very foolish,
for they would never have been undone
if they had not passed the ditch.
If one could only have seen them in the midst of the meadows
striking with lances and swords,
joining straight on, charging at a slant,
and so many lying prone,
lances shattered and shields cracked!
They can scarcely recognize each other,
so great is the press and the crowd;
that is what bothers them most,
for at the tourney the crowd is such
that one can not joust one on one
to win recognition or fame
or to be set apart from the others.
The crowd is such at that tourney
that no one can attack for himself.
But the archers do a great deal of harm,
killing many good horses.
King Adrastus sends a message to the inner army
proposing to make a truce with the archers
that they take no more shots in the tourney.
The Thebans agree to the pact,
pledging each other for their archers
because horses are being killed on both sides.
From now on, there is good tourneying,
no bow is shot.
Now no one who wants to tourney
need fear hurled darts or shot arrows;
everyone can spur in security,
with no more worry about archers.

The inner army is too arrogant,

6484 **[The king jousts]** *joste li reis*: line lacking in MS S; added by Mora-Lebrun from Constans's edition.

and the host too clever:
little by little the Greeks draw back,
and the Thebans follow them further and further;
the fools keep following them,
as the host grows larger and larger.
Now that their force has arrived,
the Greeks no longer hold back the reins;
they go on the attack.
The Thebans turn back in tight ranks
and the Greeks follow them recklessly,
chasing them with violent force.
On and on they drive them to their shame,
there is no letup in the pursuit.
Having put them in that vise,
they chase them very closely:
they press them onwards,
edging them towards the ditches.
They keep striking hard.
throw them down horribly,
and kill and slaughter them:
the fallen do not get up.
The destruction is great
and grievous and terrible and harsh.
On that field Eteoocles
has lost the best of his company;
before he has passed the trench,
he has lost the best men of his household.
There is great loss there and nothing more to be done.
He has sustained a very great burden
but despite the loss he suffers,
he does not want to cede the place to the Greeks.

Haemon comes out beside the shore,
his company is courageous and fierce.
They throw themselves wildly into the battle,
begin swiftly and endure long;
they endure long and begin swiftly,
trying to be the first to fight.
Atys comes towards them with his entourage.
He loves the king's sister
and is jousting for her sake;
for the girl who is watching him
he has joined battle with two Greeks in the avant-garde.

He knocks one down, the other flees,
everyone on both sides sees him.
Ptolemy has a black horse
Let me tell you the truth about this horse:
none in the host had so beautiful a hide,
none was so agile, none so swift;
he was an Arab from beyond the sea,
the offspring of water and a demon.
Sitting on his black horse, Ptolemy
begins to charge towards those inside;
spurring, from the side
he throws down Flori, the Duke of Anvers.
In the same charge,
he joins battle with Jugurtha of Edessa.
Haemon sits on a bay horse;
his heart is light and happy,
with his noble entourage,
that was feared and respected in times of need;
he encourages them to engage in the tourney,
but there is no need, for they are doing it already.
If one could only see them spur,
and throw themselves among the ranks!
They have no fear of darts or arrows,
nor the loss of their horses.
Haemon is the first to break rank;
he himself shows them the way,
spurring towards Tydeus on the sand;
you should know—this is no fable—
he gave him such a blow on the shield
he almost threw him down from the horse.
But Tydeus avoided that,
because his horse leapt to the side;
if the horse had not swerved,
the joust would have been very hard.
Hamon strikes him and quickly takes off,
he does not stay around.
Tydeus is distressed,
because he has never failed with his lance;
he spurs the horse in all his anger,
and joins battle with Antenor of Sardinia;
Tydeus throws him down on the sand
and leads his horse away as is his right.
Tydeus has a cousin,

a tall, thin, fine young man;
his name is Afran.
Afran drives impetuously through the ranks.
He rides towards one of the enemy
who tries to hide among the foot soldiers:
but Afran, lance lowered, spurring
follows him over the sand.
In the pursuit, Afran gets closed in among the foot-soldiers,
and cannot get out again.

Tydeus sees that the servants
have captured his man, his relative;
with more than two hundred knights,
he goes to help him against the inner army.
But as Tydeus spurs through the ranks
a footsoldier from behind a rock
wounds his horse
with a dart that goes through to its fletch;
the horse is wounded in the flank,
his blood runs out with great force.
Tydeus comes out of the press,
dismounts, and leaves his horse on the field.
He sees a young nobleman from the host
leading a swift Arab steed and calls to him;
the young man turns over the horse,
that is quick, agile, and very alert.
Tydeus mounts by the left stirrup
while the youth holds the right.

When he has mounted,
Tydeus gives him free rein
and as he runs, in small leaps,
through the field, he meets Atys.
Atys is a very large young man,
although he is only fifteen.
His hair is curly, blond and long,
very long to his shoulders,
and his head is circled
with a band of striped taffeta.
His eyes are bright, laughing and clear,
full of gaiety and wildness
and his face is whiter
than snow on a branch.

Over the white skin
Nature with great skill has set red—
that is a coloring that greatly pleases me,
white highlighted with red!
His face is clean like his chin,
with no beard or moustache.
He is quite slim in the waist
and has very long legs.
He is dressed in wool samite
with pointed sleeves narrow at the wrist,
and shod in the best silk
one could find in Thessaly,
with gold spurs
worth a thousand sous and more.
He sits astride a Castilian horse
that runs faster than a swallow flies;
his sword is girded at his side, a shield hangs at his neck.
But I think he is a fool for one reason:
he has taken off his hauberk, frivolously,
for he has done a lot of chivalry.
Now he wants to ride out around the field
to show off his body.
He spurs through the field, his lance raised,
a standard fixed at its point.
As he rides around,
he finds Tydeus in his path
and does not turn away,
but rides towards him with great fury.
Tydeus, seeing him unarmed,
avoids him and laughs at him;
seeing a child without armor,
he pities him, and he is right to do so.
"It would bring no shame to me," he says,
"if I turned away from you in this encounter,
for there are several reasons
that make me want to avoid fighting you.
You are unusually beautiful,
without armor, and young
and you must be very valiant, I think,
if you dare to ride against me;
that is why I do not want to kill you.
It would bring grief and distress to your soul.
You are too eager to carry a lance,

you should spend your childhood in other ways,
and stay at home,
it is not yet time for you to fight."
Atys answers: "You are mad!
Your pity is only cowardice!"
Immediately he spurs towards Tydeus's shield
which he cuts and breaks,
pushing the shield up to his temple,
and knocking them against each other.
Tydeus sees that he will have to fight
but he hopes to strike him only lightly on his shield;
he cannot, however, control his hand,
and strikes him full on the chest.
Atys falls from the mortal blow,
down from his horse onto the grass.
Tydeus grieves and weeps:
"Ah, God," he says, "what bad luck
to meet this child today.
I would have given my whole fief,
not to touch him with a weapon!"
He is wondrously troubled;
throwing his lance into the field,
he commends it to the living devil
and lets his horse wander loose.
He does not guide it with his hand.
Atys faints from the pain
and when he comes to, he blames himself
and pardons Tydeus for his death.
He knows he had no responsibility for it.
"Don't weep for me, friend," he says,
"I have killed myself,
but it is a great comfort to me
that I am killed by a great warrior,
not by a scoundrel
but by someone who is worth a hundred others;
I lose my life to one
who is the flower of chivalry.
Friend," he says, "I pray you for God's sake,
have me carried into the city;
death is near, it oppresses me,
I think I must certainly die."
Beside a ditch in an orchard
five young men were shooting bows.

Weeping, Tydeus calls to them,
tells them the chilling news about Atys:
"Carry the body inside," he says,
"so dogs do not eat it outside here."
The youths run quickly to get him
and carry him on his shield.
His wound is large and bleeds badly,
he is completely bathed in red blood.
The face that was so fresh and tender
has no more color than ashes.

Ismene and her sister are talking
on the upper floors of the tower,
Ismene saying a lot about Atys
and the deeds he has done,
her sister keeping a watchful eye on
Parthenopeus as he joins battles.
She recognizes him on the sand
by the peacock tail feather
laced behind his helmet;
when he spurs along the shore
the feather expands and opens in the wind
and covers him completely in the back.
The sisters joke and laugh about their lovers
and argue about their prowess
for each one, in her view,
thinks she has the best one.
Antigone says to Ismene:
"It's easy for you to talk.
you can kiss and embrace Atys
and speak to him every day.
I can't speak to my lover
or kiss or embrace him.
I can't even see him, wretch that I am,
except from here, from this battlement."
"Envy never dies," Ismene says.
"It's not my fault your friend is not with you.
If I have the chance to be with mine
and do what pleases me so much,
why does that bother you?
You would do the same if you could.
But I am very troubled by a dream I had:
God grant that it does not come true.

This morning when I was sleeping
I saw Atys's mother weeping
and she said to me: `Give me back my son,
if I don't have him I shall go mad!'
Then I looked for him everywhere
but I couldn't find him."
While they are talking,
there is a racket that makes everything tremble.
Ismene fears in her heart
that it means her great sorrow and loss.
From the city rises
the cry and sobbing of women,
for as Atys enters the city
a great crowd follows him crying.
Ismene looks behind her
and sees the bier carried below;
the ladies and the little people
howl and cry in the street.
Fearing for Atys whom she loves,
she falls in a faint on the floor.
Her sister holds her in her arms;
but when she comes to,
she falls swiftly down,
crying and howling like a mad woman.
Her sister supports her and carries her in her arms
and very gently comforts her;
but there is no place for comfort,
for her love was too strong.
They place the wounded Atys under the olive
and scold those who are weeping around him
while they try to arrange him; he keeps fainting.
They anoint his tongue with balm,
opening his teeth with a knife
they anoint his tongue with balm.
That enables him to speak a little,
but what use is it! He is not really able to speak;
but he begs them, with some pain,
to bring Ismene to him quickly.
Ismene is on his tongue,
his love for her touches his heart;
he asks often for Ismene
and Jocasta brings her to him.
"Love," she says, "here is your spouse,

miserable and grieving!"
He opens his eyes and sees her;
at that moment the soul leaves his body.
There is grief—and it was enormous—
of old men and children
who cry out and howl over the body.
They recall Atys's deeds of prowess,
they lament his beauty and his age,
his prowess and his valiant service.
Ismene hugs and embraces him,
and faints often, on that spot.
For a long moment Ismene seems
dead, without vapor or breath.
You must hear this wonder:
she does not blink,
she does not move as much as a stone;
she is green like a leaf of ivy,
with no color in her face,
she is colder than ice.
At her neck they find a vein
that scarcely beats;
her mother and sister move her,
with the help of the other ladies;
they carry her into a chamber,
prepare a bed and lay her on it.

Those who return to the tourney
announce the death of Atys to the king.
When Eteocles hears that Atys is dead—
the best of his army—
he weeps from the eyes and sighs from the heart;
it is no wonder if he is angry.
He faints on the neck of his steed
blaming himself for the death of Atys;
when he hears the news of the death
he can scarcely stay in the saddle.
The king grieves and sighs,
wondrously and sorrowfully.
He gallops across the sand
sending his men before him;
the fighting has ended for the day,
from now on there is only distress.
The battle is put off because they are all exhausted

and because night is falling,
but the truth is
the death of Atys disrupts it.
The king is sad and tearful
and sighs grievously.
The grief of the king is great,
all his talk is of Atys,
and I do not speak only of the king—
all the others do the same.
Servants and knights weep,
and young men and squires;
there is not a single man in the court
who does not weep for love of Atys.
Atys had brought with him
one hundred knights in his troop;
they were among the best of his land,
one could not find any better.
Their lament is great, you have not heard the like
described by the mouth of man.
They grieve without control,
they hate their life, they care nothing for it;
they say they have lived too long
since they have lost their lord.
They can't tear themselves away;
instead they blame themselves, they're in shock,
grieving bitterly for their lord,
whom they see lying there, dead.
They fall to the ground in a faint
and mourn him like the good vassals they are:
"Atys, our leader, so young,
With a face so handsome, so ruddy—
dear lord, now that you're gone,
who can possibly lead this great army?
You gave us our arms and armor,
our fiefs and great castles;
you molded your great following
into a fighting force valiant and eager,
for you gave us the equipment,
you gave us mules and palfreys,
our arms, our badges, our horses' caparisons
and handsome greyhounds and fine hawks;
you gave us husky steeds,
gold and silver and rich clothing.

Your retinue of knights was always happy,
because they were never in need:
you lavished wealth on them,
you granted their every wish;
you loved those knights of yours,
held them in the highest esteem;
whoever served you had nothing to regret,
he never lacked for anything in your service.
There was never a man of your prowess,
nor one so generous.
You made decisions wisely,
and thus you had the twin virtues
of strength and wisdom, found so rarely
in a person of your high station;
what a foundation for greatness!
It's a sure thing
that if you had lived a little longer,
you would have surpassed dukes and kings.
But now it's all over for you, dear lord:
and for that we can only feel sorrow and rage;
now you've left us desolate—
we have no land, no fiefs,
and not the slightest chance
of returning some day to our land;
we don't even dare talk about returning,
when we can't go back with you as our leader.
How could we ever face
the king and queen without you?
No, we have no choice but to go somewhere else;
we're too worried about going back there."
That's how Atys's men weep and groan
and express their sadness.
Ismene is shut up in her room
where she quickly regains consciousness;
her mother makes sure she's well guarded,
to prevent her from approaching the corpse,
because if she were to gaze on it for any length of time,
it would only result in her repeated collapse in a faint on top of the body.
But Ismene couldn't stand her confinement;
she quickly began to swear
that if she didn't see the body she would die at once;
sorrow would break her heart.
So her mother finally allowed her to go;

a knight parted the crowd for her
and two others led her to the bier,
where she uncovered Atys's face,
finding it pale and discolored.
Sorrow grips Ismene's heart;
tears pour down her cheeks,
wetting the collar of her robe of furs.
A hundred times she kissed him passionately:
on his eyes, his face, even his chin.
She lamented over the body in her misery,
letting her great grief pour out:
"Atys, my dear lord, can't you hear me?
Open your eyes—why are you closing them?
It's me, Ismene, who's talking to you.
Poor me—now I'm talking like a fool!
He can't hear me, can't see me;
I know he's lying there all cold.
Atys is dead; what a disaster!
All your bravery came to this bad end:
you're lying here, dead before your time.
May God have mercy on your soul!
Atys is dead, truly dead;
you hardly had time to enjoy your youth.
Those beautiful eyes of yours, open them now!
The worms are coming to eat them.
Your tender skin—what a tragedy it ever existed!
Now it will be reduced to miserable ashes.
And your body, with those beautiful limbs of yours,
will become rotten and putrified.
Aah! Death, how powerful you are!!
There's not a living thing in the whole world
that you don't have in your power,
to take away its life whenever you want.
You force a bitter drink down the world's throat,
and separate lovers forever;
to lose a lover like that brings great grief,
and all the joys of life turn into sadness.
You've certainly cut short my happiness,
and left me with enduring sadness—I'm sure of that:
I'll never know joy again, as long as I live.
Whoever may be laughing, I'll be crying;
and it's no wonder I'm weeping
when I've lost my dear lord and husband:

my husband was my heart's desire,
and I never expect to have one like him for as long as I live—
someone so wise, so brave,
and so loved by all who knew him.
I was still a young girl when I was given to you;
you loved me as your wife,
and I loved you as much as I knew how,
but I was never fully yours.
Dear, sweet lord, you told me
that after this siege you would take me with you;
when the war was over,
you'd bring me to your land:
but now you'll never see your land again,
and you'll never bring me, or anybody else, back there.
Oh! Your father's going to die of sorrow:
because you have no brothers,
he suddenly has no heir;
you were the source of all his hopes.
And what can I say about your mother?
From now on she'll always live in anguish;
the poor thing—for the rest of her life
she'll never know any joy.
When we used to have good times together,
more than a hundred times I heard you praise
a sister that you have:
you'd never known anyone so wise, so brave.
And now. . . what heavy sorrow that sister will have to bear!
Her heart will never again know joy.
Your death will plunge her
into great sorrow and confusion.
Cursed be the soul of whoever killed you,
and also of the smith who forged his weapon!
They have caused many people great woe,
and especially me, who lost the most."
This was Ismene's lament over the corpse,
and her sorrow continued all through the night.
All the people, the mighty and the humble,
attended the body of the duke with great honor;
within a circle of candelabra,
the king was seated there, and all the barons;
despite their fatigue, they stayed awake all night,
didn't even sleep a wink.

In the morning, after the hour of prime,
The sun rose, burning off the frost.
All the sages of the city
assembled, a good two thousand of them;
dressed in albs and tunics,
they processed with relics in reliquaries,
with sacred texts and phylacteries,
with burning candles and swinging censors
filled with incense and other perfumes.
Their chief priest sent the dead man's soul on its way,
and then with great honor they carried his body
into the temple located nearby, outside the castle.
The funeral service lasted a long time;
the lessons were read and the responses sung
with great care, all in the proper sequence,
followed by the burial in the cemetery.
But before the body was placed in the tomb,
the king released all the prisoners,
and before it was covered,
the king freed five hundred serfs.
Ismene falls at the king's feet,
but he quickly lifts her up and holds her close,
asking, "What do you desire, my sister?
Whatever you may have in mind,
don't doubt for a second that I will give it to you:
even if you should want my kingdom, just take it."
"My brother," she says, "I don't want anything like that,
but I do want to change my life.
I'll become a nun, and live under a rule,
because I've lost all interest in this world;
just give me enough of your riches
for one hundred women to live on.
While he lived, Atys loved you a great deal,
so found an abbey here for his sake;
he served you so loyally
that he not only fought great battles and suffered great hardships,

---

7031 **the hour of prime** *heure de prime*: The monastic hour of Prime, roughly 6 a.m.

7064 **so found an abbey here for his sake** *faiç ci por lui un abbeïe*: A similar request is made by a discarded wife in the *lai* "Eliduc," vv. 1120ff., *Les lais de Marie de France*, ed. Jean Rychner (Paris: Champion, 1969). See further Introduction, p. 10.

but he even sacrificed his life for you.
Now do right by his soul, and do it right now!
You will have done him a great favor, and earned great praise,
if his soul finds its rest thanks to you."
The king agrees; he grants the abbey extensive fiefs,
plus six hundred hogsheads of wine every year,
and as many mills and ovens
as they'll need always to have enough bread;
demesne land large enough to need one hundred ploughs;
two major streets in the big city,
the river with the fishery,
and the farmland all around it.
If the estate manager doesn't make crooked deals with outsiders
she'll be able to live very well indeed within her abbey.

Prompted by their pity for Ismene,
counts cried, castellans bawled;
everyone there burst into tears,
rich and poor alike mourned bitterly.
And for love of the young lady
a hundred more maidens of her age,
worthy and of high rank,
took the veil in the chapel, becoming nuns.
The next day, in the afternoon,
the king decided to go out onto the plain;
he called ten of his companions,
well-born and valorous, to accompany him.
But before they set out,
the king equipped himself
with the best armor that he possessed—
indeed, the best he had ever found.
So he strapped on a fine sword
that came from Babylon;
it was found in that city
in a sarcophagus made of sardonyx;
King Ninus, who had had it made, lay in that tomb,
according to the words inscribed on it.
The blade of the sword was red and violet,
and sharper than any razor;
the pommel was of gold, the guard of ivory.

7101 **King Ninus** *Ninus*: Legendary first King of the Assyrians, husband of Semiramis.

Nothing it cut into could remain alive!
Next he put on a hauberk,
one neither too small nor too big,
made of tightly woven chain mail,
very light and well shaped.
It had been wrought not long before:
the forging was tempered
in one of the rivers of Paradise,
into which it was plunged six times;
he who forged it was a master of his art,
so that whoever donned it could feel absolutely secure:
he need have no fear
that he'd lose even a drop of blood in battle.
It bore the blazon of an ermine,
Framed by long, silken strips.
He laced on a bright red-gold helmet,
that shone brilliantly in the sunlight;
it contained a good three hundred ounces of gold.
Set into its crown were two bright red gems
and in the middle an amethyst;
below, around the border,
there were beryls and sardonyxes,
topazes and chalcedonies,
and on the nasal piece in front,
a carbuncle and an enameled surface.
Then they led Hoarywhite to him,
the steed sent to him a while back by his mistress,
whose name was Galatea,
daughter of the King of Nubia.
Hoarywhite was a noble horse,
as fine as fine silver:
he was solid, thick-set, with a well-trimmed mane,
and quite famous in his own land.
He was broad in the neck and shoulders, with a well shaped head,
A large chest, a narrow saddling place
That expanded to a great breadth further down,
And thence to a round, hefty rump.
His hooves were arched, his legs straight.
He was swift and lively,
and highly praised for his ability to run long distances;
the slight sway of his back
made sitting astride him that much more comfortable.
This horse was a pleasure to gaze at:

whoever saw him had to say
that never, in all his life, had he seen such a fine animal.
His bridle was golden, his saddle of silver
And its covering all of silk.
The king laid his hands on the saddlebow—
his stirrup was held not by mere valets,
but by four counts—
and mounted Hoarywhite.
Two young retainers brought him
his great ivory shield,
painted blue with white edging;
the knob in the center was of enameled gold.
If its maker didn't lie,
The shield had a border golden in color,
and was fastened with thirty-three bolts of pure gold;
its strap, too, entirely embroidered with gold.
On its face, the king had, as a joke,
had painted his mistress's legs,
and right next to them was a great dent
that wasn't made while he was in retreat.
A knight handed him the shield,
and the king, on receiving it, hung it around his neck.
He carried a great ashen lance;
there wasn't in all of Saxony a Saxon, however big,
to whom it wouldn't be a fiercely heavy load,
but to him it seemed rather light.
Two multicolored banners were wrapped around it.
And thus armed, the king sallied forth.
Salatiel rode out with him,
a Jew from the children of Israel,
astride a grey mount
that two thieves had robbed from an island.
The wind drove them to Thebes,
where they made the horse a present to the king.
Dyogenes, the King of Assyria,
was mounted on a horse of dark, metallic gray
stolen from the emir;
it was worth two barrels full of deniers.
Teucer had as his horse Poor Ol' Shaggy,

7165–68 **On its face. . . while he was in retreat** *Devant ot fait. . . pas pris en fuiant*: A similar ribald shield decoration is attributed to Guillaume IX, Duke of Aquitaine, by the Anglo-Norman historian William of Malmesbury.

one fine beast;
there wasn't another so easily managed:
compared to him, all others were out of the running.
Helmagoras of Salamine
had a horse, white as an ermine,
that was covered, down to his toes,
in a slashed, red silken cloth
decorated with multicolored ornaments;
his range was a full thirty leagues.
Petree, the Count of Marseille,
was seated on a marvelously fine horse,
whiter than any flower;
he was fast and well-mannered.
Polidorus, he of Caesarea,
sat astride a swift dromedary
that he had covered in a brownish-gray fur robe;
he wouldn't trade that beast for all of Phrygia's gold.
Then there was someone called Nestor,
a youngster without beard or moustache;
Adrastus had denied him his heritage
and expelled him from his realm;
then he had come to Thebes,
and become the king's close friend and confidant.
He was a very fine archer,
which was why the king favored him more than anyone else.
He had a horse, a swift thoroughbred,
for whom he had paid the steed's weight in silver.
Agrippa, Count of Sicily,
was there seeking to do great deeds;
hunkered down in the city,
his goals were to fight well and win fame.
His was a steed of great worth,
the father of the famous Bucephalus
that Alexander possessed for so long,
thanks to whom he won so many battles.
Gariot from Corinth was there.
He had a really resonant shield,
fixed as it was with a hundred little golden bells;
the king had given it to Nestor.
He was mounted on a light gray charger from Slavonia,
well suited for chivalric encounters.
There was even an English warrior,
Godrich by name, brave and courtly;

a good knight, that one,
and he had very luxurious equipment—
on no one else could you find such fine gear,
except on the king's own body:
Godrich had neither bridle, saddle, nor spurs
made of anything less than gold.
He sat astride Swallow of Nicole,
who ran faster than a bird can fly:
he covered the ground with flying hooves.
You'd be a fool to look for a speedier stallion:
there just isn't one, brown or bay,
who could beat him in a race.
Accompanied by these ten paladins,
the king issued forth, across the bridge.
The women of the city climbed up
on the earthen ramparts and the city walls;
they mounted the towers to see them leave.
Now the cry went up within the besieging army:
"Here come some troops from inside the city walls!"
Tydeus didn't hesitate:
already mounted, as it happened,
he raced away from the army at full speed,
on a fine Gascon horse
that propelled him quickly into combat;
within the army his companions mounted up at once
and spurred on after him.
The king came charging
up to the ford, near the marsh,
which Tydeus had commandeered
with eleven companions, not one more.
Across the water, at the ford of the thorny bushes,
they met and clashed, twelve against eleven.
Some fell on the king's side—
perhaps three or four; I'm not sure—
but of his opponents at least one half
were unhorsed.
Tydeus and the king jousted,
landing great blows on each others' shields.
Tydeus struck the king
right on the knob of his shield,
landing a crushing blow with great force,
entirely shattering his coat of mail.
If it had been precisely aimed,

it would have knocked the king to the ground, out cold,
but in fact it slipped a bit to the side,
and didn't strike through to his body.
Now the king struck Tydeus
high up on the blue covering of his shield;
his lance was straight, it didn't waver,
and it ripped the good shield from his enemy's neck.
A servant who was with the king
had hidden himself among the rose bushes;
his name was Menalipus,
and now he gave Tydeus a mortal wound:
he was a fine archer with a powerful bow,
and his arrow brought death to Tydeus.
It struck through the flesh of his buttock,
cutting veins and nerves;
Tydeus lost blood; his heart failed;
he dismounted onto the fresh grass.
His companions did the right thing,
beheading the wretch who shot him.
Tydeus lay in the middle of the field,
blood welling out of his wound.
Now the army mounted and came charging up,
but stopped when they came to Tydeus;
meanwhile, those who'd come from the city returned to it,
rejoicing greatly over the fate of Tydeus:
all those inside were laughing and cavorting
while everyone in the besieging army cried and lamented.
Tydeus is close to death,
for all his blood is spurting out fast;
with his blood he loses his color,
and lies dying on the grass in great pain.
King Adrastus feels grief—he's never felt greater—
he mourns Tydeus and his bravery,
his prowess and his valor,
his generosity and nobility;
nevertheless, he doesn't reveal
the full extent of his sorrow:
everyone is completely shocked by this loss,
so the king has to put on a brave front.
I can't imagine a wiser man than the king;
he knows how to comfort his people—and himself.
Polynices returns from the woods
where he was having his siege engines built:

he had constructed two battering rams and four catapults
to attack the city walls.
From far off he heard the cries and laments
and was frightened by the noise;
spurring ahead, he raced into the middle of the field
where the Greeks had been in combat,
and there he heard news hateful to him,
and saw the pale and bloody body
around which the knights and nobles
were venting their grief.
When he recognized the corpse, he collapsed on it:
you can't blame him for being so devastated!
Polynices lets his extreme sorrow pour out,
repeatedly drying his eyes on his sleeve;
he weeps copiously, utters heart-rending sighs,
and feels great rage swelling inside him.
As he sighs and weeps like this,
he laments his friend's death passionately:
"Comrade," he says, "you're dead!
If I live on after you, I'm in the wrong;
Since you're dead, I oughtn't to be alive,
for even a learned scholar couldn't record
the great pain and suffering
that you've endured out of love for me.
You were a rock-solid friend;
you always promised me
that you would win me back my realm:
now you're dead trying to win it back.
You took on yourself all the hardships,
the dangers and the perils,
while you told me to rest easy.
It was your way to argue against me
whenever I wanted to go out in battle,
because you loved me so much
that you didn't want anything bad to happen to me,
or for me to get caught in something I couldn't handle.
I wanted to go to try reclaim my realm
before it came down to open war:
you heard about my plan, and you argued against it
and wouldn't let me go,
because my brother might kill me—
and now I can well believe he would have;
if he had gotten me in his power,

I wouldn't have gotten away alive that day.
You took this perilous trip on yourself
and behaved there with great courage,
because everyone of the court, in the great hall, heard you—
no one was so deaf he did not—
when you accused the king of perjuring himself,
and challenged him to keep his promise.
You then performed heroic deeds,
leaving behind fifty of them, dead—
fifty of them, done in by you alone,
leaving only one survivor that you sent back to the court:
you left him alive
so that he could testify to your exploits in battle.
Then thanks to you, and with you in charge,
all the barons of my army were brought together;
no one worked as hard at it as you,
putting yourself in charge of the whole army.
During the day you oversaw its forage operations,
and often took part in the tumult of battle;
there wasn't a night when a sentinel was needed
that you didn't keep watch in person.
To go hungry and sleepless at night on guard,
to battle and joust—
you asked for no other pleasure:
certainly not enjoying yourself in bed!
When we first entered Greece,
we argued over a place to take shelter from a storm,
under a stone vault in front of the royal residence in Argos,
and came to blows over who would have refuge there;
the king heard us from his palace,
and made peace between us:
from then on, you never loved anyone more than me—
not a first cousin; not even your brother;
with you dead, I no longer want to live."
At once he draws his steely sword,
and is ready to plunge it into his body,
when the king races to grab it from him.
The king has seized the sword,
and begs him not to kill himself.
Then all the knights try to comfort him;
they hurry him out of the crowd,
pushing him through the press
to get him away from the corpse.

The King of Thebes knew very well
from the weeping and wailing he heard,
he realized from all that grieving
that Tydeus was done for.
How much harm that man had done him while he was alive!
So now the king gets a very evil idea:
he wants to steal the body from the Greeks,
so that they can't bury it;
instead, he wants to have it fed to his mastiffs,
and to the crows and vultures.
After Tydeus's death the king wants to get his revenge
by having his dogs eat the body,
so that the Greeks will be even more distraught
when they see their hero become dog food.
Within the besieged castle the warriors armed themselves,
and came racing out at the same time:
then you would have seen a mob at the gates!
The king rushes to join his men;
in high spirits he tells them, "We're in luck!
Menalipus has landed a great blow:
with that blow he killed Tydeus—
look at the corpse, lying right over there.
Whoever wants a great reward from me,
here's what I want him to do:
let's go all out to grab that body,
because if we can carry it away
by a quick, brutal attack,
we'll really do great harm to the army besieging us.
And we'll never be happy
if that corpse isn't snatched from them and brought back here."
With that, they let their horses gallop
and try their hardest to get hold of the body.
Enormous sorrow descends on the besieging army—
many of them faint from grief—
when they see the troops advancing from inside the castle;
Adrastus wastes no time getting into the saddle—
he's not slow to mount:
"Stop your blubbering!" he cries;
"You see your enemies coming,
who've already destroyed Tydeus;
whoever is really sorry
let him show it by how fiercely he strikes back.
Avenge your sorrow here and now:

hit hard; show no mercy,
and make sure you're not sloppy
in your cutting and thrusting!"
Polynices weeps and faints,
but the king rushes to him:
"Stop crying," he commands.
"If his death makes you sad,
avenge him! Just look at them, the ones who killed him,
and are so happy about it:
your job is to turn their rejoicing
into grief.
You must avenge him right away,
and leave all that mourning to his wife;
women and children should lament,
but knights should deal great blows.
While he lived, that corpse performed
many chivalric feats for you;
in support of your war and through his great loyalty
this warrior is dead—that burdens me—
now fight back out of love for him,
not just to regain the land rightfully yours.
And even if they were ready to yield the kingdom to you,
you should never accept it
before you've avenged his death
and brought the war to a successful end."
With some difficulty,
Polynices gets a grip on his grief:
he consoles himself—it isn't easy—
and mounts his horse, who bears him away quickly;
he and the king are deeply saddened,
but today, right away, they'll land great blows,
and so will the rest of their army.
They follow the king fearlessly:
after him they race
as he launches into battle.
Adrastus closed with Creon
and threw him off his horse;
if Creon hadn't been torn away from him,
he would surely have been beheaded.
Adrastus's army cries out in Greek,
"May our king never grow old!
See how agile he is in battle,
charging ahead at full speed."

Now Polynices attacked his brother:
what a tragedy they were sons of the same mother!
Great was their mutual anger,
how intense their desire to kill each other.
But the hour for that hadn't yet come:
the two brothers hurled themselves into combat,
all too willingly raining blows on each other,
and reducing their shields to twisted, shapeless wrecks.
Those shields were truly smashed,
but their coats of mail remained solid,
their armor was firm and tight,
and it saved them from death.
Now their retainers came between them,
and more blows were proffered and repaid;
much expert combat
occurred in short order on that plain.
Great was the press on both sides,
and much the glittering of gold and silver.
The battle spread out all across the plain,
which was very long and broad:
a great league or more, I believe,
the field of battle extended,
so that those fighting on the left flank
had no idea what was happening on the right flank.
Polynices is with the king,
more concerned for the monarch than for himself.
They'll never be separated that day,
as they protect each other in battle:
they pass through the combat zone together,
sticking together in the thick of the fight;
Polynices and the king strike simultaneously,
they attack at the same moment as well.
The king fought on the left flank,
where he charged often and struck quickly.
As for Hypomedon down below on the right flank,
there wasn't a better warrior in the entire army.
He was part of the unit
guarding the body of Tydeus.
That's where you'd have seen a mob of the besiged troops
racing to grab and carry off the corpse.
The King of Thebes gave it his all
leading a large number of his men—
a great horde intent on stealing that body.

Hypomedon stood in their way;
Hypomedon prevented them from doing it,
giving and receiving great blows,
in a violent tit for tat
practically unheard-of in intensity.
Hypomedon led a large cohort
well trained in battle;
there were a thousand of them, or even more, I think,
all from his native land:
none of them could be blamed
for how they attacked, dealing out great blows.
He ordered half of them to dismount,
a good five hundred now on foot;
a good five hundred have dismounted,
and look at that: the body of Tydeus well protected!
They expressed their conviction
that their adversaries would only get the corpse over their own dead bodies;
before the attackers could seize it,
they were going to spill buckets of blood that day.
Hypomedon certainly knew all about battle strategies:
he'd been in many a tight spot before.
He has set up a cavalry troop
of the most agile bachelors:
a mounted squadron, some seven hundred strong;
these are natural horsemen,
noble, fit bachelors.
There isn't such a hard-hitting cohort in the rest of the army,
nor one so talented, so feared,
or so efficiently organized.
Now those from inside have spread out,
fighting hard all across the battlefield
and leaving behind with the king, it seems to me,
no more than two thousand men.
The king pushes all the men he has
as hard as he can,
commanding them not to turn aside,
nor to take evasive action by racing across the front;
instead they mass for a frontal assault,
and the two armies meet head on.

When their lances shattered,
they drew their shining swords:
what a violent day's end you would have seen there,

with many a blow given,
many another received,
between those trying to grab the corpse and those defending it.
The duke doesn't have a large force,
the king's is much greater;
but the duke has prepared his troops better,
so that they are deployed in a superior formation.
The king suffers great losses
among the scouts ahead of the main force;
the royal troops take high casualties,
for the mounted knights, as they attack, knock them down,
and the foot soldiers assail
and capture them; meanwhile, if one of their own falls,
the duke's men move fast to rescue him.
The King of Thebes saw clearly
that he could achieve nothing by force,
so he had brought to him a knight
whom he had previously captured from the Greeks;
he had been held against payment of a ransom,
which had just been arranged that day.
When the king saw him, he called out to him,
"Go on my behalf to those over there.
Tell them that those fighting up on the left flank
have been defeated;
the Greeks are routed and their king is captured;
if they don't come to his rescue, they've lost him.
You can make them believe this easily enough,
because it will certainly seem to be the truth.
And if, thanks to you, they withdraw from here,
I will release you from the promises you have made to me,
and if you want to remain with me
I will retain you as I ought to,
and I'll give you a fine troop of your own.
But if you won't do this for me, believe me,
by these two eyes with which I see you,
you won't be seeing any combat this year;
instead you'll live under a harsh rule
with plenty of hunger and thirst to go with it."

7603 **I will release you from the promises you have made to me** *je te quiterai de ta fei*: A noble warrior captured in battle gave an oath not to seek to escape before paying an appropriate ransom in return for his freedom (See Mora-Lebrun's note to this verse).

At which point the captive races off on his horse,
and, arriving on the other side, pretends to be coming from the king;
he comes from the king, he swears,
shouting out for Hypomedon.
He calls for Hypomedon repeatedly,
saying he has bad news for him.
Hypomedon, meanwhile, is hard at it in battle,
not even stopping for a moment to rest;
he smashes and kills those from within the city,
fighting hard and bravely.
The hostage comes up to him, gasping and sobbing,
pulling and tearing at his hair:
"My lord," he says, "what are you doing here?
For God's sake, have mercy on the king!
Help the king, your lord,
from whom you hold all your lands!
Forget about that dead body; help the living,
because the other side have captured the king.
For God's sake pity the king
who's been taken prisoner in this battle!
If you don't rush to his aid right now,
you'll never make it;
and if you let these enemies take him away,
you'll never have any chance of rescuing him."
Hypomedon heard this news;
you can be sure he wasn't happy about it.
he believed it, though,
for the one who brought it was the son of a count,
one of the best-born men in all Greece;
his father was the Count of Melece.
Hypomedon calls out to his cohort,
rallying his men around him:
"I'd rather lose my life," he said,
"than have Greece shamed like this;
I'd rather be captured with the king
than have them lead him away without me!"
He entrusts the body of Tydeus to the foot soldiers,
and, following the advice of the messenger,
with the mounted warriors at his disposal
Hypomedon advances into a valley;
racing through it at high speed
and performing feats of great bravery,
for he has only seven hundred knights

with whom to cut across the entire besieged army.
And while he is pursuing a phantom,
Eteocles doesn't lose focus:
he calls for help from all his men,
and his cohort swells accordingly;
now he has the strength needed to grab the body
and bring it back into the city.
The inhabitants of Thebes celebrate,
laughing and carrying on all around Tydeus's corpse;
the women rain down curses on it,
weeping and lamenting out of self-pity,
as they remember their loved ones
whom Tydeus has killed.
All the remembered sadness floods over them,
and they want to tear the body apart.
Only with great difficulty does the king save the body
from the women and citizens of the town
and hand it over to five hundred serfs:
if they lose control over it, it will cost them their lives.
The serfs went off with the body,
dragging it along by a cord.
The besieging army saw that from a hilltop;
you can be sure they were very upset,
when they saw them dragging Tydeus's corpse,
treating it so shamefully;
I can't begin to tell you how sad they are about it—
this is a grief they can't avoid.
The noble lords of Calydon,
who share his lineage—
his liege men by blood—
raise a lament such as you've never heard.
They send a messenger to the King of Thebes
by a brave and wise knight,
begging him to give them the body;
or, if he won't do that, at least sell it to them,
in the process gaining a substantial treasure:
ten times his weight in gold,
and they'll even include his splendid war horse:
none like it in all Greece.
The king couldn't care less about their offer;
he won't let the body be entombed,
or allow it to be buried in the earth,
no matter what they might promise to give him.

There's nothing for it; the messenger comes back
with the king's answer, which devastates them.
The troop returns to its encampment,
weeping and lamenting bitterly;
there are no games or laughter that night,
nor does anyone say anything about having fun.
He who can get to sleep does so,
but without feeling any joy or delight.
At first light of morning they awoke
and quickly donned their war gear;
they went to the king to seek his permission to leave,
for they wished to return to their own lands.
Since they no longer had a lord,
to remain in the army would only bring them grief;
he's dead; they want to go home,
having no reason now to stay there.
Fifteen hundred and more there were
in Tydeus's cohort:
they rode together
right up to the front of the royal tent,
a sad, mournful, depressed troop,
and dismounted under a yew tree.
The king came out of his tent to meet them,
and then began a fresh round of grieving:
in front of the king the barons began to cry,
their tears cascading down;
they bewailed and lamented their loss,
becoming very nearly crazed from their sorrow.
The king himself smolders and burns with anger,
and his heart all but stops beating:
he's full of sadness for his friend
and full of pity for those he sees before him.
So great a sorrow comes over him
that he would have collapsed if he weren't propped up.
Now the seneschal speaks with the king,
taking leave on his own behalf and that of his men.

Capaneus approaches
and takes the king aside;
then he says to the others, "Wait a bit;
the king hasn't yet sought advice.
My lord," he adds, "I'll tell you the truth,
as I believe and hope it to be:

if these troops leave now, you're finished,
and you've lost all your forces.
Our men are very demoralized,
having lost a very great support with Tydeus's death;
meanwhile, on the other side they're feeling very confident,
even as our side is bewildered, disoriented.
If these troops leave so promptly,
and the rest of the army follow suit,
everyone will say that you can't keep your army together,
and are willing to see them all go.
If a quarrel now breaks out among us,
he'd be a fool to believe
that we can ever be held together:
we will have come this far for nothing,
and you will see us retreat from here, I truly believe,
in disarray and great shame.
There's a really good fighting force on the other side,
a brave and substantial army.
As God is my judge, I think
you would be very foolish to part with these men.
While the sadness and the damage done to you
are still so fresh in your minds, it would be a major blunder
for you to allow these people to leave;
give them plenty of gold and silver
and keep them in your cohort
for as long as your own army is demoralized.
Once the siege is reinforced
and our sadness has lessened,
let's say within about two months
when the hurt won't be as fresh in mind,
if they don't want to stay with you ,
then you can let them go."
The king replies, "you can be sure
that money won't keep them here;
they are already very rich men,
and they want to go home.
We'll have to find another way to tame them,
by tricking them into staying here."
The king doesn't want to keep them waiting any longer;
he rides back them, and breaks into tears.
"My lords," he says, "we too are crying,
and it's no wonder that we do,
given my profound grief for my son-in-law

and yours for your dear lord.
God has done his will,
and there's no remedy for that!
I feel especially sorry for his father,
who's frail, old, and trembling;
once he hears of his son's death,
you'd better believe he will die of grief,
since he has no other heir
to inherit his lands after him.
But Tydeus has a child
by my daughter, a baby still nursing:
I will give this child to him, if there's someone who will bring it to him,
and that will be a great consolation to him:
when he will have mourned long enough,
all his attention will be devoted to the child,
and he will consider himself healed of his sorrow
now that he has his son's heir.
I'll send for the child right away,
while you stay with the army during that time;
and I assure you that when I give you my little heir
I'll also hand over substantial wealth;
and you will in turn present to your king
the money and the child on my behalf.
I also want you to communicate to him the words in which I beg him
not to be angry at me on account of his son:
it's terrible for me, and worse for him,
but I'm offering the best compensation I can;
and when you do leave me,
I promise you on my honor
that to each one of you individually
I'll make a generous gift from my own resources."
To make a long story short for you,
they did what he said they should:
they turned back and dismounted,
agreeing to remain in the army while awaiting the child's arrival.
Now I'll tell you something about that boy:
he'll take after, and avenge, his father very well indeed,
for, when he came of age,
he certainly showed himself to be a great warrior,
continually performing deeds of prowess;
his name was Diomedes.

He was in the army attacking Troy,
and in hand-to-hand combat
with Aeneas, a mighty opponent—
indeed, except for Hector, the best one of all.
(If Aeneas hadn't had help,
Diomedes would certainly have won.)
Now Adrastus summons the barons,
and asks for their counsel on a particular matter:
since he who commanded the entire army
has lost his life,
who should be chosen to succeed him?
It's now important to target one of them
who can take upon himself all the responsibility,
after the king, of leading them in battle.
All of them recommend Hypomedon to him;
in doing so, they've picked the best, in my opinion,
for he is brave and of noble lineage,
at the right age to put up with hardships,
and well trained in chivalry.
So they passed on the authority to him,
requesting him that from that point on
he will accept the charge
of being their commander in combat:
under the king they will have him as their captain.
Hypomedon consents, somewhat reluctantly.

He wastes no time in taking on himself
major responsibility for the army;
He sets up the night watch so well
that it was faultless from then on.
The barons keep watch
every night when he assigns them to it;
seven hundred strong awake and on guard,
to make sure that they aren't surprised from inside the city,
and he keeps watch with them himself,
advising them and keeping their spirits up.
No man ever complained less
to stay up all night, in full armor.

7824–29 **He was in the army. . . Diomedes would certainly have won** *En l'ost de Troie . . . Dyodemus fust la victoire*: A reference to an episode in the legendary siege of Troy by a Greek army. On medieval western Europe's knowledge of the Trojan War, see Introduction, p. 1.

During the day, he goes out in the field to guard the foragers,
bringing up the rear when they return;
when they're weighed down with booty, exhausted,
he rides slowly behind them.
He was generous, but within limits:
he finds out secretly
who may be wanting money,
and once he has discovered this,
he helps them enough, by his assistance,
to maintain an honorable status at court.
When he can't help them from his own funds,
he takes what he needs from the royal treasury;
he behaves with great generosity,
meeting the army's expenses,
and each day he advises the king
to give generously to his barons.
By means of his openhandedness and his battle skills,
he inspires them to endurance.

The campaign has lasted a long time,
with strong armies on both sides:
the besiegers seeking to capture the city,
their opponents to defend it.
A clash between such large forces laid waste the land,
making them search far and wide for their provisions:
believe it or not, you could travel three days in any direction
and not find enough food.
The people of least standing suffered badly,
but so did those of great estate,
because they couldn't get anything by right or by might,
and found little available for sale.
Hypomedon is very upset
when he sees his army in such a needy state;
he can't keep himself from crying.
So he orders the Bulgars to come to him,
and, in conference with them,
promises them a great reward from his own wealth—
a reward to include
seven mules laden with silver and gold—
if they will lead him to bountiful lands
where food is not too costly;
after all, they know this land well,
since they are natives here.

But if they won't do this, he swears an oath
that they will be signing their own death warrant.
His listeners fear for their lives:
"Quite far from here," they say, "near Russia,
on the shores of the Danube,
there is such a land of plenty;
but a great mountain blocks us from it.
Beyond the mountain a great plain stretches out:
the earth there is well tilled,
cultivated, and leveled;
there's strong Toul wine
and good marsh wheat;
the wheat is tall and neatly planted,
the vineyards large;
the orchards are such that all of us
could live on the fruit we'd find there.
There are extensive fields there
and huge herds of pigs,
pigs and also ewes, and great stags in the woods,
does and bucks, kids and boars;
there's a profusion of animals in the meadows.
They have no fear of being hunted,
because reaching their haunts is so difficult,
since there's only one entrance;
if you can force your way in through that,
you'll have everything you need for three or four months."
Hypomedon cheers up at this news,
and, laughing with happiness, says to the Bulgars,
"If you are telling me the truth about this,
I'll be giving you a great deal of money."
"My lord," they reply, "we're telling the truth;
but you should be mindful of one thing:
this is a very strongly guarded land,
rendered even more difficult by treacherous trails;
getting there will be very dangerous,
and we're even more worried about getting into it.
The roads are bad and so narrow
that you can't travel quickly on them;

7906 **"Quite far from here," they say, "near Russia** *"Bien loign, font il, prés de Rossie*: The episode, beginning here, of a search for provisions for the starving Greek army is not in the *Thebaid;* Mora-Lebrun (507) suggests the First Crusade may have provided stories that inspired this adventure.

and then the lord of the place is proud and a battler,
who has a lot of knights."
Hypomedon isn't worried about such things:
"Get yourselves armed right away," he says;
"I'm putting you at the head of my troops,
so that you can lead us there."
The Bulgars return to their camp,
where they mount their warhorses.
Hypomedon doesn't procrastinate,
but quickly gets ready,
and summons his cohort,
ordering them to saddle up
while his battle horns resound throughout the army.
He takes with him quite a large force:
he leads a thousand well-armed knights,
and he won't be back that week, for sure.
If you could have seen them press on through the host!
Most of them left their food behind,
pushing across the camp
to saddle quickly their mules and camels.
A great crowd hastened away from the army,
in order to go seek food.
Hypomedon begs the king
To take very good care of the host:
he must keep a close eye on those who remain with him,
so that they don't wander away anywhere.
Then he gets underway with the Bulgars,
sending them ahead of the rest of his men.
It's a hard slog riding through the wastelands;
whoever has bread considers it precious:
they won't find food on their way,
except for what they've brought with them.
They ride for five days, suffering as they go;
you couldn't find anyone playing or laughing
because most of them were fainting from hunger,
so they blamed and cursed their guides.
They'll have paid a terrible price for their provisions
before they actually find them.
The Bulgars greatly encouraged them,
urging them to hold out for another day;
by tomorrow they'll have reached their goal,
and found the rations they need so badly—
in the morning they'll find the promised land.

All along the road there's great rejoicing:
no need to sound the retreat now,
with help so close at hand.
The Bulgars were terrified of the army,
starving because of its long march;
if they fail in finding provisions for it,
they will doubtless lose their heads.
So they secretly
called Hypomedon to a conference:
"My lord," they said, "we need to speak to you
about this business of where we're going,
so we're going to tell you the truth about it:
if the inhabitants of this place find out what we're after—
if they hear a single word about this—
we don't want to lie to you:
they will assemble at its entrance
and deny you access
by either the mountain or the valley route,
so that you'll never set foot there.
Ride all night," they advise;
"if you get no sleep, it doesn't matter;
by dawn, before matins,
come snow or come frost,
we'll get over the mountain
and enter the land in secret."
So, to make a long story short,
as they said, so they did.
That night, they rode by moonlight;
in the morning it rained, and the day was foggy:
they passed through the entry point secretly
and spread out across the land.
Then you would have seen the countryside ravaged,
the inhabitants killed or put to flight;
whatever the army saw it wanted to grab,
but the natives wanted to make them pay dearly for it.

The King of Thebes knew what was happening
because he had his spies in the army:
at the very moment when the search party moved out,
those spies sped off to the king,
with a full report for him
about the lack of supplies hobbling the besiegers.
"My lord," they explain, "they're off

on a long journey to find food."
He asks where they've gone, and they tell him;
the king is dubious but they promise him they're right.
Now the count of that land was there with the king
with five hundred of his knights;
the king summons him at once
and gives him this news.
He was the Count of Valfaconde,
who was known as Faramonde;
"Throw me into an oven," he cried,
"if I'm not leading the parade when I return:
they can lay waste to my land,
but they can't move so fast
that I won't catch up to them—I believe that!
They won't all get back to their army,
because they'll be weighed down with their loads,
and we'll be ready to hit them hard;
in one of the passes that I'll select
I'm confident that I'll destroy them."
He asks which route they are taking
and who's in command, what troops they have.
The spies tell him, "Through Landeflorie;
their commander is called Hypomedon,
and they certainly have a good thousand knights,
along with a great horde of flunkeys."
Faramonde said to the king,
"I'll bring him to you in chains, trust me!
Just give me three thousand knights,
and I'll start out from here at once;
the army out there won't know a thing;
they won't get wind of our departure.
By the bridge near the valley
I'll head out into the meadow,
so that the swift running river
will provide a barrier between us and the besiegers.
After three days' march upstream
I'll be able to cross back without a bridge."
The king concludes this meeting
and has his troops prepare themselves.
Later that night they leave by the bridge,
three thousand strong, ready for battle,
all of them in prime condition,
and along the river they rode.

Faramonde guided them,
since he knew the passes and the guard posts
and on the third day, at the ford of Alan,
they crossed the water without needing to be ferried;
once across the river, still near the bank,
they set up camp in a lovely meadow.
Meanwhile, along this same route,
Hypomedon is returning from his mission:
his scouts ride five leagues ahead of him,
with no pack animals or burdens,
while he follows behind with the bulk of the party,
all laden with food supplies.
The scouts, from their location in the forest,
saw their opponents in the prairie below;
they reined in, estimated how many there were,
and then rode back to their comrades.
They told Hypomedon that, without fail,
he'd have a battle on his hands the next day;
they told him this in secret,
quietly and without alarm.
"We know one thing for sure," he replies,
"there are more of them than of us;
they can defend themselves better than we can;
but we don't want to make too big a deal of that."
Hypomedon sends for his barons,
and leads them out beyond the camp;
having taken them aside, he speaks with them,
but not in a cowardly fashion:
"I don't know," he says, "who these small fry are
that our scouts have just noticed;
they must be peasants who live on this mountain,
and who've come down into the plain
in order to follow us,
hoping to steal some horses from us.
Don't be too trusting, but don't overreact, either!
Early tomorrow we'll get under way,
properly armed,
and completely prepared to fight;
let's be ready to strike hard—
to win decisively, or to die."
One Bulgar had come to this council meeting,
a man wise and courtly, old and grey-haired;
"If you'd take my advice," he said,

you'd come to a very different decision;
if you're willing, I can take you
to safety by another route.
We can rise tonight, by moonlight,
and take the road to Valbrune;
the mountains are high, the valleys deep,
and there we wouldn't be afraid to take on the whole world."
But the barons said they wouldn't do that,
wouldn't make the terrible mistake
of changing their route
and fleeing because they were afraid to fight.
Whatever God had in store for them, they said,
they'd be ready tomorrow to face it on the battle field.
The council broke up; they went back down
and made known throughout the camp
what was now to them a certainty:
they will have a fight on their hands tomorrow.
The news of battle raced through the army,
and everyone was pleased about it.
They prepared themselves for combat,
and the lookouts kept even closer watch,
staying on guard against the enemy
in order to head off a surprise attack at night.
Hypomedon stayed in his tent,
[turning over in his mind ways to trick his opponents;]
in this way he stayed awake all night,
not getting even a bit of sleep;
he couldn't sleep that night
because he also knew, from his scouts,
that the other side had larger forces:
more, and also less fatigued, troops.
At first light, when dawn broke,
Hypomedon got out of bed;
he has the heralds instruct the army
to prepare itself, and quickly.
Everyone was fully equipped by early morning,
And ready to get under way.
But before they started out
Hypomedon organized them,
assembling all the squires

8136 This line, missing from MS S, is supplied by Mora-Lebrun from Constans's edition.

and choosing from among them a thousand archers;
these he placed to his left,
so that they could fire on the enemy's right flank.
He equipped them with good, fast horses
so that they could shoot from in front when the battle began;
meanwhile, he had the rest of the squires gather branches
to drag along beside the haunches of their steeds.
He had these trail far behind,
where they threw up great clouds of dust
because there were so many of them
spread out on the plain;
and side by side they went dragging their branches
and churning up that dust,
so that it drifted up to the sky,
giving the impression that a great army was on the move.
The knights were now armed and ready;
they rode well ahead, all together:
they were in good battle order,
and to the side were the archers.
They were an elegant and fierce company—
they certainly looked like a fighting force!
And I oughtn't be silent about those opposing them:
their army was much the greater;
and thus, more numerous as they were,
they went in good order across the fields—
everyone at battle stations—
wanting to make their opponents pay dearly for their provisions,
which they were prepared to sell them at a very high price:
indeed, they planned to take all these foragers captive.
In full force they came on through the countryside
to confront their enemies.
The two armies came so close to each other
that the advance guards
started feinting and maneuvering,
each one trying to outsmart the other.
This happened between the hours of tierce and prime,
just when the sun begins to melt the hoar frost;

8157–58 **meanwhile, he had . . . the haunches of their steeds** *et as autres. . . joste lor hanches*: This ruse has an ancestry that extends well back into classical antiquity as well as to the Crusades.

8187 **between the hours of tierce and prime** *entre tierce et prime*: between 6 and 9 a.m.

the day is clear, the plain is shining
and the new grass gleams bright green.
Now the two companies attack each other,
exchanging great blows;
but Hypomedon's archers
inflict great damage on the other side:
as soon as their opponents rush to join battle,
the thousand bowmen start their charge,
And, fully exposed, they shoot in unison,
wounding knights and their horses.
Hypomedon had few troops,
but though he fought hard,
he couldn't hold out much longer,
and was close to having to flee the field,
when his enemies saw the great cloud of dust
being sent up by the young men in the rear.
That cloud was so huge
that they believed the whole Greek army had suddenly arrived,
which put such a fright into them
that they ran away in complete confusion,
heading back toward their own country;
the plain was long and wide,
so they have a fine road ahead, with nothing to hinder them:
no ditches, no tree stumps, not even a curve.
One side chases while the other flees,
horses' hooves drumming loudly across the plain;
those in retreat are only concerned with getting away—
they don't forget to dig in their spurs,
while their pursuers come after them, striking as they go,
trying as hard as they can to knock them off their horses.
Whoever couldn't keep to the road,
or get to a place to ford the river,
had no choice but one of these two fates:
either he drowned or was taken prisoner.
Whoever fell couldn't get up again,
with so many enemies there to grab him.
Two out of three ended up either captured,
or drowned, or run through by a sword.
Hypomedon didn't tarry,
but gathered up his supplies and hurried back to the besieging army,
which was suffering terribly from famine.
There was so little flour left
that it took gold to buy bread:

a crust cost a *marabotin*.
They lived a painful life there;
some had lost all color:
the poorest, tortured by hunger pangs,
were sickly, pallid, and bent over;
all of which really troubled the king.
Hypomedon did the right thing:
he sent messengers ahead
to bring the king his good news.
The messengers reached the army:
to the king and all his barons,
and also to the lesser ranks
they told the whole story, exactly as it had happened.
Now there were two causes for rejoicing:
one the food, the other the battle.
The king and all his Greek barons
now set out to meet the returning troops;
he gallops with his great company
through the fields near the river bank.
Great was the celebration when the two groups met,
and joyfully they all rode back to the army's camp;
what a sight to see the army well supplied again,
with plenty of food for everyone!
The next day they assembled all the prisoners:
seven hundred of them in chains.
It seemed a great tribute to their captors' power and valiance
when they were paraded through the host, their chains clanging.
Among the prisoners, there was a young man
newly dubbed a knight,
whose captivity deeply upset his father

8232 **a *marabotin un marabotin***: an Arabic gold piece.

8259 **Among the prisoners... a young man** *En la prise . . . un jovencel*: Here begins the episode of Dares the Red[head] (Daires li Rous). It does not appear in the *Thebaid* but is present in all extant manuscripts of the *Roman de Thèbes*, albeit in very different lengths, with that of MS S being one of the longest. It offers a cleric's view of the complex issues involved in the demands and limits of loyalty to one's superior—issues considered central to the value system of the warrior aristocracy, but which offered wide latitude for legal maneuvering designed to expand the possibility of independent, self-interested action while limiting the chances of being punished for it. The episode in S features many displays of quite flamboyant casuistry. See further the Introduction, pp.8–9, 22–23, 30.

and caused his mother to cry all the time;
they both loved him very much
for he was their only son.
Polynices knew him well
and honored him, as he ought:
honored him, and valued him highly,
so that he had the lad sleep in the royal tent,
and eat and drink with him as well,
and went out of his way to flatter him.
He wanted very much to form an attachment with this young man,
strongly believing that it would be to his advantage.
One day he summoned the prisoner
and privately got down to business with him:
"My friend," he said, "until now
I have been very good to you:
I've made sure that you live well,
and allowed you to move about all day
freely, and just as you please;
you weren't kept the least bit under guard.
During the day, you go about on just your word of honor,
and come back at night to me;
I always have a good bed ready for you
and I let you do whatever you please.
I've never demanded any ransom money from you,
so you ought to be very grateful to me.
If you were to trust me about just one thing,
our friendship would be certain and true."
"My lord," he replied, "you can be sure of this:
there's nothing in the world
that I wouldn't do for you;
have no doubt about that."
Polynices gives him a big smile,
and puts an arm around him:
"If," he says, "I can conquer the land that's mine by right,
I'll give you twice the territory
that your ancestors ever held:
but you must deliver to me the tower that you control."
"Release me, then, but with my guarantee to return,
since I don't have a messenger loyal enough
that I would dare trust to do this."
So he offers a sign of his promise and takes his leave;
leaves his gage and goes on his way,
back to his father in the besieged city.

All of his family rejoices at his return;
as fast as they can they rush out to meet him.
His mother runs to greet her son,
and can't keep from crying;
she weeps over him tenderly,
repeatedly covering him with kisses.
"Dear son," she says, "tell me this:
were you released under obligation, or are you really free?"
He answers, "my release is conditional;
I've given my word as my bond,
and I've promised to return.
I can only be here for a single day."
When she hears that he will have to return,
and can't stay with her any longer than that,
"then this joy of mine is all too brief," she cries,
and falls in a faint, from which her son must pick her up.
He spent that evening with his father;
he had great hopes of regaining his freedom,
since his father promises him emphatically—
declaring it and swearing it—
that he will do everything he can
to get him out of his imprisonment.
The next day, after they had eaten breakfast,
he asks his father to be allowed to leave,
explaining that he now had to go back
to that prison that's so terrible.
He was a sly one: he cries and sighs,
and tells his parents that he wants to die;
he'd rather die, he assures them,
than continuing to live like this.
His mother cries, weeps and wails,
and his father takes him off to one side:
"I have very great wealth," he says,
"of fine cloth, and of gold and silver;
take it now, and go give it to them,
in return for letting you come back here free.
Get back there and trick them,
by offering a deal worth ten thousand marks;
if they'll let you go free for that amount,
I'll consider it no more than a drop in the bucket."
But his son answers, "you're wasting your breath;
I'll never be freed for ransom.
Polynices has made it very clear

that I've got myself into a terrible fix
if you don't turn over your tower to him;
but if you do, I'll be set free right away."
The father replies, "How could that be?
I've sworn to our king,
with my right hand on holy relics,
that I will faithfully protect him;
I won't commit treason
for you, or for your imprisonment.
My dear son," he avers, "God forbid
that I should be a traitor on your account."
The mother has come over to join the conversation,
and has heard everything;
she realizes that her husband can liberate their son
if he will surrender the tower.
"My lord," she pleads, "you should never say
that you'll let your son be killed because of a tower.
All the wealth that we've amassed—
what will it be worth to us, if we lose him?
I couldn't care less about the tower or the wealth
if we lose our heir."
"My concern isn't the tower," he replies,
"so much as the promise I made to my lord;
I would do a shameful deed,
and behave terribly,
with complete disloyalty,
if I were to betray this city."
"I don't give a damn about that," she declares,
"because you're all already perjured vis-à-vis the other side—
all you barons and vavassours
who swore to take turns, year by year, ruling the realm.
When you subsequently swore to uphold this king
then you broke faith to his brother, out there.
The way I look at it, it makes more sense
to honor and remain loyal
to a just oath
than to one taken under unjust circumstances."
"I have no desire," the father says, "to take up arms
to defend myself against the charge of perjury;
we had no choice but to betray one of them,
since we swore allegiance to both
When you have to choose between two evils,
it's best to opt for the less shameful one:

of all the crimes that one could commit,
treason is considered the most heinous.
I'd rather break faith along with everyone else
than betray my lord alone.
If I have to sin together with everyone,
no one can blame me so much for that;
greater men than I am have done the same,
so I don't think it will ever be held against me."

He was a canny man, well along in years,
who had served at many courts;
his expression was fierce, his hair reddish brown
and his tongue quick and clever.
"Go back to your jail," he told his son;
"I'll go speak to the king.
If I can find a way around this,
so that I don't actually commit treason,
I'll let you know by a servant
and hand over this fortress to you;
but if I can't do this honorably,
then there's no point in our talking about such a deal."
The mother cries and laments,
but her lord works hard to reassure her:
"I'll tell you what your son is going to do:
he'll go back into custody,
and I will talk to the king
tomorrow morning, after he's dined.
I'll tell him that it's high time
for him to reach an agreement with his brother,
because it's a bad thing, an ignoble thing,
that they are so at odds with each other.
The king is very upset,
and hates nothing as much
[as he does his brother;]
so he won't listen to advice from anyone about this.
There's no one who's of such high rank,
or comes from so noble a lineage,

8401 **his hair reddish brown** *le chief ros*: Red hair was sometimes considered a mark of untrustworthiness in popular understandings of physiognomy in relation to character. See Mora-Lebrun (535), note to v. 8403.

8423 **[as he does his brother]** This verse fills conjecturally a lacuna in MS S at this point.

who might advise him to make a treaty
that the king wouldn't curse him out;
and if anyone told him the truth about his conduct,
I believe he'd immediately strike him down.
Given that he's behaving so badly,
and so obviously perjuring himself,
I know full well that he'll pay no attention to my plea.
Instead he'll say stupid, nasty things to me;
right away, out will come words
that later he'll be sorry he ever said;
and if I can push him so far
that I'm in the right, any way you look at it,
and can make a case for my position,
then I won't let you, my son, die for a tower:
Polynices will have my tower.
and after that my entire domain.
But now I have to figure out,
if I can just arrange an angry, total break with my lord,
how the besieging army can find that out,
and by what means they can take control of the tower.
For the king has stationed his own men there,
only twenty less than one hundred;
and besides them I have sixty of my own troops
and a good fifty excellent archers, as well.
If I were to order the king's troops to stand down,
they would certainly undertake to defend themselves there,
and if they cried, "Help!"
they'd get plenty of it right away,
since everyone who is nearby
would come running to them at once;
the tower guard up above will fight in self defense,
and the rest of the army will attack us as well:
and between those above and those below
I won't be able to hold out against all of them.
But—if I could bring it about
somehow; think up some trick
that would get the besieging army inside the tower
before its defenders realized it,
and if there were enough of the invaders
that they could occupy and hold it
without having to fear the army inside the city,
that would be the best outcome;
and I think I can do that,

in exactly the way I just said.
Now I'll tell my son how they'll do it
and by what out-of-the-way route they should approach:
there's a flatboat in port over there,
between this park of mine and the garden,
that I will have prepared,
and in which I'll have them set out.
They'll enter it smartly,
and without even a murmur;
they should be equipped with good arms,
carrying swords and halberds,
wearing their coats of mail,
their swords hung around their necks,
so that if it comes to a battle
they'll have what they need to defend themselves.
They'll be able to arrive below the park;
I will have had it opened for them.
From the park they'll then come through the orchard,
between the pine and the laurel over there,
up to here, at this ditch;
they'll be packed in tight here.
As soon as I can spot them,
I'll get them in right away:
I'll have some of my men up above,
who can hoist them up with ropes;
I'll make sure my men stay awake all night,
while the king's men are sound asleep.
Before the inside forces know what's happened,
more than seven hundred of the raiders will be inside, too.
But now it's time to go;
we can't wait here any longer.
My dear son," he says, "off you go;
here's what you're going to say to your lord:
I will never know peace or contentment
until I see you again,
nor will your poor, sad mother,
who is suffering terrible anxiety over you.
Repeat all this to him just as I have told you.
You tell him too, my lady, lest he forget."
"I won't forget," her son said, "I know it well;
I won't leave out a single thing."
"Take this fine gold cup with you,
on the bottom of which a pine tree is painted;

there's marvelous workmanship in this cup
and in the lid that covers it;
the cup is worth more than seven marks,
and the lid that tops it is worth five.
Take my hare-hunting dog and my falcon,
and offer them to Polynices as a gift;
give it all to your lord,
who has treated you so well while in his hands.
In three days I'll let you know
what luck I've had in dealing with the king."
The youth took the rich golden cup
and set off with the mountain falcon;
he had his squire
lead the hunting dog on a leash:
he seeks out Polynices in the middle of the army,
and puts on a sad and downcast face.
Polynices saw his prisoner
who is bringing him the falcon;
then he looks at the hunting dog:
"Now here's a fine entourage!" he says.
"Two months from now, I promise you,
you'll no longer be in chains."
"My lord," the prisoner replies, "many thanks.
We have something special here,
to tell the truth, it's worth one hundred marks of silver."
Then he gives him the cup:
the other takes it, admiring the workmanship;
it would be impossible to describe its excellence.
As the book by Statius puts it,
the knob atop its cover was a topaz;
no one had ever seen its equal
in its setting or its brilliance.
Polynices goes on and on about it:
he has nothing that he would rather have,
more as a present for the king
than to keep for himself.
Now he takes the young man aside,
and asks him what he has done;
so lacking in cunning was the youngster
that he didn't dare lie to his captor:

8541 **As the book by Statius puts it** *si come dit le liver d'Estaisce*: On this reference, see the Introduction, p. 5–6.

"My lord," he says, "I'll tell you;
I won't lie to you about anything.
Without any fear I went right to my father,
and spoke to him about my having been given leave to go,
just as you advised me to,
and adding on some details of my own.
He answered, may it never please God
that he should commit treason because of me,
but he would go reason with the king.
If he could find a way
to turn over his tower to you
while preserving himself from the charge of treason,
he'll deliver it into your possession,
as long as he feels he's even a little bit in the right doing so.
But if he can't do it with honor,
then there's no point our talking about surrendering it."
Polynices asks, "How will we know?
When will we get word about it?"
"By the day after tomorrow, dear lord," he replies,
"I'll have accurate information for you."

The next day, before the hour of nones,
the king summons the young captive's father;
so that very day he goes to the royal court:
before he comes back, he'll make the king
sad and angry, for he will set in motion
something that will cause an angry rift to grow between them.
The king is presiding over his council in his orchard,
and three messengers are with him:
the Pinsonards have dispatched to the king
three courtly barons who share the king's religious faith,
and these three envoys speak
in their own language, with the aid of an interpreter:
they offer the king and his forces
the aid of the Pinsonards;
they will bring him twenty thousand men,
so that he'll never be defeated by the Greeks,

8581 **the Pinsonards have dispatched to the king** *Pinçonard ont tramis le rei*: The Pinsonards, or Petchenègues, were a Turkic people who invaded areas of the Byzantine empire and were eventually destroyed by the Byzantines at the end of the eleventh to the beginning of the twelfth centuries. See Mora-Lebrun 547, note to v. 8583.

on condition that he restore to them the border region
from the Danube to Usarche
that his father wrongfully took from them,
and that, after his father's death, he still holds.
The king has heard out their offer,
and the prospect of this assistance greatly pleases him;
he has the embassy brought back to their quarters
and takes up this matter with his council.
"My lords," he says, "what are your views on this?"
The first to speak out was Dares the Red,
the prisoner's father,
who needed to communicate with the king;
he was a rich and powerful retainer.
"They're asking too much from us," he said.
"That border zone should be very important to you,
for the land produces abundantly
and has many fine knights as well;
its people are formidable warriors.
It's also the gateway to our land
whenever the Pinsonards make war on us;
it's always by using that entry point
that they've been able to lay waste to our countryside.
Of all the lands you hold,
that's the one you, more than anyone else, should love.
Your father had to endure a lot
before he could take control of it;
he worked hard to possess it,
and to be recognized as its lord.
Warrior that he was, he suffered
Many a cold, indeed freezing, morning
During which he received plenty of blows
while giving many more with his sword.
If you give it up so easily now
there'll be no making up for it later,
and I can promise you that you'll never
get back anything worth it in exchange.
The Pinsonards certainly know how to lay waste a land,
and they're always willing to go off seeking treasure,
but they don't excel in a pitched battle,
where they never mount more than one assault.

8590 **Usarche** *Usarche*: An uncertain place; various possible locations have been proposed.

Having them with you against the Greeks
[won't give you an army that's any better;
once you've added twenty thousand of them
to those already in this city,
you still won't have a force]
that can do battle with the Greeks out there in the open.
Our city is strong enough for us to hold it;
we don't need other men to come help us.
We have plenty of people to defend it,
so it's not a good idea to give up our frontier.
But let's get this whole dispute over with
by making an agreement with your brother:
you're making him miserable and he you,
and because of this you make bad, foolish decisions.
Thanks to your war, there isn't a neighboring land
that hasn't been able to grab some of your lands,
and as a result you're losing a lot of the realm
that your ancestors were able to control;
each neighbor has peeled off his bit,
without any concern for the consequences to us—
whichever of you two ends up with the land—
as long as they will retain what they have taken.
If you lose enough hair, you're left bald:
you have a very large realm,
and once upon a time people were accustomed to fear you,
so now you have to get back to that.
Settle this quarrel between you now;
it's time to change your tune!
Make an end of this with your brother—
then everyone else will bow to your wishes."
The king didn't like this advice;
he turned red with rage, and exclaimed,
"I know very well why you're saying this:
it's so you can set free that son of yours!
You can go tell that story to a deaf jackass!
You're wasting your breath
with such worthless arguments.
You'd be great at using someone else's hand
to pull a snake out from under a rock—
do you think I don't know you?

8630–33 **[won't give you. . . won't have a force]** *n'avreiz. . . pas tale comaigne*: An obvious lacuna in MS S; lines supplied from MS C.

You could certainly pull the wool over a lot of peoples' eyes,
but I'm not so stupid
that I'd give up part of my inheritance
for the son of some stinking vavassour;
you'll have to find some other way to get him back
than through me or my land!
You'll need to use some of that money
of which you have more than enough:
if you want to have your son back,
try buying him back from your own resources."
To whom Dares responded, "I'm speaking for myself,
and also for the others I see here,
and for our children and relatives,
more than seven hundred of whom have been captured.
They've been captured, yes, and killed on your account:
it's for their sake that you ought to make peace—
for them, yes, but even more for you,
and for your brother, and for us.
Because you swore to him, without deceit,
that he would possess the realm during the year allotted to him,
and we can't deny to him
that we also subscribed to this oath:
so now to release us from perjury
you really ought to grant him his rights."
The king's temper flared;
in his anger he almost lost control of it:
and hearing the accusation of perjury,
his rage exploded:
he went to strike Dares in the head
with the short rod of office he was holding.
But his mother uttered words of reproof,
so the king restrained himself and didn't touch him.
"Get out of here," he cried, "get out of my sight!
What an example of good faith you are!
Out of fear for your money—
and I know you've got two hogsheads of it—
you've dreamed up this scheme.
You have my absolute permission to leave,
and that means I give you leave to do your worst:

8669 **pull the wool over a lot of peoples' eyes** *Bien savreiez maunger oue luis*: Literally, you like to eat with myopic people (so that you can steal their food without their noticing).

a curse on anyone who tries to hold you back from it!
You redheaded, worthless bastard,
do your worst—it's fine by me."
The other heard these words,
and you can be sure he won't forget them;
he intends to take advantage of them
and quickly avenge his shame.
The king gets angry and argues forcefully,
but he knows very well he's in the wrong;
since he can't defend his position by law,
he chooses to do so by fighting.
Dares stands his ground in the middle of the court
little worried by the king's threats;
"There isn't a baron in your court
who, if he knows how to think things through,
wouldn't perjure himself with respect to your brother
all the while knowing that your brother has justice on his side."
"We've perjured ourselves, is that what you're saying?
That's not what I know; you're spreading lies.
You lousy, redheaded good for nothing,
you're just full of hatred:
I never met a redhead
who wasn't evil and bursting with envy."
Now Othon intervenes, complaining
that the king shouldn't say such foolish things to his baron.
The king answers, "What do you want from me?
Why is it a surprise if I'm furious?
This underling has wrongly picked a quarrel with me:
who would have such great patience
that he wouldn't be upset
by hearing someone accuse him of perjury?
He says that we are all perjurers,
and as I see it, he's not telling the truth:
with your approval I offered my brother
part of my father's territories;
when I offered him that
he refused it—wouldn't consider accepting it;
and instead, with haughty arrogance,
he's invaded our country,
leading an army of foreigners,
in order to defeat and conquer us.
If you don't take offense on my behalf,
I whom you've raised from my childhood,

at least each of you should worry about himself,
since, by the faith that I owe you,
if he can conquer us by force,
there'll be only one outcome:
you can have absolutely no doubt
that they'll kill us first,
then they'll have their way with our women,
and the children will face only slavery."
"My lord," says Dares, "on my word,
you're wrong to be angry with me;
what I'm saying to you isn't said with evil intent,
but instead to offer you loyal advice.
We want to see you make amends
for the fault of which you've been accused:
there isn't a knight in this entire company
who'd argue against me in this.
You made an agreement with your younger brother
about the disposition of this realm;
if he now wishes to deny the deal,
and violate the old agreement,
we should all side with you
and he should truly get the worst of it.
But if you propose a new agreement,
voiding the one previously ratified,
and he doesn't like it, he won't accept it,
and he'll stick with the old arrangement instead;
and you know in your heart
that we're not released from our obligation to honor that pact.
You've perjured yourself on the record,
as everyone knows very well;
so I'm upset for your sake,
for the loyalty that I owe you, and for all of us."
This speech irritated the king,
who snorted angrily and leapt to his feet;
he struck Dares on the head with his rod:
the blow left a great open wound.
The barons rushed to get between them:
they restrained the king by surrounding him,
and hustled Dares out of the court;
he and his followers fled quickly.
Dares goes back to his dwelling;
he thinks he now has good reason
to do harm to the king, if the latter will let him,

and if he can come up with something that will really crush him;
he really believed that if he could wreak vengeance on the king
he had every right to do so.
He sends a messenger to his son
explaining how things stand,
how he's left the king's service,
and doesn't owe him any more loyalty;
so now he's ready to hand over the tower
in order to liberate the son from prison.
The messenger travels to the besieging army
and is soon able to tell everything to Dares's son,
who commands him, "Now tell me how this change came about,
and in what atmosphere it all happened."
"My lord," says the messenger, "I'll tell you,
and I won't leave out a word.
Your father spoke to the king,
advising him in good faith
to come to terms with his brother,
with the king's mother listening carefully.
That's all there was; the king got angry,
and struck your father right in the head
with a rod of oak,
so that blood came spurting out.
And my lord wanted to hit him back for that,
which would have led him to be humbled right away:
if he had returned the blow even once,
I don't believe he would ever have escaped;
this was not a recipe for an even fight:
give one blow, get a hundred back.
He hadn't brought enough of his men with him
to mount a good pitched battle."
The young man kept all of this in mind
and recounted it all to Polynices:
that his father has cut his ties to the king
and owes him no further loyalty:
"Now he's ready to turn over the tower,
so that he can get me out of your prison.
My dear, sweet lord, when he left me today,
this is what my father told me:
he was going to tell the king to reach an accord with you
and abide by the oath
that he swore to you a long time ago—
a good seven years, in my opinion.

When he said that, the king hated him for it,
and struck him in the head
giving him so many blows with a rod
that the blood ran down to his heels.
My father has a really great fortune,
and that bothers the King of Thebes a lot;
so just now he showed him
that he doesn't give a damn about his affection.
If things go badly for him now, it's only fitting—
let him be disgraced!"
"My dear, sweet friend, how will we accomplish this,
and how can we go about getting that tower?"
"My father has thought all that through,
told me his whole plan, and charged me
to tell you how to do it
and exactly how you can take control of the tower.
Near his manor house he has a woodland park
which is chock-a-block with deer,
stags and does and bucks,
as well as with boar and other savage beasts.
Your men will go through that park,
getting started just at the moment when people get drowsy,
guided by the messenger who will come,
having been sent to us by my father;
so they'll encounter no obstacle
until they get to the tower,
except for a ditch around it,
filled with water from the castle moat.
Rising above the ditch is the surrounding wall
which is very solid;
the ditch is marvelously wide
and its water of great depth:
it's sixty meters deep
and sixty wide all around,
and from this body of water a channel runs off,
the water drawn into it by a clever device.
Across this channel there's a rotating bridge,
made and placed there.
The troops will go across the bridge,
and they'll turn it around after them,
so that if anyone wanted to enter across it later
he would first have to call for it to be straightened;
by the bridge: that's where they must enter,

for the chain blocking the way in will be undone,
and once inside they'll proceed directly ahead,
without any difficulty.
They will halt at the foot of the tower
without saying a word,
so that the soldiers of the king aren't awakened,
and start wondering what that noise was;
because they sleep on the stairs,
with the door closed on them:
no one can enter through that gate
without having to speak with them first.
My father will be waiting for them:
when the moment comes that he hears them,
he will at once pull back the lock;
he knows exactly how it works.
He won't be able to let your troops in by the front door,
instead he'll hoist them up on ropes,
to prevent those inside from knowing what's happening
until our men chase them down and kill them."
Polynices, having given this news his full attention,
chose part of his men
and sent them down to the riverbank,
where they found the messenger
who led them to their goal
in the best, most direct way possible;
he took them to where Dares said he should,
without, I believe, any missteps.
From his station high above, Dares recognized them
from the moment he first saw them,
so he threw down ropes and cords
that he had ordered to be linked together with considerable effort;
with the help of half his men,
he quickly pulled them up to himself;
when the first half had done enough pulling,
the others, who had done nothing so far, took over.
Inside, the royal troops snoozed on,
and in the other towers the watch took their turn,
completely unaware of the trick
that Dares was playing on them;
before the troops inside the tower knew what was happening,
he had hoisted up more than seven hundred fighting men.
But before daybreak they were seen
from other, nearby towers;

the watch in those towers sounded the alarm:
"Noble knights," they cried, "what are you doing over there?
Get up! Get up and get your armor on:
it's certain we've been betrayed;
Dares the Red—he's the traitor!
The Greeks are already in here with us."
The tower guard are fully armed—
the noise they make reverberates throughout the city—
and they head up into the tower to mount a defense,
only to see the invaders coming down to meet them:
peering up through the beams
they make out at least two hundred Greeks there.
They race back down the stairs,
and quickly unlock the tower door;
there was great panic,
with everyone frantic that the doorway was so narrow.
So intense was the crush at the exit
that many a bone was broken there.
They escaped, but painfully:
more than a dozen bodies were shattered.
Their enemies ran after them to shut the door,
and slid the bar into place;
then, having evicted the royal troops,
they all went back up to the top of the tower,
which the king's men had now abandoned,
so that not a single one of them remained there.
Instead, they stopped at the foot of the tower
And cried out as loudly as they could,
"Valiant knights, get up, get up!
Arm yourselves quickly!
Arm yourselves and come running:
the tower has been occupied by the invaders."
In fact there were seven hundred soldiers waiting on the bridge
Who wanted to get inside,
but they couldn't do so all at once
because each troop turned the bridge when they came to it;
having turned it, they got on it,
and after crossing, turned it again.
The noise spread throughout the city;
more than twenty thousand knights armed themselves,
and they all rushed to the tower,
attacking it very fiercely.
Those in the tower defended themselves vigorously,

while from below their assailants called on them to surrender:
the forces from within the city have now grown greatly,
with twenty thousand already in a front line;
they swarm around the tower,
placing it under heavy assault.
The attackers intend to take their enemies by force,
but it's a foolishly wasted effort,
since the defenders have everything they need to resist;
the others will never defeat them,
and in the process will suffer great losses:
those above kill many of them
as they raise the hue and cry from where they stand below—
death rains down on all too many of them.
Then the dawn came,
revealing that the tower was well stocked with troops,
who launched spears and arrows down on the besiegers' positions,
demonstrating the strength of their arms.
From many down below the shout went up to climb the walls
To keep the army outside from attacking them;
if the Greeks could take the ramparts
it would become very difficult to defend the city:
the king will be in terrible straits
thanks to what Dares the Red has accomplished!
So the king has some serious thinking to do:
he sees his enemies right on top of him,
and he's also very afraid of his own men,
because he knows that his people don't love him—
they're deep in mourning for their country,
which has been ruined by this war,
and he's worried that Dares may have their sympathy,
may even have undertaken this treachery with their help.
But, look! From the citizenry comes an engineer
who now tells the king that he will recapture the tower for him.
The king says to him, "How can you do that?
its foundation is sunk twenty feet into the ground;
it's useless for you to get involved with this,
for you'll never succeed in capturing it—
still, I'd be very grateful to you if you could retake it."
"Now go send soldiers to defend the walls,
because I'm telling you the honest truth
that I'll have that tower back in your possession before nightfall,
including everyone in it, either dead or captured:
I'm absolutely certain of it—there's no chance I'll fail."

Half the troops now go to the walls,
carrying lances and swords;
quickly they clamber up to the ramparts,
urged on by concern for the besieging army.
The besiegers were stirred to action
by all the commotion they heard from the city;
they hastened to mount up
and, spurring hard, they raced through the gardens:
a hundred thousand of them came on, all arranged by rank,
right up to the city walls.
Most of them pounded on the locked doors,
valiant (?) knights
who want to perform brave deeds
in order to win praise from their friends.
Meanwhile, those manning the battlements
lace up their hauberks all the way to the top, protecting neck and face,
and shower sharp spears down on the invaders,
piercing all their shields;
and forcing them back, away from the wall,
at a safe distance from such an assault on them.
Then the besiegers regrouped,
and this time in one wave they launched themselves at the enemy,
racing toward them in great haste;
those within put up a strong defense,
launching a well-timed fusillade at their foes below.
A hundred of the attackers died then, without benefit of confession.
The defenders shattered swords, crushed helmets,
splintered shields, snapped lances;
such was the barrage they unleashed
that they made the attackers retreat yet again, at least a little way.
They pulled back a bit,
however much against their will.
The besieged kept up their attack on the besiegers,
causing many a soul to vacate its body,
while those on the outside returned the favor,
killing more than seven hundred of the defenders;
they shot arrows and fired bolts

9020 **valiant (?) knights** *Cil chevalier dodueour*: the meaning of *dodueour* is unknown.

9034 **without benefit of confession** *desconfés*: One of several Christianizing touches in the poem; those who die without confessing their sins risk eternal damnation if the sins were serious.

thick and fast from all sides.
No matter how great this surrounding offensive,
all the hue and cry came to nothing:
they'll never capture the city by frontal assault—
it's not a tactic by which they'll accomplish anything.
Meanwhile, the King of Thebes stayed near the captured tower
with twenty-three of his barons;
with them were seven thousand warriors,
drawn from the best troops in the city,
who assailed the tower's occupiers;
that day they killed four of them,
but from above the occupiers killed fifty in return—
only ten less than sixty.
Those down below yelled to them, "Give up,
you're sure to be captured."
But instead they continued to defend themselves fiercely:
they were, after all, fighting for their lives.
They shout back that they'll never surrender;
they prefer to sell their lives at great price.
A curse on anyone who gives up
instead of selling his life dearly.
"Buying our lives will be a terrible bargain;
you'll have to pay the highest price of all:
we're not selling out so soon,
not before there are skulls cracked,
hauberks pierced and helmets split—
and, worst of all, a lot of corpses."
They continue to do great damage to the royal army,
which drives the king himself all but mad.
So the king summons the engineer,
who explains what needs to happen,
and the order is given to bring there whatever he needs,
since he's the one who knows what has to be done.
The engineer, out of devotion to the king,
tells him that he will capture that tower,
and so he did, well and truly,
and now you'll hear by what device he did it.
He started burrowing down underground,
looking for the foundations of the tower;
once they discovered them,
he hacked away at them with pickaxes until he breached them.
This was one smart engineer:
he hollowed out the foundations from underneath,

and then pushed into place wooden stanchions
to hold up the weight of the tower;
then using tow and quicksilver
he created Greek fire
and, having applied it to the stanchions,
quickly got out from under there.
Then he called up to the troops in the tower,
to give them the bad news:
if they didn't vacate quickly,
they'd all be dead—he wasn't lying.
The tow burned, the tower split apart,
its defenders rushed out and the king took them;
the tower broke into two halves,
its base having collapsed beneath it.

Dares is brought to the king,
a prisoner bound and isolated.
"Ah, you old traitor," said the king,
I'll have you burnt right this minute
and then have your ashes scattered to the winds,
because that's the end a traitor deserves!"
Dares said, "You can certainly do that,
since yours is now the greater power;
but there isn't a man in your household
who could accuse me of treason;
rather, I could make a much stronger case
that you had done me wrong.
I counseled you in good faith,
following the customs of the day as I understand them;
then you struck me with a rod,
so that blood ran down to my heels;
you thereby gave me leave, in all truth,
to do all in my power to harm you.
I arranged the best scheme that I could,
and thought I could bring it off, but I failed.
I tried as hard as possible to accomplish it;
it just distresses me that I didn't succeed."

The king answered, "I know all that.
Now you should know this:
I'll pay you back for this,
I swear to you, in such a way
that whoever loves you the most

will be left full of sorrow when this is over,
and you'll never thank me for it
once I've finished with you."
The full court had now assembled in all its strength;
Dares never once lowered his eyes from them,
but despite this show he was by no means sure he'd survive,
taking nothing for granted.
He certainly couldn't beg the king for mercy,
because he recognized his crime against him.
The king is livid with rage:
he wants Dares executed,
either burnt to a crisp or dispatched by the sword;
in fact, they were all furious at Dares,
and were ready to burn him at the stake.
Othon hears this, and it didn't please him;
pushing through the ranks of courtiers, he comes before the king:
"Sire," he said, "listen to me.
First, have him tried,
and judged in a proper, legal manner;
you'll be shamed and blamed
if you have him killed without proper deliberation.
First put him on trial,
And have him brought to justice legally."
The king replied, angrily,
"He's already judged himself;
judgment has already been passed
on a man who has so violated his trust.
no one could ever prevent me
from having him hanged or burnt at the stake."
Othon answers, "By my faith, sire,
I can assure you of one thing:
if Dares is burnt or hanged
and your unjust action should become known,
you'll come to repent it later;
I guarantee you won't be able to avoid that,
for Dares comes from a powerful kindred,
and is possessed of a great fief:
within this city he controls a main street,
and a hundred knights from his holdings
whom he can call on, should he need to,
and not one of whom would excuse himself from defending Dares.
Many of the barons of this realm
are his kin, as well;

there isn't anyone who's not aware
of being related somehow to him,
either through father or son,
through sister or brother.
They'll all be very upset
if you burn him without a trial;
They'll say that you have little love for them,
that you consider them of little worth
if you're willing to burn their innocent kinsman,
who's committed no treason against you.
Together they're offering you the chance for a trial
and by my faith, as it seems to me
you haven't the right to refuse them.
Set up a legal process
with these, your barons who are here,
who will render a judgment without lying;
and if among themselves these barons decide,
in accord with the laws and with reason,
that a sufficiently great crime has been committed
to allow you to impose a punishment,
then you can do what you like,
first to him and then to his supporters:
then there won't be one of us
who isn't on your side,
or who will ever dispute it,
because everyone will know that it was done correctly."
Then everyone chimes in to make the king understand:
"Indeed, sire," says Othon, "take my word for it,
it's best that you do it that way,
for you'll never lose anything by it."

"By my head, I know very well
that I won't lose anything by that.
Go ahead and judge—see if I care:
I know very well that it won't do *him* any good,
nor will I consider it as establishing
that I shouldn't have him roasted just the same."
Then Othon spoke in response to the king:
"If the barons can get to the bottom of this
if they come to the decision
that his was such a heinous crime,
whatever its precise nature,
that he can't make amends for it—

then you'll be able to punish him severely:
and you won't hear any complaints about it
from his cousins or other kin,
since you'll be carrying out a judgment fairly made;
but this will be a strange punishment of a crime
if Dares can't argue in his own defense."
The king takes Othon by the hand;
"What," he asks," is the law concerning treason?"
"Indeed," replies Othon, "I know it well,
and, if you wish, I'll repeat it to you.
Whoever accuses someone of treason
had better be sure it's an accurate charge;
and if the person accused
can't be proven guilty,
so that he has the chance, if he wishes, to deny the charge,
he can then challenge his accuser to a duel.
So no one should ever charge another
if he can't finally prove his case,
or call upon someone else
who will undertake to do it for him [in battle].
Then if the accused won't defend himself
it's right to burn or hang him.
And if I'm certain that I'm right to make the accusation,
and the crime is so obvious,
then I must mete out justice for it right away,
without the risk of anything bad happening to me in return.
And if, in spite of all, the accused doesn't admit guilt,
and you advise me to accept his denial,
don't blame me at all.
In fact, I'll tell you what I advise:
you should judge with your barons present and listening,
and you should do what they advise.
If they decide that justice requires
that Dares, having done you such a wrong,
should burn or be hanged for it,
then you can pass the sentence you want;
if it seems good to you, indeed you can do it,
and if it pleases you, you can in fact do nothing;
but you certainly won't be blamed
if you act on the basis of a legal judgment.
So help me God, just as I believe it to be
I'm advising you, in all good faith."
All the barons chime in:

"That's right, sire; believe Othon."
The king charges his barons
by name, one after the other:
"All right, then, go and do your duty to judge;
get on with it—don't keep me waiting."
The barons get up and go off to render their judgment,
most of them full of anger inside.
Dares was a man of highest rank,
and some of those who were to judge him were related to him;
his many friends at court
were worried that this wouldn't turn out well for him:
they were afraid the king would do him in
before he could get away from there.
Leaving the great hall, the barons adjourned upstairs,
and had the windows opened;
then they seated themselves on the stone floor
and discussed their decision.
Great confusion now erupted:
everyone else was talking at once, but Othon fell to listening.
He thought to himself for a while
about how he could save Dares,
and then he spoke up again, after a moment had passed:
"You should all know," he said, "one thing:
if you condemn Dares to death,
since my lord the king is filled with anger
it seems to me, as far as I can tell,
that you will see him killed at once.
There will be great grief for Dares the Red
if he's killed among us:
he's one of us,
by kindred and rank.
Let's ask for a delay until tomorrow
in making our judgment;
this will give the king time to calm down,
and his anger will cool.
Tomorrow we'll reconvene here
and we'll ask for mercy for Dares:
if we let this go until the morning,
we'll be able to seek a better outcome;
right now I don't see a chance for that,
as long as the royal fury is still red hot."
"By God, my lord Othon, that's a great idea!
Go right now and ask the king for this."

"I've spoken to the king about Dares a lot,
to the point where he's angry with me about it;
instead, you should go, please,
three or four of you;
he'll do it for you sooner than for me."
They all agreed with this advice,
so they sent three barons to the king:
the embassy came downstairs,
Creon leading Ither and Alon,
and they asked their lord
to give them a day's postponement.
The king was very resistant to this request
and decidedly angered by it:
"You're tiring yourselves out for no good reason;
from my perspective you're violating the law,
for I'll never concur in tolerating for one more day
the harm and the dishonor
that this traitor has caused me,
nor will I hear any argument about it.
You want me to grant him a postponement—
and then you'll beg me to pardon him!
Judge him for me according to the law,
for his crime will be as fresh in my mind
a year from now as it is at this minute.
I couldn't be bribed with a sack of gold
not to be avenged,
and I know very well what judgment
our ancestors would have delivered:
burn the traitor at the stake!
I will rightfully affirm that judgment:
and I will not be gainsaid in this court!"

Creon said to him, "Sire, you should do this;
don't allow yourself to be ruled by your anger.
Accept our counsel and you'll be doing the right thing.
Give us a delay until tomorrow—
take our advice; let us postpone!
Tomorrow you'll mete out your justice
the way you'll have been advised to do:
and a curse on anyone who wants to pardon him!"

The king swears by everything he knows
that there will never be any such delay.

Creon was fiercer than a lion:
he attempted to talk sense to the king.
Creon had a large retinue in the city,
he was a man rich in gold and silver;
he and the king were kinsmen,
for which reason he spoke with assurance:
"I really hate," he said, "hardheadedness
and the arrogance that springs from great power.
May God curse an obstinate lord,
for he'll never govern his realm well;
he'll be universally hated, by rich and poor alike,
for persistently opting to be unbending.
Sire," he says, "as I see it,
a young warrior who's lacking in wisdom
should trust the counsel of wise men—
then, sure enough, you'll find him on the right track.
But whoever lacks knowledge and abstains from seeking good advice,
well, it's not surprising if he loses out when it matters."
The king listens to Creon's speech,
gets up, moves toward him, and gives him a hug.
While embracing him,
he says, chuckling, "Leave me be;
because, for the life of me, it's not an option
that I refrain from committing this folly.
You want me to accord Dares a delay,
and then you'll ask me to pardon him:
you're giving me the advice of a child—
let me have my vengeance."
Lord Creon says to himself,
"I'll get the verdict I want—innocence—for Dares."

The three barons took their leave,
seeing that there was nothing they could do.
They leave the king and return upstairs,
full of misgivings about their comrade—
very worried about their comrade—
because they've not obtained any delay, or acquittal, for him.
Othon asks, "did you get an extension?"
"Not at all, to tell the truth; we only have until tonight."

9350 **May God curse an obstinate lord** *Deus maldie enrievre seignor*: Obstinacy and arrogance were distinguishing marks of a tyrant, as opposed to a just ruler, in medieval political theory influenced by Aristotelian thought.

"For God's sake," he replies, "calm down now;
it would really look bad for us to be in an uproar over this.
We should all let each other talk
politely and quietly,
so that those who may have nothing to say
can hear what the others have to offer."
So they all sat down to discuss the case,
and there's no one there who isn't worried;
they sat quietly for a while,
none among them ready to speak first.

Ither, who was well versed in legal matters,
opened the discussion:
"Let's consider if this lamentable act
performed by Dares really constitutes treason.
If you judge him to be a traitor
for having delivered his tower to the enemy,
then you can see very clearly
and know with absolute certainty
that he was lacking in love for the king.
His behavior showed that he felt little or no loyalty to the king:
he didn't want to remain here any longer,
nor did he manifest any reverence for his lord,
or give any evidence of unbounded devotion
when he turned his tower over to the enemy;
he wanted to strip the king of his inheritance,
assure his capture and his deliverance to the foe.
He's to be given the same treatment
as if he had caused the king to be hanged;
and it's no credit to him
that he wasn't able to hand the king over to the Greeks;
he certainly did everything in his power to that end,
and now he should pay the price for it!
It was not for him to give up his tower
without his lord's warrant:
Dares has committed a great crime,
and deserves to lose his limbs and his life."
Othon spoke after Ither,
sweetly and without malice:
"My dear lord Ither, don't talk like that ;
please, find something better to say to us.
You have hit the mark on one point,
and I can't blame you at all when you say

that he oughtn't to have turned his tower over to the enemy
without the king's permission;
you're telling the absolute truth,
and I completely agree with you.
But now you should certainly know,
without any doubt at all,
that Dares would never have thought of doing that
had the king not given him permission."
"The king did what? Gave him permission to do that?
By my faith, he never even thought of doing so."
"And by the trust that you owe me,
just listen to me a little bit,
and let me talk for a minute.
When you were speaking, I shut up,
and never once did I interrupt you;
you said what you wanted,
every bit, until you had finished.
now it's your turn to listen to me."
"Fine! Say what you want;
I won't interrupt you."
"I'll start from the beginning:
Dares indeed came to the king,
right to where he was in the palace,
and spoke with him in a peaceful manner.
As he was speaking with the king,
as many as three messengers arrived,
who came from beyond the border area
between the Danube and Usarche;
they were counts of that land
and they had come to ask the king
to grant them the entire marches
from the Danube to the bridge of Ute.
They would make a covenant,
sealed with oaths and promises,
that as soon as they had the land,
and were officially sealed in its possession,
they would enter the king's service with good archers
and ten thousand knights;
that way the king could know for sure,

9453 **the bridge of Ute** *al punt d'Ute*: Again, an unidentifiable location.
9459 **ten thousand knights** *dis mil chevaliers*: At v. 8589 the number is 20,000.

eschewing any further doubt,
that his city, however besieged,
would never be taken by the Greeks.
They said further
that it would be a good thing, were they to possess this land,
for the king never to take any interest
in what happened there:
if he thereby lost even the value of two sous,
they would compensate him that much more.
Now, there isn't any one of you
who doesn't know without a doubt
that it's the custom of the Pinsonards,
one they'll never abandon,
that whatever one of them promises you one morning
he won't hold to the next.
These are people it makes sense to be fearful of,
and to avoid their company,
because they will not keep their promises
nor hold to their word.
It's a sure thing that Dares knew them;
he doubted their word, and he was right to do so.
He spoke partly on the kings' account,
even more on his own:
he said, 'Hold on;
you should never even listen to them;
let this whole business go,
and make a deal with your brother.
You're destroying each other;
instead the two of you should come to an agreement.
He should give some of his and you of yours;
And ours will be diminished.
It would be a great thing, were you willing,
if, before any greater evil comes of this,
you would send for your brother
and make a settlement with him,
for this realm is now such a wasteland

9468 **the value of two sous** *deux soldz valiant*: A not inconsiderable amount of money in the poem's age; a *sou* was 1/20 of a *livre*, the equivalent in theory of the worth of a pound of silver (cf. the former English "pound sterling").
9490–91 **He should give some of his and you of yours; and ours will be diminished** *le son en done et vous le vostre,/ et molt y par perdront li nostre*: meaning unclear; translation conjectural.

that it will never be restored, in my opinion,
neither in your lifetime
nor in your children's.
Now these other types are coming to ask for the border land,
all the best part of your realm:
of all the land you possess
the part to which you should be most attached.
I could never advise you, no matter what your needs,
to loosen your grip on it.'
Those words made all the trouble between the king and Dares;
he hardly said anything else,
except that he did add later—
which upset the king even more—
that he should surrender to his brother the marches
between the Danube and Usarche,
since it would be better for him to have it
than someone else who had no family connection to the king.
This is why the king became so angry with Dares,
and I know that is what happened, because I was there;
nor was I there alone;
others of you were there as well
and you heard the argument very well:
you know who's wrong and who isn't.
You must know that what Dares said
he did for the king's advantage;
but the king didn't care about that at all;
instead he got his hands on a big rod
with which he would have struck him on the head,
had not his mother held him back.
Then right in front of me the king said,
'You wicked, redheaded low-life,
I give you leave to do
all the evil that you can,
and to redeem your captive son
with whatever gold and silver you have;
as God is my witness, I don't give a damn
what you use to do it.'
Once the king had said that,
in my estimation he granted to Dares
permission to surrender his tower

9513 **than someone... connection to the king** *que autre que rien ne li fust*: The text does not mention this suggestion earlier.

in order to free his son from captivity:
either his tower or his other possessions—
whatever it took to get him back.
But he couldn't free him with gold
or any other treasure;
for that reason he had to turn over his tower,
with the permission of his lord.
If you're willing to exert yourself on his behalf,
you can prevent his execution."
Sicart spoke next, after Othon,
who knew how to argue superbly;
he was wearing a cloak of Frisian cloth,
edged in gray fur;
he pulled it around his shoulders
and held out his right arm;
"My lords," he said, "even if you grant it
among yourselves, in agreement
with Othon's judgment,
that Dares was justified in the transgression
he committed against the king,
by my faith, there's no way I'll go along with you.
And I want to show you why
you shouldn't agree with Othon either;
because I know very well how this situation originated,
since I was there for the whole thing.
My lord Othon has spoken very persuasively,
but he's left out a few things.
I, on the other hand, will immediately tell you the whole truth,
which is that Dares began all this because of his son.
He considered himself dishonored,
as good as dead, and totally outraged
because the Greeks had captured his son
and showed no inclination to release him;
so the father thought to himself—
like the tricky, malicious, vicious person he is—
that he would concoct a scheme
allowing him to rescue the boy.
So the day before yesterday, after he had dined,
I don't know how carefully he had planned it,
but I do know that he left his dwelling,
came to the court on horseback
right up to here, at this mounting block,
where he dismounted, along with his retinue;

and then he went right up this staircase
and entered the great hall,
seating himself right next to me,
because I was sitting very near the king.
Soon he engaged the king,
in the hearing of all of us who were there,
saying, 'Now you should make an arrangement
with your brother; it's a terrible thing
that you should be enemies
who should be such good friends,
engendered as you were by the same father,
and borne by the same mother.'
This was very good advice,
had the king been willing to follow it;
but in fact the king knew very well—
was certain of it, in fact—
that the peace that his vassal was advising him to make
was just a way of getting Dares's son out of prison.
Now listen to what the king said to him,
and how Dares then transgressed.
The king said to him, 'leave me alone!
If you have something else to say
that seems to you appropriate, get it off your chest,
but don't ever talk to me again about *that*.'
And after giving him that order,
should Dares have said another word about it?
No, by God, not according to the rules;
but Dares was instead looking for an excuse,
that I know, an opening that he could seize,
one thanks to which he could surrender his tower.
He didn't obey the king and back off,
but started in again:
'What will we do about our children,
of whom the enemy has captured I don't know how many?
They've died and been taken fighting on your behalf,
and for their sake you really should make a treaty.'
'Ah! For God's sake, Dares,' said the king,
'You're far too great a noble
to argue like this with me, even if it annoys me;
you're doing a lot just to aggravate me.
Why not take some of those funds that you have—
so much that you don't know what to do with it—
all that white silver and red gold

that you've amassed in your treasury,
and use some of it as ransom
for your son in captivity,
if you really want to redeem him,
and just leave me out of it from now on.
If it's what you want, go ahead and ransom him,
or leave him there, if you prefer;
I couldn't care less by what means
you get him back, believe me.'
Now Dares grabbed at that straw,
namely, that the king said to him
that he really didn't care
how Dares might choose to ransom his son;
but since the king was speaking as if in council,
and as a lord addressing a vassal,
he didn't expect that vassal to betray him
by twisting to his advantage something the king said to him.
This trick that Dares played,
arguing heatedly with the king,
with the sole purpose
of leading him on
to say a certain thing
which Dares could use for his own purposes—
isn't that, in your opinion,
exactly what he wanted to happen?
Shouldn't he instead have just listened to the king,
let him speak his mind freely,
and say what he wished, as the lord?
In that way he would have preserved his lord's honor,
through friendship and through vassalage;
after all, since they're not equal in rank
he ought not quarrel with the king
nor by his insistence anger him.
And if he wanted to request something,
he should willingly have granted the king a delay
until a more convenient time
and in a more appropriate place,
rather than arguing about it right away,
as if he were some gauche burgher.
Dares has transgressed badly against the king,
and by God, that really upsets me;
he's also offended everyone here.
That's all there is to it: he should now be at the king's mercy:

if he wishes to burn or hang him,
by my faith, you can't justly forbid him
from deciding to do with Dares
whatever he desires,
entirely at his will and pleasure—
in short, exactly as he wishes, and as a lord can do to his vassal."

Othon says that he doesn't concur
in Dares's being placed in the king's power,
not because he denies
the king's power over him,
but because the king should not do anything worse to him
than to the most powerful baron in the court;
for he hadn't done anything to the king
that would justify the monarch's going beyond the law in reprisal:
and he, Othon, is prepared to show how this is true
according to reason as well as the law.
So Othon says, "According to the law,
whatever the status of a baron,
if he seeks advice from his lord,
through friendship and for the lord's honor,
the lord should certainly counsel him;
and if the situation is reversed,
and the lord requests counsel from the baron,
it's plain as the nose on my face that, acting reasonably,
the baron should not hesitate,
but instead should do the right thing:
namely, offer the very best advice that he can,
and dissuade his lord from doing anything foolish.
The king sought counsel from lord Dares,
asking his advice on what to do
concerning this agreement that he was being offered,
requesting him to say what he thought about it.
Now milord Dares knew very well
that this was in no way to the king's advantage,
so he didn't want to advise accepting it,
but instead counseled him to refuse it;
for he knew in his heart
that it would be harmful to the king's interests;
I assume that he would not have hesitated to endorse it
if it was a thing the king should undertake.
Now let's see, in accord with reason,
which one was wrong, which not:

lord Dares counseled the king
in the best way he knew how,
and gave him the loyal counsel
he owed to his natural lord;
and he's ready to swear an oath
that he wouldn't know how to give better.
The king is wrong, in my opinion,
for since he asked for advice
he shouldn't have insulted him
just because he didn't say what the king wanted to hear
about what was in his heart
and what he really wanted to do:
since he wanted so badly to do it,
why did he ask Dares for advice?
But the king should then have done,
—and would have done—the courteous thing,
to listen to what his vassal had to say;
then if he wished to do it,
and if he saw that it was to his advantage,
he could do it, if it pleased him to;
and if he saw, and believed,
that Dares was giving him bad advice,
then he could easily say to him
that he had no intention of heeding his counsel.
As soon as the king said that to Dares,
I don't think he would have spoken about it anymore;
but if he had, then I'd have blamed him for it;
and you can be sure that I wouldn't have spoken about it now.
But that's not how the king acted, for he didn't deign to do so,
given that he didn't hold his baron in enough esteem.
Instead, he began to quarrel,
and to mistreat him vilely
and call him 'wicked, red-headed,
venomous low-life,'
so loudly that there wasn't a serving boy at the court,
even if he were deaf, who couldn't hear it all.
I'll tell you one thing from my perspective:
by the good faith that I owe you,
if the king sought my advice
on any subject whatsoever,
I'd be scared out of my wits about it
before I could say anything.
He will come to me, his faithful vassal,

asking me to advise him,
and I'll willingly do it,
as best I know how,
with a view to his advantage and his honor,
as I ought to do for my lord.
But if I don't tell him what he wants to hear
concerning something about which he'll already have decided,
and which he would want to have happen right away,
he wouldn't desist, no matter what we all might advise,
and instead he'd abuse me as vilely,
in the hearing of as many people,
as you heard him do to Dares,
a man similar in rank to me.
By the faith that I owe you, that's not right,
and you've no call to say it is,
nor can anyone justly deny
that my lord is guilty of major wrongdoing."

Salin de Pont was very wise;
which was appropriate, for among his ancestors
were men of truly marvelous wisdom.
I doubt that, all the way to Rome,
there was in any land—take my word for it—
a man wiser than his father.
"Lord Othon," he said, "that's enough!
The question I want you to answer
is whether lord Dares was in a position
to advise the king to make the accord."
"Oh yes; on my honor, in a good position to do so,
if he saw in it an advantage for the king."
"What you say may well have been the case;
but he still isn't home free.
I put it to you that he did wrong:
before he left his dwelling to come to the court,
he gave considerable private consideration
to how he could make the king angry,
and then he came here the day before yesterday
with the intention of arguing with him;
he thought about what he could say
that would get the king all upset.
He didn't fail; he did what he had to do—
thought through what he needed to say and then said it;
he argued with the king just the way he wanted to,

as if he were disputing with someone he didn't respect,
whom he didn't consider to be his lord,
saying such dishonorable things to him
that he even accused him of perjury,
and wouldn't stop, even though we were all present.
And if the king was angry with him for that,
furious at his language,
I must tell you that I'm not at all surprised,
because he spoke very wrongly to his lord.
Now let me tell you one thing about me,
whose status doesn't equal that of a king:
I can't think of any man, if he spoke to me that way,
who wouldn't find out right away that he was wrong to do so;
certainly, if I had the power,
I would quickly take him apart.
Now, think about what Dares did,
and then what the king said to him:
whoever wants to come to a just judgment will see
that the wrongdoing here falls squarely on lord Dares's shoulders."

Othon answers, "That's what you think;
now it's time for you to prove it;
and if Dares is to be blamed,
It would be good for you to make the case."
"Yes, this is the right time for me to proceed further,
now that you are aware of my opinion
concerning this crisis that he brought about—
what happened, and where it stands now.
This vassal, overflowing with bitterness and evil,
in the wrong and ready to argue,
came to see the king, who was in his palace—
where he thought he'd be left in peace,
having no desire for conflict—
until Dares came before him
and started telling him
that he should make peace with those besiegers out there.
And because he knew very well
that my lord would never do that,
and the king said to him, laughing,
that he had not forged his alliance with friends
in order that he could then make a treaty with his enemies,
and didn't say any more than that.
Dares realized that because of the king's conviction

he would pay no attention to his vassal;
from the king's expression, Dares could tell
that he couldn't care less what he had to say.
So now Dares addressed him more bitterly;
in order to prick the king where it hurt,
he began to argue with him,
to blame him for all his losses—
for all the land he'd had to give away
in order to finance his war;
for everything he'd ever had
taken from him by force of arms—
in order that he should feel self-hate,
anger, and heaviness of heart."
"What are you saying?" interrupted Othon, "is that why he said what he did?
Dares, if you don't mind, never did such a thing!!"
"Why, my lord, are you in such a hurry to speak?
I've not finished talking yet;
you can speak next, if you know something else,
but first you have to listen to me a little longer:
I can assure you that I'll never fail
to do the right thing in deciding this case before us.
From beginning to end of this affair,
Dares was guilty and must be judged so:
if we all keep our mouths shut about this,
we would commit a great treason,
even if condemning what he did to the king
weighs heavily on you and me as his peers.
What could anger a man more
than to be blamed for his failings,
and what's more troubling than having to recall them?
He couldn't have imposed a worse shame on him,
and it's certainly true that Dares was aware
that his strategy would make the king very mad;
and when he thought this plan up
before coming to see the king,
he would certainly also have realized
that it would not please him at all:
that was certainly no secret,
and it would protect him from a charge of treason
when he would use it as a reason to surrender his tower
in order to have the king expelled from his realm.
The king had neither said nor done anything to Dares

that they couldn't have been reconciled over
before he left the king,
if he'd been willing to do it.
Instead, he then accused the king of perjury:
as God is my judge, he was very wrong to do that.
So let the king have his revenge,
and get back what he's owed for this treason,
for, by my faith, if that's what he wants
he has the right to burn or hang him."

Othon can't keep quiet
about his own proposal concerning this case:
"Salin de Pont," he immediately answers,
"the judgment you're asking for is stupid.
This outcome that you're so sure about
and that you insist is the correct one—
if someone wanted to challenge it,
would you be ready to settle it in a duel?"
"I don't yet know what I might do,
until I see the need to do it,
or have that need thrust upon me."
"Trust me, you're not very far from that moment right now.
As you want God to bless you, don't do this:
don't make a mountain out of a molehill!
You're reading much more into this than was really the case,
including things about which Dares never said a word:
that he may have accused the king of perjury,
and that he did so correctly,
but only in a sense that I'll explain to you,
is true; you can be sure I won't lie about this.
Cursed be Othon if he lies about this;
may he be sure, to his knowledge,
that he tells the whole truth and nothing but the truth,
with respect to the king and to Dares.
Dares knew very well
that the king had perjured himself,
and he said to the king, truthfully,
that he should honor the oath
that he swore toward his brother,
shortly after his father's death,
and then, by God, he should turn his attention
to how he could free himself and his brother from the oath:
since this was the larger intention behind his saying what he did,

you should think again about whether he did wrong."

Salin answered, "I can't ask anything better,
since you cannot deny
that he accused the king of perjury,
and that it wasn't a just accusation.
Now just watch what you're going to do,
how you're going to manipulate all this;
don't worry about a thing, my lords:
cursed be Othon, if he doesn't defend the accused!
Thanks to you, the court will always be kept busy;
but go on, say all you want, we'll listen to it."
"If you really want to listen to me,
and the court wants to do the right thing
whether to the king's brother or someone else,
which is what I promise to do together with the court,
then you're speaking well, and I thank you.
My lord barons, pay attention to this.
If my lord makes an agreement,
by oath or promise,
and has me swear to it also,
to make the agreement more binding,
and because it's not appropriate
that he alone should give his word,
now listen: if he's summoned
on the day that the contract comes due for execution,
and he then tries to escape from his obligation,
because he doesn't want to honor it,
you can be sure that someone will call him on this,
while another will beg him
to make peace with the person
with whom the oath was made.
If he releases me from the agreement as he earlier bound me to it,
I won't be able to complain if he's upset;
he'd be able to come down still harder on me
if he wasn't willing to absolve me of the obligation.
And if I keep trying to get him to release me,
after I will have explained in great detail
how important it will be for me
not to break my word,
it should be clear to you that I'm right to do so,
and that I'm not committing treason.
And if someone wants to contest that understanding,

I'm ready to defend it in battle."
Not a single one of them wants to stand up
out of a desire to challenge him.
Then one of them comes forward:
that was Alis, who says at once:
"My lords," he said, "why are you quarrelling?
Listen to me for just a little while.
What ought lord Dares to have done,
if he wanted to and felt it to be worthwhile?
Before he surrendered his tower
he should at least have offered the king a challenge.
So help and bless me God,
he fell short in his loyalty,
for the king wasn't aware
that he would behave as he did, just because he wanted to."
All the others say that Alis is right:
"Now answer that, lord Othon," they cry.
Othon took Alis's hand:
"Let's talk, my lord Alis.
Why have you given the king
the gift of becoming his man, your hands joined within his?
Tell me; don't leave anything out."
"Certainly: I did it to reinforce and assist him."
"Was there any other reason? Please keep talking."
"Yes, if you really want to know, there was also this:
that he protects me as he does himself,
and vice versa."
"And if the time came that he let you down,
that he broke faith with you,
if he issued a formal defiance of you, what then would you do?
Would you continue to hold faith with him?"
"Do you think I'd keep faith with him
since he violated his with me?
A curse on whoever would have anything to do with him,
when he broke his word to me!"
"By my faith, the king broke his faith with Dares;
who therefore didn't know how to deal with his sworn allegiance,
once the king behaved in this way,
so he escaped from there as quickly as possible.
He didn't dare say to the king, 'and I defy you, ending my allegiance,'
for he was quite alone,
and he saw, if he uttered a defiance,
what couldn't fail to happen to him, immediately:

the king would have him arrested
and, if it pleased him, abused and mistreated,
and then he would have commandeered Dares's residence,
denying him the possibility of ever setting foot in it again.
And I want to say, furthermore,
that you're fully aware, if the lord
leads his vassal into a violation of the law,
then the vassal no longer owes him his loyalty;
from the hour that the king defied him,
as God is my judge and protector,
Dares no longer owed him any faith or allegiance;
if he turned against him, it was his right;
since his lord abandoned him, he could behave in the same way,
in order to look after his own needs."
"By God, my lord Othon," says Alis,
"Dares has behaved really badly.
Since he had come so far
as to leave the king after a rupture between them,
he should then have waited two or three days
—indeed, it really ought to be a month—
or at least until the next day, before doing something rash.
He should have kept possession of his tower,
not surrendering it to anyone else;
then he should have carefully considered his circumstances:
even if the king didn't offer to set right
the wrong and dishonor he'd done to him,
didn't move quickly
to offer him redress of his grievances—
even so my lord Dares should have taken counsel with himself
as to what were best for him to do
by way of accepting or refusing a royal offer;
he could certainly have pondered that.
And if the king didn't think enough of him
that he would consider doing right by him,
then *that* would have been the right time
to do what he instead did in an untimely fashion:
then he would have had justice more on his side,
because at that point there was nothing else he could do.
Now he has neither this nor that,
and nothing with a scrap of value;
but anyone who has a grain of sense
and can understand what's reasonable
should easily be able to comprehend

that the whole thing was just a ruse on lord Dares's part,
since he wasn't willing to wait to surrender his tower
for at least as long as I've suggested he might have.
And now one thing is certain:
he can't make up for the loss of the tower,
nor can he offer back to my lord the king his troops,
more than two hundred of whom have been captured,
all as a result of this quarrel
that Dares concocted and carried out—
an act of treason
from which he can never escape blame.
Let the king have his vengeance
on his body, in accord with his power as his lord,
be it by hanging or burning,
since he has certainly deserved it."

Othon replied angrily,
heaving himself up on his feet;
everything that has gone before
was nothing compared to what he'll now say:
"My dear lord Alis, change your tune,
because I'm not about to agree with any of it.
You spoke well, except for one thing;
I can't blame you for anything;
everything you say is entirely true,
so I'm on your side with respect to all that.
If he did commit treason toward the king,
then he hasn't got a legal leg to stand on;
but I intend to defend him against this accusation
by appeals to the law and to reason.
A man who condemns another to being torn apart
should make absolutely sure
that his judgment is such
that he can make it in accord with the law.
For, since you will have killed a man
as a result of your judgment,
you will not be able to protect him later,
or bring him back from death to life,
however much you might wish to do so;
in that case, you'll repent later for what you do now.
Your obligation should be to put down evil
and uphold and exalt the good.
The king has greatly dishonored his baron,

when he struck him with his rod
and gave him, as I heard him say,
complete leave to do him harm;
and if Dares proceeded to do that at his earliest opportunity,
since he had the king's leave to do it,
he didn't thereby cede life or limb,
for he didn't commit treason."

Creon, the old—indeed, the ancient—
was well schooled in legal judgments:
he stands up in the court
He was hardy and valiant, especially for his age,
and of high nobility;
tall, with white hair,
but by no means sickly;
and well schooled in reasonable argument.

"Lords," he says, "listen to me!
It is wrong to consent knowingly
to a bad judgment.
Othon has given his opinion,
and we have all listened to it;
but, by the faith I owe you,
I do not agree with it.
If the king insulted his baron,
Dares was silent and accepted it,
he did not question the king,
he did not assert his rights;
he did not challenge the king,
nor did the king deny his rights.
He was the king's man and the king his lord:
he should not, it seems to me,
want his lord to lose land,
over a dispute or out of anger
nor certainly seek
to disinherit him so lightly.
He should have set forth and claimed his rights
and then waited forty days;
he should have sought and offered his rights,
and endured for forty days.
If the king did not do right by him,
then rather than commit a crime
he could well have done something less rash

and simply withdrawn from his service;
even if the king wronged him,
he should not have sought his death.
He sought the king's death when he set
his mortal enemies on him —
they would willingly have killed him,
if they could have gotten hold of him.
We should not lie about rights,
nor consent to treason.
Dares committed a great felony,
he has no right to keep his members nor his life;
and I do not think that there is anyone here
who is more distressed by this than I am,
but I shall not, for love of him, distort
the judgment I must make.
A man who loves another in good faith
does not want to harm him anymore than himself."
Othon says: "I have no interest in love,
when it leads to dishonor!
If you loved him at all,
you would not make such a judgment.
Sir Creon, you should amend your position,
for I cannot agree with it.
If my lord takes my land or my possessions,
I must either claim my rights from him,
or, if he does not give them, wait
forty days before I transgress;
but if he should strike my body,
cursed be anyone who would just challenge him!
He has forfeited his right over me,
he has belied his faith to me.
I then have a right to take vengeance for the blow,
and he must defend himself from my lance!
I do not know how to assert my right against a physical attack
except by taking vengeance with a sword."
The court was greatly troubled;
it was close to coming to blows,
for the discussion was not going
as they wished,
when Amon rose to his feet.
Amon was a powerful man with a good reputation:
"Lords," he says, "calm down:
your quarrels are getting ugly.

We have listened to the points
you have made here.
Let us recall all the points that were made
and then make the judgment,
for by the faith that I owe you—
and I say this as much for myself as for anyone else—
we can never make a judgment,
if we do not first make peace among ourselves.
But let us remember the discussion,
and then let us make the judgment.”

Why should I stretch this out further?
No judgment is made.
For while they are arguing this way
and the court is waiting for them,
Jocasta takes the king aside
and speaks secretly to him:
“Son,” she says, “moderation is more valuable
than judgment or legal right.
It might be legal for you to destroy this felon
but you would be doing too much harm to yourself:
he has relatives who will avenge him
and they will be able to avenge him forcefully.
You can see your enemies before you here
and, by the faith that I owe you,
I assure you they will bring them inside here one night;
if they are determined, they will not fail to take revenge.
Trust me and make a truce with him,
but have him give security that he will keep his word.”
As her mother is speaking,
Antigone, the king’s sister
comes to her brother,
bringing the daughter of Dares with her.
Do you know what the daughter of Dares is like?
Her body and her countenance are lovely,
her face fresh with high color;
she has a small mouth well-formed,
and lips that are suitably full—
Nature made them for kissing.
Her eyes are bright, laughing and loving:
it is a great shame that they are now weeping!
Her flesh is tender, smooth, and soft,
her heart pure, her speech sweet.

She is not too large nor too small,
of medium height
and very thin in the waist;
she is wearing a silk gown,
a colored silk
minutely worked in a floral design,
and over her shoulders she has
a new gray cloak.
Her hair is long, fine and blond,
wrapped around her head.
But she has taken no care to prepare herself,
and that is no wonder,
for the girl is grieving
and in her sorrow she is very beautiful.
With a mournful face she moves humbly
and weeps quite attractively;
her face is wet from weeping
but her tears seem like another woman's smile.
Her face and her bearing
cause many of the men there to suffer;
there is no one who does not grieve for her
when he sees her grief.
The king loves her beyond measure
but she has been very harsh towards him;
he loves her more than any living being
but she is quite aloof to him.
When the king sees her coming towards him,
he can scarcely keep himself from
going towards her with a smile;
the sight of her tempers his anger.
If he felt more confident
he would immediately go to speak to her.
Jocasta smiles at the king:
"Son," she says, "you have no right in you,
no right by chivalry,
if you do not make this girl your love.
Have you ever seen such a beauty,
so lovely and so modest?
Give her back her father and let her be your love —
that would be an act of great courtesy."
The king likes the idea and smiles
as his mother talks.
The girls come forward,

both of them weeping;
they fall on the ground
at the king's feet and weep tenderly.
One asks mercy for her father,
the other begs it of her brother.
The king turns towards his sister
who is sad and grieving for the other girl:
"Sister," he says, "you know perfectly well
that I have always courted her in vain;
why should I have mercy on her
when she never had any on me."
Antigone answers: "Now you have the advantage,
you do not have to beg any more.
You should show mercy to each other,
you to her and she to you."
The girl promises it, but
the king says "I don't know how I can believe you."
Jocasta says: "It will be all right,
I am your pledge for this deed."
She does not say this
foolishly;
Jocasta is a very good lady,
charitable and chaste,
and she wants to save Dares from death.
It would be wrong to blame her for it.

As the king is sitting at one side,
taking counsel with the three women,
the bachelors, the soldiers,
come up to ask mercy for Dares.
They feel pity for Dares's daughter
and they all go to the king for her sake;
they all seek mercy for Dares
and they will find it, I think.
Their request pleases the king very much,
but he keeps a somber face,
wanting to hide the pact
the girl made with him.
He is pretending to be intractable
but it is hard for him to delay
since he is now sure of his beloved
who is weeping and crying for mercy.
Troubled by the tender face

that he sees wet with tears,
he longs to show mercy to her.
I should not make you wait any longer either:
with some difficulty the king grants them
that he will accept the counsel of the barons.

A messenger is sent to the judges
to tell them what the king has done.
Most people rejoice over it,
and bless their lord
for pardoning such a great wrong.
They cherish him more for it.
But Creon says: "I don't mind saying
a young man can be quite foolish!
I say this because of the king
who refused you and me;
he refused me and you,
he didn't want to do anything for us,
not even give us a delay.
Now he is pardoning Dares
at the request of a girl!
I don't say this out of hatred
or because I don't like the fact
that the king has forsaken his law,
but if he were going to do this,
he should have done it for his barons."
Othon replies: "That is not the way it is
with love and chivalry.
That is what he cares about;
you should not be surprised
that he holds it great courtesy,
though you consider it folly.
There is no man from here to Syria
more ready to uphold courtesy."
The barons come to the king
and give their judgment on Dares;
he comes forward, offering as his surety
all the barons of the city.
Dares stands before the king,
with his friends around him.
"May God bless me," he says,
"I acknowledge my mistake.
I did what I should not have done,

that is what started the adventure.
That is why you have put me in prison,
and you have the law with you to some extent.
But if you pardon me this folly,
you can send me into battle
with the most loyal friends
you will have while you live.
I committed folly, as I say,
but I do not admit to treason;
I am prepared to absolve myself
from treason and deception."
Creon answers him contentiously:
"Sir Dares, calm yourself.
The battle will be waged
but another will fight it for you!"
None of them knows what he means
except the king who is furious
for he is alluding to the daughter of Dares.
The king looks down
and lowers his head to his cloak —
you can imagine that he was not pleased!
If he had been alone with Creon,
he would very willingly have fought with him,
but he did not want to argue in court
nor to give importance to those words.
All the barons beg him so hard
that he grants their plea.
He takes hostages that Dares will keep his word
and gives his entire fief back to Dares.

In the Greek host they grieve for their friends
who were killed and captured in Dares's tower.
The son of Dares is much hated among them;
they say he has betrayed them
and because of that treason they want
to hang the prisoner on the gallows.
Twenty thousand of them
go to Polynices's tent;
they want to take Dares's son by force,
kill him and hang him on the gallows.
A knight named Ponce
quickly announces this to Polynices.
But Polynices, who was a noble man,

puts the young man on his horse;
on a horse worth one hundred pounds,
and lets him go free into the city.

It is some time since the inner army and the outer
have done any harm to each other
although they have no love for each other,
but only hate and fear.
Hypomedon does not rest,
he is always thinking, plotting something,
always on the watch to see how
he might cause trouble to the inner army.
He thinks a great deal
about how he can harm them.
He goes to consult with the king,
taking Capaneus with him;
they descend to the royal standard
and draw the king to one side.
Hypomedon speaks first:
"This wait," he says, "is driving us crazy;
we have sat here for too long
and have conquered very little.
We have been too long in a strange land
without conquering anything.
We will never take the city this way,
never force their hand this way.
You cannot starve them
because ships come to them by sea
that bring them enough to eat;
they have no fear of an assault.
And we can't go on the salt sea,
because we have no barges or galleys;
we did not come by sea
but through the deserts of Nemea.
They have the great river of Ismenos
enclosing them on the other side;
in the prairies beyond the bridge
their great flocks of cattle pasture.
The land can be reached
through the hunting reserves and the sand.
That is where the grains and the wines come in
on mules and camels and pack horses.
Across this bridge under our very eyes

the train of supplies comes at a good pace.
We see them gathering the wheat
but we can't cross the water.
These people cannot not be besieged,
they will never be taken by force;
we will not be able to do anything to them
if we can't draw them outside here.
But I can show you
a way to trick them.
Soon, when there is bright light,
have the knights armed,
thirty thousand and more,
and let them set an ambush at Malpertus,
while others stay back,
and take up arms in the morning.
Have all of them armed,
have the squires strike the tents
and send the cry through the host
to load the chargers quickly.
Let the pack animals go ahead
and the knights follow behind;
let the infantry set out
fully equipped for battle.
Inside the city there are many knights
that are quite annoyed with you.
Their king is proud and fierce,
but very fickle in his heart;
he will gather a great force of knights,
and follow us.
You can be sure
they will immediately enter the field with us.
But I will make up the rearguard
where there will be no pack animals or baggage;
we will be twenty thousand of the elite,
knights who were born to it.
We will let the Thebans approach us
and insult and humiliate us.
By the faith I owe you,
there will be no confusion;
there will be no charge
until we catch sight of our ambush
The men we have hidden in the woods
must not make any noise.

They should put themselves deep into the woods
in the valley beneath the mountain
and take care not to come out too soon
so they don't cause us to fail.
They must let the others pursue us along the road,
let the whole great crowd of them come,
until our thirty thousand can get themselves
on the road between the Thebans and the city.
As long as we do it well,
we who are in the rearguard,
I don't think they can escape us
for they will not have the strength."
Capaneus does not want to delay
or hold back from this affair:
"I tell you truly," he says,
I shall be in the ambush.
Let the king summon
his barons immediately but secretly."
Hypomedon says: "I will not fail in this.
I take this labor on myself;
this labor I take on myself,
I shall summon them as I usually do."
"My lords," says the king, "you know
I have no two barons so close to me
as you are, nor whom I trust so much.
I will adopt this plan through you,
carry it out as you know best;
you shall win great praise and glory from it.
You will win great honor
for the love of your lord.
You have done well so far
and I thank you for it.
Now give your attention to this matter
and take the burden of it on yourselves
for the plan suits me
just as you have outlined it."

The night arrives, Hypomedon has summoned
the barons for the affair:
they get ready to ride,
they mount and go to set the ambush.
With him go ten or more like him,
each one a king or count or duke.

Partenopeus goes out first
with his company that is fierce and ferocious;
they are five thousand
and you may be sure that they have noble equipment.
Anyone who sees them might well say
their sire is not a bad man.
Capaneus goes next,
taking the whole burden on himself;
he has three thousand bold men,
well instructed in chivalry.
The Duke of Amycles has come out
with only two thousand shields,
but those two thousand are worth
four thousand to their lord in valor.
Meleager of Amphigenia,
a noble duke of great power
and first cousin of the king,
brings a noble company with him;
they are three thousand men of great pride,
all armed in the French manner.
The King of Crete had just that night
come into the host with a great force.
He does not hold a fief or land from the king
but the king had sent to him for help.
He was a childhood friend,
by oath and by his word,
and does not want to fail him:
the king prepared himself very quickly
both to help his friend, and for the pleasure of it,
and brought a great company into the host.
The King of Crete is called Minos,
worthy and with a noble body
and a strong reputation for courage.
He goes out with the men of Crete,
seven thousand men of fierce deeds;
where they go it is worse than a storm.
From Anuques there is Count Agenor;
who has great wealth of gold and silver
and is not slow to ride out,
leading one thousand five hundred men.
Laertes of Lacedemonia
asks no excuse for his wound,
but gets himself up with some effort

and leads a thousand armed knights.
Pyrrhus, a count palatine,
who renders justice and counsel,
has no more than a thousand knights,
his son Tryptolemus has five hundred more.
After them comes Palemon,
a powerful duke of high birth
who holds Carmin and Azon;
his company is all of the same young age,
bachelors, a lively people
who will be the first to strike blows.
They are three thousand, people without restraint,
who have no interest in anything but fighting.
Antenor is the one from Troy
with a blond and well-built troop;
they wear flowing clothes with long trains,
hauberks will be no burden to them.
They torment the enemy on the flanks,
with strong lances of cutting iron,
but they are not very effective
at throwing knights to the ground.
From Africa, from that people of evil law,
there is the son of a king
who brings two thousand Almoravids,
skilled and wise in tourneying.
He crossed the sea for love of the king;
I heard he was called Salomand.
With the others I have named,
he completes the thirty thousand.
They all ride out under the moon
and lay their ambush in Valbrune,
in the forest of Malpertus
where Tydeus fought and killed
the fifty men that were sent to ambush him,
except for the one he sent back to Thebes.
In the morning they are wet by the dew
that falls from the trees under the leaves.

[The remaining men of the army get up in the morning,]

10591 **[The remaining men of the army get up in the morning]** *[Cil de l'ost par matin leverent]*: This verse, omitted from MS S but required for the sense of passage, is added by Mora-Lebrun from Constans's edition.

pick up their arms and put them on;
the squires strike the tents,
they give all their attention to the departure.
They load their pack animals without rushing,
and then set out.
Hypomedon stays behind
to make up a fierce rearguard;
there are twenty thousand in the rearguard,
not counting squires or baggage.
There has never been such chivalry,
so select, so well equipped;
they have helmets, hauberks and caparisons
and standards of a thousand kinds.
The day is beautiful and clear and lovely:
the gold and silver shine
and the countryside
and the mountains sparkle.
The countryside is deep and broad.
All is in order in the rearguard;
even among the four troops of Roland,
about whom these minstrels keep singing,
there was none as handsome and richly appointed—
anyone would be mad to claim it.
The baggage train goes in front of the host,
the king follows with his battalion.
Four companies ride behind him
along the riverbank,
five thousand in each,
slowly following the host.
Polynices rides in one of them,
Hypomedon in the next;
in the third, the men from Aquilonia,
and the barons of Calydon;
in the fourth, the men from Mycenes.
The companies stay very close;
side by side they go through the meadow,
with little space between them.
The inner army sees the host depart,
and they scarcely believe it
until they see that their lodgings were struck,
which convinces them that it is true.
In the city there is great tumult;
each man runs to his lodging,

taking up arms as best he can—
there are a lot of them!
They do not wait for an order
but chase out in confusion.
Eteocles spurs after to hold them back,
but when they see him coming,
they press their spurs for a long distance
so the king cannot catch up to them.
The king rides a marvelous horse,
that leaps from the path onto the grass
and races across the field
to catch the men in front.
As the horse rushes with great force,
he stumbles on a rock.
The horse falls and the king flies off him;
if he had not fallen on soft earth,
if he had fallen on the hard road,
the king would have been killed.
The king bore heavy arms
and his lively horse
ran very swiftly without control;
if he had fallen on hard earth,
by the faith I owe you,
he would have broken all his limbs!
The king falls on soft earth,
on the thick grass near a swamp,
and the others who come after him
stop where the king lies.
They have the king disarmed
and the foot that the king had twisted
is quickly treated with charms
by a Moor.
The king is completely disarmed,
and mounted on a palfrey;
he leads his people with difficulty,
with great difficulty he sits in the saddle
for he has badly dislocated his foot
and broken and bruised his body.
They move slowly and laboriously.
The king has his people drawn up close;
if, out of the corner of his eye,
he sees anyone break ranks,
the king gives him such a look

that he quickly returns.

The ones in front have gone far,
riding in such haste in pursuit of the departing Greeks
that they pass the ambush but do not notice it.
Those who are in the ambush
do as they should,
and keep well hidden.
They have a sentinel on a tall pine
and he sees the Thebans coming along the road.
He sees them and watches
as they approach the rearguard;
he estimates
they are ten thousand, and he is right.
But he does not see the ones behind them,
coming along the shore,
who are still two leagues and more
away from the forest of Malpertus.
"Move out," he says, "I don't see any more,"
and they rush out all at once.
They rush from the mountain,
come spurring across the plain,
and thrust themselves after the Thebans;
riding hard, they take the road behind them.
When the pursued realize too late
that these are not their men,
they know that they were fools,
to come out in such disorder.
Hypomedon sees them come,
recognizes them, and says to his men:
"Turn around, our men are coming!"
and they join battle with them.
Immediately they go to strike
and the others can not withstand it;
they strike them suddenly,
in back and in front.
They flee towards the water nearby,
but Hypomedon follows them.
There used to be a ford there,
the Thebans knew it well.
Whoever can flee enters it
and Hypomedon throws himself after them.
They wade easily to the middle of the ford

but then they find it very deep
because there had been a flood
that had caused the water to rise.
When the ford fails them, the ones in front
begin to drown.
Then they turn around in the ford to attack;
rather than die miserably,
fleeing and drowning in the waves,
that are so deep,
they will die defending themselves,
giving and taking blows.
All twenty thousand went into it,
the thirty thousand stopped.
But Hypomedon is not afraid of the ford,
he leads the whole rear guard into it.

Those who were in the ambush
see the king coming;
they ride spurring towards the king
and the royal company joins battle with them.
The king who had heard the tumult
when he got down from his palfrey,
looked for his steed, and it was brought to him.
He mounted it with some effort
but he could not bear
to put his hauberk on;
he was badly wounded from his fall.
He took his shield, laced on his helmet,
on which he hung a motley sleeve
which Dares's daughter had given him.
He expected to deploy his people,
to cut off the fighters in front;
but they are already fighting on their own
and can do nothing for their lord.
On the bank by the meadow
the battle is intense;
the forces join immediately, they smash their lances,
break and shatter the shields.
There you might have seen such splintering of shields,
so many knights thrown from their saddles,
so many fatal blows dealt,
so many strong hauberks torn apart!
Those in the Greek host are a good thirty thousand

and there are as many from the city
so the battle is equal,
one cannot tell which will lose.
They are all intent on striking
and they have no heart for flight,
but then Adrastus comes along the road
leading a huge train.
When Adrastus sees them fighting
he rides very quickly towards them.
The inner army will not be able to last,
the host has too many people;
they are seven to one against them.
I will not make a long story of it:
Eteocles turns back,
he flees, he can take no more.
The victory goes to the host,
they have routed the inner army.
As for those who got themselves into the water,
I will tell you what end they met:
they fight well on both sides,
they go at each other in the large ford.
The Greeks go after them fiercely,
striking with their swords;
as they join battle, they lose their lances,
so they are down to bare swords.
The Thebans defend themselves well,
fighting for their lives;
each avenges himself as best he can
when he sees that he must die.
By force and great prowess
they push the Greeks from the ford to the shore
and, if they had been equal in number,
I think they could have defended themselves.
But they were not equally matched;
those in the host were twice their number.
And yet as long as they are fresh,
they continue to fight with them,
but they cannot endure
the great attack for long.
On the field they defended themselves strongly
but they died a double death.
You might have seen many drown at the ford,
dying by the sword and thrown down:

those who remain die of their wounds,
those who flee try to swim,
but when they come to the deep part
their heavy hauberks
drag the wretches down to the bottom.
There is no help for them.
Once they have plunged in
there is no way to come up,
the water pulls them down.
Floating on the surface are aspen lances,
and many standards,
and pennants and painted shields.
The horses do not know what to do,
because the reins tie up their feet;
plunging, they bend their necks and go down with the current.
They drown there with their lords.

Hypomedon, rejoicing,
cries out until he is hoarse;
sword drawn, he goes to strike,
and cuts up as many as he pleases!
He sits on Tydeus's horse,
that is worth a hundred gold pounds and more.
No horse like it was ever born of a mare:
he has no trouble swimming a league,
even swimming a full league
does not shorten his breath.
There was no horse that could bear such effort,
yet Hypomedon presses him so hard,
he does not notice
that he is not on hard ground.
He trusts strongly to his good horse
and moves through the ford as if on a ship.
He bears great anger against the Thebans
and makes every effort to kill them.
What can I say? He drives the horse so hard
he cannot breath.
The peasant says: "Who lives by the sword
must die by the sword."
He must drown with the others,
there is no better reward for him.
Hypomedon, the bold and wise,
drowns there, that is a shame;

he drowns in the deep water.
God confound anyone who would rejoice at that!
Since God first formed the world,
no man like him ever drowned in the waves;
and the horse drowned under him.
Ah, such a bad end for both!
By the light of the sun
one could not find such a noble pair
of knight and horse,
nor two that were so well suited.
And of the inner army, not one escaped:
whoever was not killed drowned.

The king is happy and
filled with love for Dares's daughter.
And she deserves to be loved:
there is no one so beautiful on this side of the sea,
on this side of the sea, there is none so beautiful;
the girl's name is Salamander.
The king loves Salamander very much,
secretly and without scandal;
he is very worthy and for his love
he does frequent deeds of chivalry.
The king is bold:
he knows how to slip out of the city,
with only two companions, secretly,
and charge towards the host with his lance raised.
Lance raised, he charges towards the host
and joins battle with the Greeks to their discomfort;
often he throws knights down
and returns with their mounts.
Salamander recognizes the king
from his horse and his armor.
From the wall as she looks down on the valley,
she is very pleased with what he is doing.
Now when the two are alone,
she sleeps more willingly with him.
One day the king makes a sortie,
mounted on Hoarywhite,
a horse that had been sent to him from Nubia
and was very good for chivalry.
The king wears a helmet, shield, and lance;
he has a purple silk emblem,

speckled purple indigo,
minutely worked in gold.
He rides lightly on his horse
but he has left his hauberk behind.
He had boasted to his love
in his vassalage and recklessness,
that he would meet the enemy without body armor;
but he was not quite quick enough.
He leaves by the postern
beneath the northwest tower,
bringing two knights with him
and they go alone, the three of them.
One is called Alexander,
a first cousin of Salamander,
and for love of her
the king held him in great honor;
he had recently knighted him
richly and with great joy.
Alexander was a young boy
and quite beautiful.
The king who loves him very much, brings him along
and makes every effort to praise him;
he brings him to the combat
and begs him to join it.
So he does, he should not be criticized;
he joins the battle completely unarmed.
The other one with them is Dryas;
he is very courtly and good-humored,
a powerful man of high birth
and very great valor.
He is well-instructed in chivalry;
when the occasion arises, he does not hesitate.
Under heaven no man charges better,
nor joins battle more willingly.
He is big and broad and vigorous,
with an open face and red hair.
He strikes great blows with his lance
and, when he is on foot, with his sword.
I have seen no man better at defense—
if anyone were to tell me of one, I would think it was a fable.
These two come out with the king,
all three unarmed;
the other two would willingly have worn armor,

but if they had put on hauberks
while the king did not,
they would have committed a great fault.
The king comes out of the city
as thirty thousand watch him from the walls.
Each one would like
to be outside with his armor,
but the gates are strong iron,
well closed and well fortified.
Though they search above and below,
no man can get out on a horse.

The king rides spurring through the meadow,
where he encounters an adventure
from which will come great sorrow and harm;
he will die with great valor,
he who was King of Arcadia,
the bold, the wise, the courtly.
Parthenopeus by chance
comes riding towards them at a smart pace,
with one companion, no more.
His companion is Dorce.
They go shouting at the men from the city
and, you should know, they are unarmed.
Parthenopeus rides towards the three.
Then the king does something impressive.
He does not want to let his three joust with the other two:
"Dryas," he says, "stop here;
let me take this youth
and teach him his trade.
Let me instruct Alexander;
we will fight, whether we live or die."
Dryas stands back and the other two spur forward
and join battle equally one on one.
Antigone and Salamander
are sewing a silk from Andros for the king,
on the wall in a tower
called Blanchefleur,
sewing at a window.
They look down to the left,
they hear the horses whinny
and see the vassals come
towards one another across the meadow

spurring, with their lances raised.
Antigone recognizes her brother, the king,
and her lover, and is torn between the two.
As she sees one riding towards the other,
she does not know which she cares for more,
but she knows in her heart
that she will not escape loss.
Salamander fears greatly for the king
because he does not have his equipment;
he is unarmed, so she is very much afraid for him.
That is no wonder, since she loves him so much!
The two kings joust together
and Antigone trembles in fear.
Eteocles is vigorous
and very chivalrous;
he has a rigid lance and a sharp sword.
He strikes Parthenopeus on the shield,
tearing it violently from his neck
as if it were a cabbage leaf.
Parthenopeus not wanting to kill him,
spares both his shield and his body,
but strikes the horse in the middle of his forehead,
knocking both down in a heap.
Alexander and Dorce
throw each other down from their horses;
they are on foot on the flowered grass
and preparing for combat.
Dryas sees the king knocked down:
"I will belie my loyalty," he says,
"if I don't help my lord."
Then he spurs his steed worth a thousand sous,
brandishing his lance.
He comes towards Parthenopeus, threatening him:
"If I find you in the saddle," he says,
"I shall strike you beneath the armpit."
Parthenopeus does not know what to do,
he sees him coming and threatening him
and he has no shield or lance.
Though to turn away would be base,
he would turn away,
even if it makes him a coward, but it is too late!
He does not want to let himself be killed foolishly
so he turns his horse with too great force.

The grass is thick, it catches the horse's feet,
and he falls right there.
Meanwhile Dryas arrives
and stops over the king,
who shouts to him
not to strike nor kill Parthenopeus.
But Dryas comes spurring,
and strikes Parthenopeus suddenly —
to great harm and great wrong
he strikes him dead through the chest.
Dryas comes towards Dorce;
having broken his spear, he draws his sword,
strikes him in the shield and shatters it.
Alexander captures him on foot.
The two of them have taken Dorce unharmed;
Alexander takes the sword
from his hand and Dorce surrenders it in faith;
running to his horse, Alexander takes that as well.

Meanwhile the king runs to the wounded man
who is lying on his back in the meadow.
The place is red with blood;
his face is discoloured,
he has lost color,
he faints from pain.
The king runs to him where he lies;
he knows him well by his face,
having seen him many times
in battles and tourneys.
The king grieves for his great lineage,
his goodness and his age;
the king laments his great nobility,
his beauty and his prowess:
"It would have pleased me greatly," he says,
"if I could have kept him alive,
if I could have taken him alive
and could have rendered him alive.
Then my war would have been finished,
my land well freed,
for he would have, very easily and swiftly,
made the host turn back."
The King of Thebes sorely laments
the noble man who is now suffering.

He is bleeding badly because of the great heat,
so the king cuts a piece from his tunic,
and binds the wound
to staunch the flow of blood.
When it is bound, the bleeding slows down
and Pathenopeus turns on his side.
As the bleeding is staunched, he comes to
and recovers somewhat from his faint.
He opens his eyes and sees the king,
weeping hard over him:
"You should," he says, "be distressed for me,
for I tell you in good faith
I would have made peace in this war
if I had been taken without a mortal wound.
I would have resolved all this trouble.
But I am dying, there is nothing to be done.
I beg you for my companion here
that you not hold him in prison;
he is a bachelor from my household,
and would bring little ransom."
Even if he had been the son of an emperor,
the king frees him for love of Parthenopeus.
Dorce faints over his lord,
weeps and grieves until he can do no more.
"Dorce," he says, "do not weep;
listen to me while I can still speak.
Don't weep, fair friend,
but return to my country.
Go straight to my mother —
you will bring her a cruel message.
If you tell her what happened to me
when she speaks with you,
I am afraid she will die straightaway.
So tell her I was wounded in the combat
and that is why I am sending you to her.
Beg her not to grieve for me.
You should not unleash her great grief
and her great rage too soon;
don't tell her the great sorrow all at once,
uncover it little by little.
You can mediate her grief for her;
speak first of the wounding,
then she will work out for herself

her great grief, her great sorrow.
Mother, (he says), you told me
I would not return alive
when I was so eager to come.
You tried to hold me back,
but that was not destined to be.
When I left my country
with my fierce and fearsome household,
that remains here distraught,
you accompanied me for one day.
We parted in a meadow,
where you remained in a faint,
like one who had been abandoned.
Dorce, tell my mother
to take a husband soon.
She has great land and great domains;
deceivers will try to steal it,
they will make war on her,
then they will lay waste her land.
Tell her to take a lord quickly,
a king or duke or rich count;
there is no king or duke from here to Troy
who would not take her with great joy,
for she is beautiful, worthy, and wise,
and she is a queen and very young.
She is queen by royal lineage,
and still very young;
she is of high birth and young —
we were almost the same age.
She was eleven when she had me,
she could not have had me any earlier than that.
She didn't seem like my mother
but my sister and I her brother.
I send greetings to my household in faith,
my seneschal in whom I have great confidence:
tell him to divide my treasure,
to give my gold to my whole household;
all my gold and my plate
he should give as a gift to my household.
Let him richly make knights
of my young men and my squires.
I gave them a lot during my life,
as long as I was a knight;

now I ask them not to forget me.
Let them cry always 'Parthenopeus,'
when they are at big events,
at tourneys and great combats;
I leave them my name as a war cry
and let them keep it from now on for love of me."
So they did and do it still;
they have this war cry in Arcadia.
The baron raises himself on his elbow
but his wound bursts open again.
Dorce sees that his lord is dead,
he is in grief, no one ever felt greater;
but yet he thinks he might have
a little respite: he fans the body
with a broad ermine sleeve
that Antigone and the queen
had given him for love,
the day she became his love.
There are four shields there:
Dorce takes two and makes a shade for him;
he takes off his own precious Eastern cloth,
puts it under his head,
along with the saddlecloth of a steed,
the only pillow he can find.
It is a gallant act, but to what purpose?
Parthenopeus does not feel cold or heat,
he no longer feels anything that is done to him,
he is rigid and cold as ice;
he is rigid, though his color is white,
and fresher than snow on a branch.
That is why Dorce hopes for a sign of life;
but when he finds the flesh cold
then he knows well that he is dead,
that there is no more comfort for him.
With Eteocles and Alexander,
who was Salamander's cousin,
you might have seen great grief there,
pulling and tearing out of hair.

Dryas has long since fled.
He did not dare stay there or wait,
because his lord was so afflicted;
he feared that he would be hanged,

because he knew that though he had been forbidden,
he had killed Parthenopeus on foot in the field.
He was wise to flee,
for if they had caught him,
or if the king had found him nearby,
he would have hanged or killed him.

The king grieves, he makes no pretense,
he laments Parthenopeus wondrously.
Finally, the fallen
Dorce, who has fainted,
comes to
and jumps up like a mad man;
he begins to mourn for his lord,
whom he loved so strongly:
"Sire," he says, "what will become of me,
when I cannot speak with you?
When your mother hears it,
she will feel a lot of grief and anger;
she will lose her position,
when she has no son or lord.
Your land will have no heir
and will be plundered frequently.
Sire, what good was your bounty
and your great nobility,
your beauty, your prowess
and the lovely riches
you possessed, lord, in your land,
when you came here for conquest.
The death that has taken you by surprise
here in this strange country
has badly discomfited me;
I shall never again see my realm."
Dorce grieves fiercely,
he weeps, cries, laments, and wails;
he strikes his face hard with his fists
and begs death to strike him.
The king feels grief and anger
for the laments and words he hears.
The men of Thebes are aroused
by the weeping and the wailing;
they come spurring towards the cries
where the combat was, all astonished.

The king calls to his barons:
"Lords, what shall we do?
Now my friend Parthenopeus
has been killed;
I expected to give my sister to him.
I am in grief, I don't want to hide it.
Dryas killed him though I forbade it;
but if I can as I intend,
I will have him hanged or killed,
burned in fire or dismembered."
They answer appropriately:
"Good lord King, let that go.
If you are grieving for Parthenopeus,
have him brought inside;
if you ever cared about him
have a sepulture made for him."
The king answers: "You are right."
The Thebans dismount from their palfreys;
they have Parthenopeus placed on a shield,
and carry him thus into the city.
They have chosen the most beautiful temple,
in which to bury him with great honor.

A messenger came racing to the army
to announce the news to the king right away.

When he heard it, King Adrastus
became sadder than he had ever been;
his heart almost broke out of grief.
He drew Polynices apart:
"My friend," he said, "what are we to do?
If we don't go after them now,
if we don't finish this war right now,
we don't deserve ever to control any territory."
He sent for all his barons,
and sought advice from those of his inner circle:
"My lords," he said, "counsel me.
For God's sake, I beg you, grant it to me
that we take the fight to those

11252 The version of the *Roman de Thèbes* in MS C inserts at this point a long episode recounting the violent death of Capaneus, struck down by the gods as he seeks to climb the walls of Thebes.

through whom we've sustained this terrible damage:
we've lost Parthenopeus,
the best sword and shield we ever had.
If you advise me to do so,
before noon tomorrow
I'll have my troops prepare
to ride out against the enemy in battle."
The barons, speaking with one voice, said,
"In our opinion, that's the best thing to do;
anyone who fails you by refusing to be part of this
should be denounced as a traitor for as long as he lives."
Early the next morning, as dawn was breaking,
King Adrastus arose from bed
and secretly summoned his warriors
to dress and arm themselves quickly.
The king armed himself first,
together with one thousand knights;
the rest of the army followed suit,
and then they all rode out in proper formation.
Drums, horns, and trumpets sounded,
marvelous brass choirs;
the mountains and valleys resounded
with the hue and cry as well as with horn calls;
everyone within the city walls sounded the alarm
in response to the noise being made by the Greeks.
Out came Eteocles:
out from the city streets, far out into the fields,
near a beautiful meadow, beside a pond,
and on to the cypress fountain;
a full twenty thousand, and even more, came with him.
On against them came King Adrastus.
Once the two armies caught sight of each other,
they made a great show of being ready to fight;
what a sight, to see the army stir itself to battle,
to see the knights racing back and forth!
Each knight called loudly for his squire
to prepare his arms;
they laced on helmets, donned hauberks,
and brought out their trenchant blades.
If you could have seen them attach the banners
and pennons to their lances,
watched each knight attach his shield to his arm
and grasp his steel sword,

you'd certainly remember this fierce company,
so eager to do battle.
All the plain shimmered and shone
with the reflection of all that brilliant armor;
when the sun's rays struck the polished metal,
the entire field gleamed.
Polynices and his troop,
extremely well armed
and all mounted for battle,
galloped ahead quickly and in closed ranks.
They were twenty thousand and more;
Polynices was their duke.
and Eteocles had banished them
from his land and disinherited them.
My lords," said Polynices, "now we'll see
who will do well when it really counts:
whoever wishes to earn a fief from me,
now's the time for him to come conquer it!"
They immediately spurred their mounts,
having them wheel about on grassy field;
indeed, they soon had them leaping,
so that they made the earth shake.
As they charged, they raised their lances into position,
then they struck hard against the shields of their opponents:
the lances shattered with a great, cracking sound,
their shards and fragments flying up into the air.
Among the attackers and the defenders,
more than two hundred fell from their steeds,
but as soon as they had remounted,
they began dealing great blows with their naked swords.
There you would have seen, lying on the plain,
so many dead horses, so many exhausted bodies,
so many trunks of bodies, sundered feet, exposed entrails,
so many heads cut off below the helmet's neckpiece!
Great was the lamenting and moaning,
and the dreadful, dolorous cries
of the wounded who lay there dying,
as well as of those who were still battling.
A knight named Nestor,
son of the duke of Châtillon,

11348 **son of the Duke of Châtillon** *filz fu al duc de Chasteillon*: The Dukes of Châtillon were a noble lineage of Champagne during the eleventh and

had left his native land and come to this war
seeking to perform chivalrous deeds;
his arrival was by no means shabby,
as he had brought with him a retinue of a thousand men.
He was a very young nobleman:
only twenty years old but very handsome;
if he only believed in God and God's power,
a more attractive knight would never have borne a lance.
He had a well-shaped head and a long face,
a shapely, well-apportioned nose,
a strong, big-boned body
but slim in the waist.
As for his equipment, let me say this:
the king couldn't command better for his own use;
the excellent hauberk was made of very finely woven chain mail
with well-shaped flaps;
he had a light but strong helmet,
which could protect him well from death;
and a good, very sharp sword—
none worth more in the entire army;
he carried his lance in his right fist,
very handsome to look at.
He had a fine ivory shield,
and was seated on a long-haired warhorse
quite swift of foot—
strong, rapid, and reddish-brown in color;
its caparison, bearing Nestor's emblem, was of brown silk,
imported from Thessaly:
the animal was well covered down to the ground.
Now Nestor spurred his steed, loosening his hold on the bridle,
and Alexis saw him coming;
They charged hard at each other,
constantly whipping and spurring their mounts,
and each landed great blows on the other's shield.
Count Nestor didn't miss his mark at all:
he drove the soul out of his opponent's body.
The dead man's nephew saw this; he gave the unprotected Nestor
a great blow, without first challenging him,
in the middle of his chest, under the nipple,

---

twelfth centuries with connections to the First Crusade (including the Pope who preached it), the implied reference to which here and elsewhere in the text is designed to serve as a putative exemplar for the *Roman de Thèbes*.

so that he knocked him backward from his horse, dead.
When Polynices saw that,
he galloped toward him at full speed,
astride his swift charger;
with a fine, sharp sword
he struck Agenor at the point of his helmet,
splitting him in half, right down to his saddle bow.
In the midst of the battle lines such was the congestion
that no one could demonstrate personal valor
however brave and renowned he might be,
nor stand out from those around him;
lances splintered, shields split,
and the archers let loose volleys of arrows.
Polynices, riding at the head of his knights,
led them into battle;
Eteocles, on the other side,
recognized them from the moment he saw them.
The two approach to within two acres of each other;
one of them, whichever it may be, will soon know grief.
Both now, without further ado,
rain down great blows on each other,
charging fiercely;
now the king misses, and the other runs him through,
right through the body, with his sword;
throwing him down from his horse, Hoarywhite.
Polynices, when he sees
that his brother has fallen,
and is mortally wounded,
dismounts quickly;
he does this because he knows
that the king cannot survive his wound.
He goes to him and looks at the wound,
and at the crimson blood that spurts forth from it.
He takes pity on his brother—he can't help it—
and goes to comfort him:
he hugs him tightly,
kisses his eyes and his face,
and then says to him, "my dear lord and brother,
it was an evil hour when our mother bore us;
now your pride has brought you death,

11393 **Agenor** *Agenor*: Not the same Agenor as the Theban warrior mentioned in vv. 5948ff, above.

and there's no way out of that now."
Eteocles was extremely angry
and deeply upset in his spirit;
he knows very well that he must die,
and that no physician could possibly heal him.
He was full of evil ideas,
and wanted above all to take his brother's life:
secretly grasping his sword,
he carefully composes himself a little;
he raises the flaps of the white hauberk,
and thrusts his steel blade into Polynices's side.
Polynices realizes he's been wounded;
he falls, sprawled out on the ground,
and says, "Brother, why have you killed me?
You know very well that you've done wrong here.
I dismounted to come to you in good faith,
out of pity for you;
now you have finished our war:
neither you nor I will claim this land."
He can no longer speak; he looks at his brother
and dies there, his soul leaving his body;
the other now begins to sob:
whether he wants to or not, he must die;
the brothers have certainly been enemies,
and now they've killed each other.
When King Adrastus sees
that Polynices has fallen,
and that both brothers are dead,
there's no good that can possibly comfort him;
"My lords," he says, "I don't know what to say;
from now on I care nothing for my life.
If we don't assail them now,
we'll never in our lives defeat them.
Follow me to the city,
and let's throw at them everything we've got!"

They all answered in one voice
that they would do what he asked,
for they knew very well, thanks to the predictions of their oracles,
that they were all destined to die.
He led and they followed him,
spurring on in a full cavalry charge;
but their opponents from within the city now fled,

getting away as fast as they could,
with the others hard on their heels,
going all out to kill them.
The Greeks were the invaders,
before whom their enemies beat a hasty retreat,
fleeing as fast as they could back within the walls.
The besiegers pursue them as long and far as they can,
chasing them right to the city gates
and immediately assaulting them;
but the Thebans battled their way into the city
displaying great valor,
and the gates slammed shut behind them,
tightly closed and strongly barred.
Once they are safely inside the city,
together they mount the walls,
carrying stones and sharp-pointed spears,
swords, lances, and shields;
they take up positions at the embrasures,
looking down through them at the troops
who are trying so hard to attack them;
but from above they rain down death on their assailants,
who now bring up ladders and climb them,
landing some nasty blows on the defenders,
who repel them, hurling them down to the ground.
Whoever takes that fall will not be able to get up again:
others come crashing down behind them
and they pile up, one on top of another.
Anyone watching would have seen many great blows struck,
and many a fine knight meet his end;
those atop the walls put up an intense fight,
killing and striking down the others,
thanks to their being above and the others below;
they struck relentlessly at the massed troop below
until they had felled them once and for all;
a thousand died there unshriven.
The besiegers regrouped and attacked again,
and the defenders again struck back,
killing many and disabling more;
those struck down would arise no more.
There's no other way to describe the attacking army
but as men delivered up to martyrdom;
the city's defenders, from its walls,
have killed so many of the besiegers,

and corpses lie in such heaps at the base of the wall—
and as far away as an arrow could fly—
that no matter in what direction such an arrow was shot
it would land on a knight
who was either dead, wounded,
or thrown from his horse to the ground.

When those within see how the Greeks
in all their pride have been laid low,
they all rush out from the city
and fall on them at once.
So brutally do they slaughter them
that they're all dead except for three:
one of those three was Adrastus
a second was Capaneus,
and the third was a knight of Greek birth
who had a deep body wound.
When these three realized that they alone survived—
just two of them besides the king himself—
they withdrew a little way from the killing field;
the wounded Greek addressed the king:
"My lord," he said, "I'm going to go
and bring the bad news to the rest."
Said Adrastus, "Go, my friend;
tell the whole story in my land."
He mounts and spurs his warhorse,
and comes racing to Argos;
he tells the chilling news to the Greek women;
you can imagine how little they like such tidings!
The messages he brings them
cause great pain and sorrow:
the entire army has been wiped out,
with no one left alive
except the king and Capaneus;
he's the third; no one else survived.
The women suffer the most profound grief
when they hear that their lords
have been defeated in battle,
and all destroyed, as the messenger says.
They nearly die of fear
and are entirely distraught from their great sorrow.
Throughout the city
their boundless mourning resounds,

as wives lament their husbands
and mothers their sons,
sisters their brothers,
and daughters their fathers.
The blood fled from their faces, transforming them
into creatures of ghostly pallor.
They wept and keened hysterically;
no way could they restrain themselves
from grieving and lamenting
over the loss of their dear ones.
They wring their hands, break their rings
of beautiful silver and gold,
tear at their hair and pummel their faces,
expressing their sorrow in every possible manner.
Some four thousand faint dead away
and never recover:
they're the lucky ones,
whose souls have left their bodies.
At Thebes, meanwhile, they experienced both joy and sorrow,
albeit their happiness didn't last long;
they rejoiced over all the dead Greeks,
but profoundly mourned their fallen comrades,
whom they gathered up, prepared properly for burial,
and interred with the great honor due them.
By contrast, wild dogs fed on the Greek dead,
along with hunting hounds, vultures, and crows;
the Thebans had no desire whatsoever to bury any of them,
choosing instead to have them treated shamefully,
because they had no fear
that the slaughtered Greeks would ever be avenged;
they firmly believed the king to have died
along with all the other Greeks.

There came a day when all the Thebans assembled
in order to choose a new king for the city.
They chose a king from among them
by careful consideration and discussion:
it was old Creon whom they crowned,
for they could not find in the entire city
a man of higher birth
nor of greater power.
He was of the royal lineage,
but was not given to great arrogance;

he was also a much praised knight
and a worthy, noble judge—
and let's not forget that high lineage of his.
They couldn't find a man of equal rank and qualities
to choose as king,
so they crowned him most solemnly.
There was great joy over this in the city,
but it certainly didn't last long.
For meanwhile, the women of Argos,
who, as I've told you, were mourning their loved ones,
when they had finally lamented them long enough,
convened a parliament:
they couldn't bear their situation any longer,
and for advice they proposed to seek the assistance
of the daughters of King Adrastus.
So they mounted the stairs leading to the royal palace,
and found there the two sisters
to whom the king had given as their lords
the two vassals whom he had heard fighting
beneath the portico in the atrium,
and went to separate.
It pleased him greatly to retain them as his vassals,
since each of them was a king's son:
they had in fact come to him in order to serve him.
Adrastus gave one of his daughters to Tydeus,
who was Duke and King of Calydon;
then gave the other to Polynices,
Eteocles's brother.
These two warriors led the companies
now lying dead on the plains outside Thebes;
these two were in the battle,
now both are dead, without a doubt.
The two sisters feel completely abandoned,
now that they are severed forever from their lords;
they weep, proclaiming their misery
and regretting that they're still alive.
When all the women have gathered,
they number more than twenty thousand;
the assembly of these poor, sad souls

11602 **so they crowned him most solemnly** *molt hautement l'ont coroné*: The description of the choice and coronation of Creon as King of Thebes does not appear in the *Thebaid.*

lasts all day.
The consensus of the meeting
is that they will go together, all of them on foot,
right to Thebes to seek the bodies
of their dead loved ones
who've been abandoned in the roads
to be eaten by birds and wild dogs.
Completely barefooted and with disheveled hair
they now take their way.
The great host of women moves along,
but not very quickly,
since they have not been trained for such expeditions;
they suffer because of their bare feet.
On they go, over the hills and through the valleys,
mournful and beside themselves.
They had already traveled for three days
when they passed through a great forest,
and found some plains on the other side
that were very beautiful, but stretched far into the distance.
Then they undertook to speed up,
to increase their pace:
the company proceeded at a rapid clip
for as long as the plain lasted.
Now they looked far ahead,
toward a hill next to a meadow,
and suddenly they saw two knights
advancing very quickly on their horses:
one was King Adrastus,
and the other Capaneus;
they were coming from the battle.
No one else had escaped,
except the king and his companion,
who now spurred toward the women.

Adrastus saw them first,
his eye caught by the women's white garments.
The king said to Capaneus,
"Look up the road:
you can see a whiteness,
greater than any man has ever seen.
Are they sheep, my good friend,
who make the whole countryside shimmer?
Or are they girls, all set to dance,

who've come to play in this meadow?"
Even as the king was speaking,
he came quite near to the women;
his two daughters had moved ahead,
because they recognized the king very well,
from his eyes and his white beard,
from his nose and his noble mien.
Then they began to cry,
expressing their great grief,
and all the others in this female host did the same:
the result was a great outpouring of shared sorrow.
When King Adrastus, having recognized his daughters right away,
hears this commotion,
a great sadness imprints itself on his heart,
and from that sadness he faints.
When he recovers consciousness,
he exclaims to himself,
"God, I am such a wretch;
It's terribly wrong that I should still be alive!
Why wasn't I killed the other day,
when I was thrown off my horse
and lost my entire army?"
Then he drew his naked blade:
he wanted to thrust it into his body.
Capaneus, seeing this, goes to take the sword from him;
he wrests it from the king's fist
and tosses it far away down the road.
Now the king faints from sorrow yet a third time;
he can't help himself: he collapses.

I confess I don't know how to express adequately
the cries and lamentations
of the women, or the way
their grieving mingles with the king's.
He camped there that night
with the women he'd met;
he spoke with them all night,
counseling them as best he could.
The next morning, he took to the road again,
but now he set out back to Thebes.
He wanted to bring the women with him,
in order to show them their dead,
so he led them straight back, retracing the path

along which he had come the day before.
The troop of women became very exhausted—
so worn out, in fact,
that it couldn't go any further,
no matter in which direction, forward or backward.
The king became very upset
when he saw his troop stuck in place;
it didn't seem to him a wise decision
for the women to set up camp there.
He looked to the right, across the plains,
and saw great armed companies approaching:
mounted knights and infantrymen,
with lances and banners,
they came on accompanied by a great, roaring sound:
the noise made by such a large company.
Their helmets shone in every direction
as did their shields, painted with the device of a lion;
the countryside glittered
thanks to the armor worn by this troop;
and the earth beneath them trembled
even as the countryside resounded.
Whoever leads that army is certainly very powerful,
fierce and ready for combat:
it's the Duke of Athens.
There was never another such army assembled,
either by pagans or Christians,
out of power or arrogance,
such as this duke had raised,
in order to go destroy a country:
he was out to punish a king who was his vassal
who had broken his oath of loyalty.
This king ought to have held his realm from the duke,
and have paid him the tribute owed his lord;
but he didn't wish to attend the duke's court
nor to hold his land from him,
for which failings the duke was on his way to conquer the offender
and to take his land;
he wanted to overthrow him, even burn him alive—
throw him in prison or kill him outright.
The duke rode along proudly,
leading well his army and all his followers;
King Adrastus examined them carefully,
but, not knowing who they were, also fearfully.

The duke rode well ahead of his men,
seated on a steel-grey horse;
as he approached, Adrastus
finally recognized him, and rode toward him
quickly leaving behind his travelling companions:
nearing the duke, he begged him for aid and comfort.
When he had come quite near to the duke
he dismounted and went on foot;
in fact, he ran the rest of the way
and threw himself humbly at the duke's feet.
When the duke sees Adrastus kneeling in this way,
he in turn got down from his horse,
greatly surprised by what he had there,
since he didn't know his suppliant.
King Adrastus fell to the earth,
grabbing onto the duke that he might seek his aid;
he cried out humbly for compassion,
all the while crying tenderly.
"Sire," he said, "for the sake of God, have pity now!
I'm sure you have heard a lot
about the besieging army and the great confrontations at Thebes,
about the battles and grand melees,
and about the suffering undergone
by the residents of the city of Thebes,
as well as the slaughter of our Greeks attacking it—
they're all dead except for just three survivors.
I'm one of those, my lord; now just a poor wretch,
whom they call a king.
Two feuding brothers were the cause
of that monumental slaughter:
Polynices and Eteocles, Oedipus's sons.
The Greeks battled on behalf of one brother,
the defenders of Thebes for the other,
who played havoc with the Greeks.
For the sake of God, help me now in my great need:
men call me the lord Adrastus;
let me tell you why you should come to my aid,
why you should have mercy on me.

11768 **nearing the duke, he begged him for aid and comfort** *al duc en vient, mercie li crie*: In MS C the Duke of Athens is enlisted by the daughters of Adrastus—not by the old king himself—to have the Greek dead properly buried.

Look up there, atop that mountain:
there are women there suffering enormous sorrow;
lamenting and distraught,
wretched and crushed by grief
for their loved ones, all of whom are dead.
They're going to Thebes, at great hardship,
to see and then to bury them,
and by burying them to protect their bodies
from being eaten by dogs and pigs.
That's all they want: to bury their dead.
The Thebans won't let them do it;
I know very well that they will forbid it.
That's why I'm appealing to your goodness
and your great nobility:
give these women back their loved ones,
slaughtered by the Thebans;
avenge them on their enemies,
and show your compassion for wretches such as we."
The noble duke heard everything Adrastus said;
it prompted him to feel great pity for them.
Taking Adrastus by the hand,
he raised him up from the ground:
"My lord king," he said, "do get up;
you may have whatever you desire;
if the Thebans refuse to give you back your dead,
they'll suffer great devastation."
He called two knights,
named Girart and Engelier:
"My lords," he said, "come here;
carry the message I'll give you as quickly as you can,
right to the King of Thebes,
old Creon, who's behaving like a fool;
tell him he is immediately to return
the bodies of the Greeks to their women folk,
and allow them to be buried honorably.
If he doesn't surrender the bodies right away,
his city will be destroyed,
and he himself will be killed."
Then King Adrastus, the Greek, said,
"Is Creon then King of Thebes?"
"Yes, indeed, my friend;" said the duke,
"the truth is that they made him king;
the inhabitants of the city decided

that Creon should be placed on the throne."
Then the messengers mounted,
and got underway on their journey.
They galloped on at full speed,
coming straight to Thebes.
They found King Creon,
and presented their message to him.
First they greeted him courteously,
and then said their piece:
"Oh, King, warmest greetings
from the Duke of Athens.
The noble duke, your neighbor,
has sent us here to you,
to tell you to give up all the Greek bodies
now lying outside your walls.
You should understand that if you do not surrender the bodies right away,
the duke and his army will be on your doorstep;
they will destroy your city,
and kill you."
When King Creon heard all this,
he became extremely enraged:
"Underlings," he said, "get out of here
before I completely lose my head!
If you don't disappear very soon,
it'll be your heads that are lost.
I'll arrange to have you severely tortured,
then burnt alive or dismembered.
Tell your lord the duke
that even at the cost of his entire realm
he could never have the bodies of the Greeks who died here;
I won't surrender them, no matter what he attempts.
Let him go take care of his own cities,
his castles, and his redoubts;
as for this place, I'll defend it well against him:
if he comes here, I won't run away from him."
So the messengers turned back;
returning to the duke, they told him everything that had happened.
Now the duke began to get mad;
his anger blazed, his rage boiled over:
he commanded his army to arm itself quickly
and get ready for battle;
first of all he donned his armor
right in the midst of his knights.

All the rest of his troops followed suit,
and then they rode, bracing for combat,
and the noise of the trumpets sounding the charge
resounded through the countryside.
The duke led his cohorts right to Thebes,
where they quickly surrounded its walls.
King Adrastus followed,
guiding the army of women,
all of whom, like the Athenians,
now organized themselves into serried ranks.
The duke proceeded very valiantly
to assault the city with all his forces,
who, aided by a siege engine,
collapsed the city walls on all sides.
What a sight it was: the women clambered up,
attacking the walls with steel hammers,
or clawing at them frantically with their nails,
making more than one hundred holes in them ;
they didn't care who might kill them,
or might do them harm;
they fought with great ferocity.
The other assailants had great sympathy for them,
crying uncontrollably about the women
even as they strove to carry out their assault.
Now came Capaneus,
spurred on by his great anger:
"God will never protect them," he cried,
"nor will he save even one of them
from giving up the ghost thanks to our attack."
He attempted to climb the walls,
but as he climbed toward the top
a boulder thrown from above struck him in the forehead,
and so smashed in his face
that it toppled him down, dead.
The Duke of Athens, so valiant himself,
shouts encouragements to all his followers:
"What are these knights doing, my barons?
You can be sure of this: we're going to take the city!
Come on—your fathers were great knights; be like them!
Make sure Thebes has no wall left in one piece!"
And so they did, with great strength,
and supported by the infantry.
Those within the walls vigorously defended themselves,

while those outside strove to take the city.
The duke was a superb knight,
and his assault on those within was that of a seasoned warrior;
he fought like a lion,
the model of the effective fighter;
he constantly urged on his men
and threatened the Thebans,
brandishing his sword
and waving its point back and forth;
he leads the attack against those within the walls,
while inspiring his own army to great deeds.
The attackers' mobile turrets were on the other side of the city,
and the city's defenders weren't paying attention to them;
but those manning them have so knocked and scratched
as to puncture that strong wall;
they made holes in it from their side,
causing the fall of one whole section.
A crossbowman standing in the city's tower
was the first person to see this;
he began to shout loudly
that the attackers have now come very close to the city:
"Look! See the walls collapsing,
and the besiegers entering the city!"
The noble duke, when he heard that,
pushed forward strongly right to the hole made by the mobile turrets;
"The fire! bring the fire!," he starts to yell,
and then spreads it throughout the city,
engulfing all the inhabitants,
who now suffered the great agony of being burnt alive.
The falling towers
and the collapse of the high walls
would bring great sadness to any spectator
who saw it happen.
The duke destroyed it all:
he ordered the walls and the towers completely leveled,
had the men of the town imprisoned,
and gave orders that they be well guarded:
he proposes to lead them to Athens
with him, when he's ready to head back there.
All those who had resisted surrendering
he commands to be taken at once,
and drawn and quartered,
burnt alive, or otherwise killed in his presence.

He ordered a thorough search for the two brothers who started this war,
whom he wished to behold, and then bury.
his men searched and searched until they found them,
entangled among all the other corpses.
King Creon had refused to surrender
so the duke had his head cut off while he watched.
He then turned over to the women the bodies
that had been rotting away outside the city walls;
the women wept bitterly over them
and voiced their sorrow over their loss with great pathos;
then the duke, a man of honor,
had them honorably buried.
He had a search mounted for the two brothers,
in order that he might see and then bury them;
they looked so long that they finally found them,
in a heap with the other corpses.
The duke had a tomb made for them,
and has his clergy perform a great memorial service;
the brothers are placed in two coffins,
and buried with appropriate ceremony.
But the bodies wouldn't permit
the earth ever to hold them;
they were found above ground,
as if they'd never been buried;
and the corpses actually wanted to fight it out,
each one trying to knock the other one over.
This marvel was observed
by a large crowd that assembled there.
The duke, thunderstruck,
ordered that the bodies be burned:
he had them carried to two separate high piles of kindling,
to avoid any further contact between them;
as soon as the bodies were set on fire, however,
great flames spurted out from the two pyres;
each one flared against the other, making it appear
as though they wished to fight once more.
When the bodies were finally reduced to ashes,
the duke ordered them to be taken
and sealed in two separate vessels;
then he undertook to watch them,
to see if the vessels tried to move
and attempted to continue fighting.
But the urns couldn't hold onto their contents:

which wanted above all to escape:
compelled by the ashes, the urns sprang at each other,
giving every appearance of mutual hatred.
The noble duke stared at them,
recognizing what an incredible event this was;
then he commanded the two piles of cinders to be extracted
and sealed together in a single tomb;
and thus they were reunited, dust to dust:
their destiny, eternal vengeance.
Once he had had the brothers' remains locked away,
the duke had no wish to stay longer in Thebes;
he took his prisoners with him,
and didn't stop until he reached Athens.
The women also turned back,
under the leadership of Adrastus;
having had their grievances redressed
quickly, and to their satisfaction;
nonetheless, their great lamentations persisted,
as did their weeping and wailing,
over the loss of their loved ones,
dead and gone at Thebes.
Their grief would continue, as would their expressions of it,
for as long as they lived.
So ended the war
over who should rule Thebes.
This was how the great and famous battle
for the city came to its conclusion,
as did the animosity, so vicious and finally mortal
between the two brothers,
which left the kingdom without an heir,
as well as ravaged and laid waste.
Many were the crises, the torments,
and the maledictions that descended on their children,
which their father had bequeathed to them,
prophesying them beforehand.
Therefore, here's my final advice to you: "Take good care
that you move through life justly and with moderation;
do nothing that goes against nature,
lest you come to a bitter end."

EXPLICIT HISTORIA DE THEBES

Appendix: Passages from the Original Text, *Le Roman de Thèbes*

Polynices's Journey and the Storm
(vv. 674–97)

Tant chivalcha par lez montaignes,
Par les combes et par lez plaignes,
Et par chemyns et par sentiers,
Set jors chevalcha touz entiers.
Joust un meere vait chevalchant,
Dont l'eve vait fort tempestant:
Nuls ne set ne ne poet counter
Quels ele esteit ne porpenser.
Tout la noet plut et gela,
Gresle cheit et neif vola,
Et corurent li doze vent
Par tout le monde a lor talent.
Onc nes poet tenir Eolus,
Qui ert lour sires et lour dus;
Parmy cel aer vont torneiant,
Combatent sei et vont bruiant.
De totes parz tone forment,
Fouldres cheeient espessement,
Chancelant vait li firmamenz,
Et la terre qui est dedenz;
Li grant arbre sont esracié,
Et li petit tout debrisié,
Li flueve sont tout fors eissu
Et par les champs tout acoru.

Tydeus Ambushed
(vv. 1701–7)

Cil se defent come leons;
Mais il est sols, si vait lassant,
Et cil le vont fort enpressant.
1704 Jouste vit un haute rochier,
Qui molt ert bons a guerreier;
Sus y monta, lez oilz veiant:
Or orreis mais bataille grant.

(vv. 1762–73)
Il saut amont et puis aval,
Envaïst les come vassal;
1764 De touz parz lez abat morz,
Par vasselage et par efforz.
Et quant li autre se restreinent,
Pas avant autre amont le meinent;
1768 Il le quiderent amont prendre;
Cil entent fort a sei defendre,
Et neporoc gaires nes dote,
Aincés les ruse, aval les bote.
1772 Molt grant bataille lor tendeit,
Por la roche qu'il defendeit.

Monster Devil
(vv. 2848–69)

2848 Figurot sei en lieu de vielle,
Et ert tant vert come d'ierre foille;
Chiere ot hidouse et effreé,
Bien ot de nés une cotee;
2852 Les denz ot granz et retornees,
Jusque detrés le col tornees;
La dent qui li saut fors la bouche
Jusque detrais le col li touche;
2856 Les [oils] ot rouges come lepart:
Onc homme ne vit tant laide regarde;
Li surcil que sont desus
Vos closissent trestout un us.
2860 Mais uncor est maior merveille:
Toute se covre de l'oreille;
Les oreilles sont grantz et lees

Et velues et effreés.
Les bras ot gros come uns trés,
La bouche neire et tout le nés;
La main ad grant et les deis lons,
Les ongles semblent de leons:
Cui ele ferra de la main
Ja ne mangera mais de pain.

Jocasta and Eteocles Undertake the Mission Refused by Men (vv. 3886–905)

Jocaste fu miere le rei:
Son filz acole et trait vers sei.
Por amor Dieu mercie li crie,
Qu'a son friere face partie:
« Filz, fait elle, por Dieu merci,
Creie ceus barons que tu veiez ci.
Ja ne te forsconseilleront,
Fai ceo que il te loeront.
Ore ont Greu ceste ville assise;
Aincés avras ta barbe grise,
Si tant te poeiz deffendre,
Que ja s'en torgent sanz le prendre.
Quant tu ne poez touz sols tenir,
Mielz te vient oue autre partir
Que tout coveitier et voleir,
Et tout perdre sanz rien aveir.
Oue tout iceo tu li juras;
Si tu onques de tei cure as,
Ne te parjurer ja por terre,
Ne por coitïé d'onor querre ».

Jocasta and her Daughters Undertake the Minimum Refused by Men (vv. 4094–107)

Jocaste fu et proz et sage:
« Jo irai, fait ele, el message;
Mes dous filles merrai o mei,
Quant vos tuit en falez le rei;
Et por sofraite de prodomes
Iert cist messages faiz par domes.
—Granz est, fait Otes, li periz:
Ne nos guarreit ja vostre fiz.

Mais ore alez al parlement,
Vos et voz filles senglement:
4104 Se il agreent ceste fin,
Apreisment sei jusqu'a cel pin;
Entresque la iron nos bien:
Ne cuit que nos i cremon rien ».

Partenopeus and Antigone
(vv. 4192–209)

4192 Partonopex fu l'un des treis:
Riches homme fu, d'Archaide reis;
Molt fu sages et bien corteis,
Vestuz a guise de Franceis.
4196 Un mul chevalchot espaneis,
De pur bealté semblot bien reis:
Soz ciel n'ad dame, s'ele li veit,
Que molt vers lui ne se soupleit.
4200 Antigoné, quant ele le vit,
Forment en son cuer li covit.
Rien ne coveita tant come lui;
Molt fuissent bien jousté il dui,
4204 Car il dui sont bien d'un aage,
D'une bealté et d'une parage.
Partonopex vit la pucele:
Soz ciel n'en ot un tant bele;
4208 S'il la covit, ne m'en merveil,
Soz ciel n'eüst tant gent pareil.

Antigone's Answer
(vv. 4237–60)

Partonopex pas ne s'oblie,
Molt li preie qu'ele seit s'amie.
Ele fu molt et proz et sage,
4240 Al chivaler dist son corage:
« Par Dieu, ceo respont la pucele,
Cest amor serreit trop isnele.
Pucele sui, fille de rei:
4244 Legierment amer ne dei,
Ne dei amer par lecherie
Dont l'en puisse dire folie.
Issi deit l'en prier berchieres

Et ces autres femmes legieres.
Ne vous conois mais ne vous vi,
Ne mais ore que vous vei ci;
Se or vos done d'amer parole,
Bien me poez tenir pur fole.
Por ce nel die, celer nel quier,
Ne vous eüsse forment cher,
Si esteiez de tiel linage
Que vous fussez de mon parage,
Et ceo fust chose destiné
Que vous feusse a femme doné.
Car beals estes sur toute gent,
Onc ne vi mais homme tant gent ».

Ecphrasis of the Chariot
(vv. 5144–59)

El curre fu ceste peinture,
Vulcans l'entailla par grant cure.
Et a pierres et a esmals
Fu faitz darriere li frontals,
Et enlevees les sept ars:
Gramaire y est peinte oue ses pars,
Dialetique oue argumenz,
Rethorique oue jugemenz;
L'abaque tint Arimetique,
Par la gamme chante Musique:
Peint y est diatessaron,
Dyapenté, dyapason;
Une verge ot Geometrie,
Un autre en ot Astronomie:
L'une en terre mette sa mesure,
L'autre es esteilles ad sa cure.

Ismene's Lament
(vv. 6957–72)

« Athes, beals sire, tu ne m'oz?
Ovre tes oilz, por quei les clos?
Ceo es Ismeine que parole.
Maleüré, bien sui fole!
Il ne m'entent ne ne me veit,
En la biere le sent tout freit.

Morz est Ates, ceo est damages:
Mar fu veüz tis vasselages;
Avant tes jors gis mort yci:
A l'alme face Diex merci!
Morz est Ates, tout veirement:
Molt as poi usé ton jovent.
Ces toens beals oils, car les ovrez!
Ore les mangeront colovrez.
Come mar fust ceste char tendre!
Ore deviendra povre cendre ».

The Trial of Dares the Red
(vv. 9979–9999)

« Ore parlez oue mei, sire Alis.
Por qu'avez fait le rei cest don,
Qui jointes mains estes sis hom?
Ditez le mei, nel laissiez mie.
—Certes, pur force et pur aïe.
—Et a i plus? Dites avant.
—Oïl s'il vous pleist, unquore tant:
Que il me guart si come sei,
Et autresi lui come mei.
—Et a l'heure qu'il vous faudra,
La sue fei vous mentira,
S'il vous defie, que ferreiz?
La fiance si vous tendreiz?
—Quidez que li tienge fei,
Des qu'il ne la tiendra a mei?
Dahé qui s'en entremettra,
Des qu'il a mei ne la tendra!
—Par fei, li reis desfia Daire;
Et de s'amour ne sot que faire,
Des que li reis le defiot,
Mais torna s'en come il ainz pot ».

(vv. 10008–24)

Et si vous voil jeo aprés dire,
Ceo sachez bien, que [si] li sire
Meine son homme estre lei,
Il ne lui deit puis nule fei;
En es l'iure qu'il le defie,

Si Deus me gart et beneïe,
Fei ne fiance ne lui deit:
S'il le purchace, il ad bon dreit;
Des qu'il li falt, oue tiel se tienge,
Si il ad busoign quil maintienge.
—Par Dieu, sire Otes, fait Alis,
Molt par y ad Daires mespris.
Puis que taunt avenu esteit
Que il par mal del rei partit,
Car attendist ou deux jors ou treis,
Que il deüst bien faire un meis,
Ou sevals jusque l'endemain.

(vv. 10036–39)

Et si li reis tant nel preisast
Que dreit faire ne lui deignast,
Idonc peüst estre ainz tens
A ceo qu'il ad fait trop a tens.

(vv. 10050–57)

Et ceo est ore bien chose certe,
Il ne poet pas rendre la perte,
N'a mon seignur rendre sez genz,
Dont y ad pris plus de dous cenz.
Et tout sont pris por ycest plait
Que Daires ad basti et fait,
Et la traïson qu'il ad fait
Li serra mais touz jor retraite. »

(vv. 10088–95)

« Li reis laidi molt son baron,
Quant le feri de son baston
Et li dona, ceo oi retraire,
Tout plein congié de li mal faire:
Si cil le fist come il ainz pot,
Puis que il le congié en ot,
Vie ne membre n'ad forfait,
Ne traïson il n'i ad fait ».

(vv. 10111–24)

« Si li reis son baron laidit,
Daires se tut et le suffrit,
Ne le rei a raison ne myst,
Ne de ceo dreit ne li requyst;
Ne il le rei ne defia,
Ne li reis dreit ne li vea.
Il ert son homme et li reis sire:
Por tençon ne pur un poi d'ire
Ne deüst pas, ceo m'est vis, quere
Come sis sires perdist terre,
Et certes issi freschement
Querre son desheritement.
Dreit deüst offrer et dreit prendre,
Et puis quarant jors attendre ».

Jocasta's Intervention in the Trial
(vv. 10189–200)

« Filz, fait elle, mielz vaut mesure
Que jugement ne que dreiture.
Cest feloun a dreit destruireies,
Mais trop grant damage y avreiez:
Il ad parenz que lui vengeront
Et venger assez le purront.
Tes enemys veiez devant tei
Et, par la fei que je te dei,
Un noit ça enz lez mettront:
Si li voilent, ja n'i faudront.
Fait plait oue lui, et si m'en crei;
Seürté doinst de porter fei ».

Battle and Drowning
(vv. 10753–60)

En la riviere, par le pree,
La bataille est molt aduré.
Lungement manais ces hastes frusshent,
Et cil escu fendent et freussent;
D'escuz veïssiez tant astele,
Tant chevalier chaïr de sele,

Et tant bon cop doner a mort
Et enfoundrer tant hauberc fort!

(vv. 10801–20)

En champ se defendissent fort,
Mais ils morent de double mort.
Al gué veïssez maint neier,
Morir de glaive et tresbucher;
Cil qui estait y muert de plaie,
Et qui fuit a noer essaie,
Mais puis qu'il vienent al parfont,
Li pesant hauberc que ils ont
As funs aval les chaitis traient,
Sanz socours que ja puis y aient.
Puis qu'il y sont plungié la enz,
Del resourdre amont est nïenz:
Al funz aval l'ewe les emble.
Amont flotent hastes de tremble,
Et molt y flotent entreseignes
Et gomfanons et escuz peinz;
Li cheval ne sevent que facent,
Car les rednes les piez lor lacent:
Plungeant vont aval oue le cours,
Illoec neient oue lour seignurs.

Grief of Women
(vv. 11554–59)

Par les rues de la cité
En font duel molt demesuré:
Les dames pleinent lour marriz
Et les mieres pleignent lour filz,
Et les sorurs plaignent lour friers,
Et les filles plainent lor pieres.

(vv. 11566–73)

Tortent lor puinz, fruissent aneals
Qui sount d'or et d'argent molt beals,
Rumpent lor crins, batent lour chiere,
Grant doel fount en toutes maniers.
Tiels quatre mil se pasmerent

Que onques puis ne releverent:
Mort sount les benurez,
Les almes ount des cors sevrez.

Women's Attack on Thebes
(vv. 11902–11)

Donc veïssez femmes ramper,
Oue mails d'acier les murs falser;
As ungles esracent forment,
Pertus y fierent plus de cent;
Ne lour chaleit quis oscist
Ne qui unques mal lour fist:
Molt se combateient forment.
Grant pitié en aveient gent:
Por les femmes forment pluroient,
De l'assaillir molt se penoient.

List of Proper Names

Abas, 5809, Argive warrior
Abiram, 5235, Old Testament figure buried alive, like Amphiaraus
Acamus 5799, Theban warrior who kills Iphis.
Acheron, 5257, 5258, 5265, underworld river in classical mythology; 5268-69, companion of Charon, the underworld ferryman of souls
Achilles, 962, Greek hero, cited as exemplar of friendship (with Patrocles)
Achillor, 3158, 3574, 3594, 3600, 3606, a knight of the castle of Monflor captured by the Greek army
Acopars, 3797, barbaric race from the East (possibly the Ethiopians are meant), allies of the Thebans; often noted for ferocity in *chansons de geste*
Adrastus, 524, 723, 866, 926, etc., King of Argos, ally of Polynices, father-in-law of Polynices and Tydeus
Aeneas, 7826, 7828, Trojan hero of Vergil's *Aeneid*; future adversary of Diomedes in Trojan War
Aeolus, 688, Greek god of the winds
Afran, 6607, 6608, 6611, 6613, Greek warrior, cousin of Tydeus
Africa, 10579
African of Mycenes, the, 2089, a baron of Adrastus, warrior in the Greek army
Agenor, 11393, Theban knight, nephew of Alexis; killer of Nestor, murdered by Polynices
Agenor, 5948, 5965, 5968, 5978, 5982, Theban warrior, the nephew of Dryas
Agenor, Count of Anuques, 10547, Greek baron
Agreus, 5778, Greek warrior
Agrippa, 7215, Count of Sicily, companion of Eteocles
Alan, 8071, place of a ford across a river
Alemande, 3565, a land, not precisely identifiable, from which come two of Hypomedon's knights
Alexander, 7221, Alexander the Great, Greek conqueror
Alexander, 10901, 10907, 10961, 10997, 11030, 11032, 11034, 11179, companion of Eteocles and cousin of Salamander, Dares's daughter
Alexander of Mont Cenis, 4911, Theban ally killed by Capaneus
Alexis, 11379, Theban knight, killed by Nestor
Alexis, 5862, 5875, 5912, 5928, 5931, powerful Count of Arcadia, allied to the Greek army

Auphrigenia, Duke of, 2087, one of Adrastus's barons
Aymon, 4670, Greek (?) warrior
Azon, 10561, city/fortress ruled by Palemon, a Greek baron

Babel, Tower of, 2803, the biblical exemplar of pride punished and linguistic confusion
Babylon, 642, 7098
Bearne, 4803, region of southwest France
Benevento, 3126, town in Italy, home of one of the knights guarding the castle of Monflor on behalf of Eteocles
Blanchefleur, 10968, name of one of the seven towers over the seven gates of Thebes; from it Antigone and Ismene watch the battle outside the gates
Blaye, 5973, city on the estuary of the river Gironde, France
Bucephalus, 7220, the horse of Alexander the Great
Bulgars, 7894, 7930, 7947, 7967, 7979, 7987, 8109, Bulgarian troops who help the Greeks to replenish their food supplies

Cader, 2088, ruler or inhabitant of Archemenie, warrior in the service of Adrastus
Cadmus, 5673, founder of Thebes
Caesar, 2084, Julius Caesar, Roman ruler
Caesarea, 7201, eastern Mediterranean port city, homeland of Polidorus, a companion of Eteocles
Calydon, 747, 757, 923, 2105, 3230, etc., city of which Tydeus is duke
Capaneus, 2101, 2138, 2150, 2238, 2329, 2488, 2520, etc., one of the leaders of the Greek army besieging Thebes
Carcodet, 249, a name for the Devil
Carmin, 10561, one of the fiefs of Palemon, Greek baron
Castile, 4882, 6661, a Spanish kingdom and region
Charles, 4648, Charlemagne, King of the Franks and Holy Roman Emperor
Châtillon, 11348, city of Châtillon-sur-Marne, France
Chthonius, 1663, 1699, leader of the fifty Theban knights who ambush Tydeus as he returns from his embassy to Thebes
Cicero, 6, Roman philosopher, rhetorician, and politician
Cocytus, 5272, the river of the underworld in Greco-Roman mythology
Corinth, 7223, city in Greece, place of origin of a companion of Eteocles
Creon, 5658, 6296, 7481, 7483, 9309, etc., old but powerful Theban baron, kinsman of Polynices and Eteocles, crowned King of Thebes after the death of the brothers.
Crete, 10531, 10541, 10544, important Greek island
Culmina, 5716, one of the seven gates of Thebes, controlled by Menoeceus; the name is probably the result of a misunderstanding of a phrase from Statius; see note

Danube, 7907, 8590, 9449, 9453, 9511, the river Danube
Daphneus of Sadocia, 5815, 5825, Theban warrior
Dares the King, 6115, 6117, first cousin of Menoeceus, holder of one of the seven gates of Thebes
Dares the Red (Daires li Rous), 8598, 8679, 8697, 8719, 8759, etc., Theban lord who seeks to betray Eteocles in order to free his son from Greek captivity; he is tried for treason but not convicted
Dathan, 5235, biblical wrongdoer swallowed by the earth, like Amphiaraus
David, 3264, biblical King David
Deipyle, 1196, 1325, younger daughter of King Adrastus, wed to Tydeus
Diana, 1050, Roman goddess of the hunt
Diomedes, 7826, 7832, son of Tydeus and Deipyle, future Greek warrior in Trojan War
Dirce, 5719, fountain near Thebes
Dorce, 10956, 11001, 11031, 11035, 11085, 11087, 11159, etc., companion of Parthenopeus, at his side when Parthenopeus dies
Dorylas, 1742, one of the fifty Theban warriors who ambush Tydeus
Dryas, 5698, 5828, 5842, 5858, 5948, 5974, 5984, Theban baron in charge of protecting one of the gates of Thebes
Dryas, 10915, 10958, 10962, 10967, 11001, 11019, 11023, 11027, etc., Theban warrior (different from preceding entry), companion of Eteocles, killer of Parthenopeus
Dyogenes, 7185, King of Assyria, companion of Eteocles

Eblo, 4792, Theban warrior, killed by Polynices
Edessa, 6576, city in Mesopotamia; home of Jugurtha, an ally of Eteocles
Electra, 5694, the fifth of the seven gates of Thebes, controlled by Dryas
Engelier, 11828, Athenian knight sent by Theseus to Creon to order him to allow the dead of the Greek army outside Thebes to be buried
Estevenel, 4727, young Theban who brings to Antigone the warhorse won in battle by Parthenopeus, (his master?)
Eteocles, 21, 535, 646, 1208, 1224, 1276, 1332, 1410, 1474, 1497, son of Oedipus and Jocasta, brother of Polynices; refuses to turn over rulership of Thebes to his brother as per agreement, causing war between them
Eurymedon, 5707, 5993, Theban baron who holds the sixth gate of Thebes as his fief

Faramonde, 8034, 8051, 8069, Count of Valfaconde, where the Greeks go to resupply the army with food
Flori, Duke of Avers, 6574, Theban ally
Flori "the old", 4376, uncle of Adrastus, 4767, 4771, 4800, 4802
Florin, 4807, 4816, 4832, 4838, 4840, 4862, Theban warrior killed by Garsy

Fortune, 667, 759, the goddess of chance
France, 6298, 10530, the country of France
Frisia, 3658, 4594, 4854, 7204, 9548, [Phrygia?]
Galant, 1675, weaponsmith; probably Wieland, blacksmith to the gods in Germanic myth
Galatea, 7133, daughter of the King of Nubia, mistress of Eteocles
Galeran of Sypont, 1798, 1836, 1866, 1876, 1883, one of the fifty Theban warriors sent by Eteocles to ambush Tydeus on his return journey from Thebes to Argos
Gariot of Corinth, 7223, companion of Eteocles
Garsadoine, 3231, seneschal of Tydeus
Garsiavar, 4758; Garsy, 4767, 4771, 4800, 4802, 4859, 4861, ally of the Greeks; his expanded name suggests an origin in Navarre
Gascony, 4805, 7253, French region
Girart, 11838, messenger sent by Theseus from Athens to Creon; cf. Engelier
Gironde, 5973, estuary of French river
Godfrey, 5184, Duke of Bouillon, leader of the First Crusade
Godrich, 7230, 7235, English knight, companion of Eteocles [name omitted from MS S]
Greece, 641, 651, 671, 1535, 1909, 1910, etc., the kingdom of the Greeks, ruled by Adrastus
Greeks, passim, the army led by Adrastus to attack Thebes on Polynices's behalf

Haemon, 5681, 6552, 6577, 6587, Theban baron, in charge of the third gate of Thebes
Halys, 1741, one of the fifty Theban knights who ambush Tydeus on his return journey from Thebes to Argos
Hector, 7827, Trojan warrior, chief defender of Troy during its siege by the Greeks
Helmagoras of Salamine, 7191, companion of Eteocles
Herga, 4186, King of Armenia; his son leads Jocasta to the Greek camp for negotiations
Hoarywhite, 7131, 7135, 7156, 10888, 11412, the name of Eteocles's horse
Homer, 5, legendary Greek poet; in fact, the audience of this poem did not know the epics attributed to him
Homoloia, 5670, third gate of Thebes, controlled by Haemon
Hypomedon, 2097, 2140, 2995, 3181, 3310, 3323, 3514, 3524, 3536, 3551, 3558, 3742, 7523, etc., one of the leaders of the Greek army, brave and resourceful
Hypseus, 5690, 5760, 5767, 5774, Theban baron, responsible for one of the gates of Thebes
Hypsipyle, 2400, exiled Princess of Lemnos, nursemaid of King Lycurgus's son, Archemorus, killed by a serpent

Hypsista, 5702, sixth gate to Thebes, controlled by Eurymedon

Ion of Pisa, 5812, 5822, warrior fighting with Greek army
Iphis, 5799, a Greek warrior
Ismene, 4157, 4161, 4169, 4181, 4475, 4481, 4490, 4774, 6743, etc., sister of Polynices and Eteocles, in love with Atys, a Theban warrior killed by Tydeus
Ismenos, 10417, river that runs near Thebes
Ither, 9309, 9390, 9416, 9418, a Theban baron, one of the judges of Dares
Itys, 4676, Theban warrior, killed by Parthenopeus

Jocasta, 24, 391, 420, 567, 3886, 4082, 4094, etc., wife of Laius, mother and wife of Oedipus, mother of Eteocles and Polynices, Antigone, and Ismene
Jordan of Africa, 4748, 4764, ally of the Greeks, killed by Eteocles
Jugurtha of Edessa, 6578, Theban ally
Jupiter, 590, 604, 5072, 5102, 5121, 5143, chief of the Roman gods

Laertes of Lacedemonia, 10551, baron in the army of Adrastus
Laius, 37, 43, 102, 153, 244, King of Thebes, husband of Jocasta, father of Oedipus, who kills him in ignorance
Laliche, 5748, Laodicea, city in Asia Minor; see note
Landeflorie, 8047, area through which the Greek troops under Hypomedon must pass on their return to Thebes after revictualing
Langia, 2313, stream at and in which the Greek army can quench their thirst after traveling through the Nemaean desert
Lemnos, 2403, 2404, 2421, 2580, Greek island, home of Hypsipile, where women murder all their menfolk
Lombardy, 4914, region of Italy
Lucien, 6024, 6031, knight of Capaneus, cut to pieces by the Theban infantry after his horse is killed
Lycurgus, 2182, 2257, 2265, 2643, 2650, 2680, 2686, 2714, 2753, king through whose realm the Greek army passes on their way to Thebes

Malpertus, 10438, 10585, 10694, forest where the fifty Theban knights ambush Tydeus as he returns from his embassy to Thebes, and where the Greeks in turn set an ambush for a Theban force
Mars, 5074, 5104, 5132, the Roman god of war
Marseille, 7197, French city, residence of a companion knight of Eteocles
Melampus, 5586, 5592, candidate to replace Amphiaraus as archbishop after his death
Melampus, Duke of Baille, 5742, 5754, 5766, 5776, fighter in the Greek army
Meleager, 5850, 5856, Theban warrior, closely related to Eteocles; killed by Parthenopeus

Orgive (or Orto), 5654, 5655, The first of the seven gates of Thebes, controlled by Creon
Othon, 3846, 3968, 3978, 3999, 4003, 4029, 5038, leading Theban baron, Plato's cousin, major defender of Dares against Eteocles's wrath

Palemon, 6184, 6195, 6204, 10559, Greek baron who loses a hand in battle with the Prince of Aquileia
Pallas, 1052, 5074, 5105, 5132, goddess of wisdom (Athena)
Pancras, 6131, 6132, Duke of Russia, fighting with the Greeks against the Thebans
Parma, 5191, Italian city
Parthenopeus, 2092, 2141, 4192, 4207, 4227, 4237, 4261, 4297, 4399, 4488, 4676, 4684, 4714, 5843, etc, King of Arcadia, one of the leaders of the Greek army, and lover of Antigone
Patrocles, 962, exemplar of friendship, (with Achilles)
Pennevaire, 6135, horse ridden by Pancras, Duke of Russia
Periphas, 4671, Greek warrior
Persia, 641, 4377, 5784, kingdom of the Persians
Petree, 7197, Count of Marseille, companion of Eteocles
Phaidimus, 1742, one of the fifty Theban warriors who ambush Tydeus returning from his embassy to Eteocles in Thebes
Phedymus, 5793, 5795, Greek warrior killed in battle
Phegeus, 5782, 5790, Theban warrior
Pheres, 5808, Theban warrior
Phoce, 209, city where Oedipus kills his father, Laius
Phoebus, 5110, 5116, 5127, 5130, other name for Apollo
Phoroneus, 722, ancient King of Argos, ancestor of King Adrastus
Pinsonards, 8581, 8586, 8608, 8625, 9472, Turkic nation that sends an embassy to Eteocles promising aid in return for a grant of land
Pirithous, 960, in Greek heroic legend, the faithful friend of Theseus
Plato, 5, 3847, Greek philosopher, cousin of Othon
Pluto, 5306, ruler of the underworld in Greco-Latin mythology
Poinson of Meletant, 6028, Theban warrior
Polidorus of Caeserea, 7201, companion of Eteocles
Polynices, 22, 536, 647, 657, 658, etc., son of Oedipus and Jocasta, brother of Eteocles, besieger of Thebes with Adrastus's Greek army
Pompey, 2084, Roman general
Ponce, 10381, Greek knight who warns Polynices of his army's desire to kill the son of Dares
Poor Ol' Shaggy, 7187, horse of Teucer, a companion of Eteocles
Porphyrus, 6172, 6181, Greek warrior
Proetia, 5686, fourth gate of Thebes, controlled by Hypseus
Ptolemy, 6565, 6571, Greek warrior mounted on an Arabian stallion

Pylades, 961, in Greek heroic legend, the faithful friend of Orestes
Pyrrhus, 10555, Count Palatine, baron in Adrastus's service in the Greek army

Roland, 835, 1789, 10611, legendary hero of Charlemagne's army, compared to Tydeus and Hypomedon
Russia, 6132, 7906

St. Agatha, 4913, city in northern Italy, near Vercelli
St. Thomas, apostle, 5045
Salamander, 10864, 10865, 10877, 10902, 10965, 10981, 11180, daughter of Dares the Redhead and beloved of Eteocles, who acquits Dares because of her
Salatiel, 7177, Jewish knight, a companion of Eteocles
Salin de Pont, 9768, 9888, 9920, one of the judges in the trial of Dares the Redhead
Salomand, 10580, son of an African king and leader of the Almoravid Moors who come from Africa to assist Adrastus
Salonica, 4749, city in Greece, today Thessaloniki
Saracens, 5187, Islamic enemies of Christianity, in epic fictions and crusade narratives
Satan, 5297, a devil
Saxon, 7172, native of Saxony
Saxony, 7172, German Duchy
Semiramis, 990, Queen of Egypt, according to *Roman de Thèbes*; Queen of Assyria, wife of King Ninus
Sicart, 9546, Theban baron; one of Dares's judges, urging his conviction
Sicily, 7215, island of origin for one of Eteocles's companions
Sidon, 643, 3736, 4666, ancient Asia Minor city and trade center, today in Lebanon
Slavonia, 7228, land of the south Slavic peoples
Slavs, 5680, south Slavic people, allies of the Thebans
Solomon, 3264, biblical King of Israel
Sphinx, 281, 287, 299, 360, 370, 412, 1607, 1710, 1984, 2845, legendary creature who tests all who encounter her with a riddle; Oedipus, on his way to Thebes, solves the riddle and kills her; then a devil named Astarot takes the place of the Sphinx.
Statius, 4824, 4854, (or Eustace), Count of Turin, allied with the Thebans; Floriant's cousin
Statius, 8541, Roman author of the *Thebaid*
Styx, 5289, in Greco-Roman mythology, river running through the underworld
Swallow of Nicole, 7237, horse of Godrich, English knight, one of Eteocles's ten paladins
Sybaris, 4672, Theban warrior killed by Hypomedon

Syria, 3163, home of barons helping to defend the castle of Monflor against the Greek army

Tarsus, 4378, ancient city in Asia Minor; now in Turkey

Teucer, 7187, a companion of Eteocles

Thebes, 29, 38, 201, 207, 234, etc., city ruled first by Laius and Jocasta, then by Oedipus and Jocasta; occasion for and prize of the war between Polynices and Eteocles, the sons of Oedipus and Jocasta

Thenelas, 4666, native of Sidon, ally of the Thebans; killed by Tydeus

Theodamas, 5581, 5597, 5600, 5613, successor to Amphiaraus as Archbishop of Adrastus's Greeks of Argos

Theron, 1741, Theban knight, one of fifty who ambush Tydeus on his return journey from Thebes as a messenger to Eteocles from Polynices

Theseus, 960, 11743, 11751, 11753, 11755, 11759 etc., legendary hero and, in medieval story, the Duke of Athens; leads his army and the army of grieving Greek widows against Creon and Thebes, but is never mentioned by name, only as "Duke," in this last section of MS S

Thessaly, 2735, 6658, 11376, city in Greece

Tisiphone, 591, 604, 5292, one of the Furies whom Oedipus invokes to curse his sons

Troy, 2085, 7824, 10567, 11123, famed city of legend and history, now in Turkey; homeland of Antenor, an ally of Adrastus

Tryptolemus, 10568, son of Pyrrhus, a baron in the army of Adrastus

Turin, 4825, city in northern Italy

Turks, 3797, 5185, 5680, 5747, allies of the Thebans, helping to garrison Thebes against attack

Turpin, 5186, heroic Archbishop of Charlemagne's army in medieval French epic and pseudo-history; compared to Amphiaraus

Tydeus, 746, 752, 776, 790, 792, 830, 848, 922, etc., Duke of Calydon, son-in-law of Adrastus and close friend of Polynices; killed in battle outside Thebes and possession of his body fought over

Usarche, 8590, 9449, 9511, region of uncertain location

Ute, bridge of, 9453, place of uncertain location

Valbrune, 8116, deep valley between mountains, proposed as a safe route for the Greek expedition, to return to Thebes with the food they have obtained for the army

Valbrune, 10584, different valley, in the forest of Malpertus

Valcolor, 3421, 3504, valley where Tydeus and his troops hide in order to set a trap for the protectors of Monflor Castle

Valfaconde, 8033, land where the Greek expedition seeks to obtain food for the army

Valflorie, 3012, 3028, 3781, territory controlled by Eteocles on which stands Monflor Castle; also where the Greek army pitches camp before Thebes

Venice, 3175, 3380, 3570, 3608, 3697, 3738, Italian city and marine empire; four Venetian counts are members of Adrastus's army and help him take Monflor

Vercelli, 4913, northern Italian city

Virgil, 6, Latin poet, author of the *Aeneid*

Vougrin of Naples, 1831, one of fifty Theban knights sent by Eteocles to ambush Tydeus on his return journey from Thebes to Argos

Vulcan, 1676, 5046, 5145, Roman god, armorer to the other gods